The Monk and the Philosopher

~

THE MONK AND THE PHILOSOPHER

A Father and Son
Discuss the Meaning of Life

JEAN-FRANÇOIS REVEL
and MATTHIEU RICARD

Translated from the French by John Canti

Foreword by Jack Miles

Schocken Books   New York

Originally published in France as *Le Moine et le Philosophe: Le
Bouddhisme Aujourd'hui* by NiL éditions, Paris, in 1997. Copyright ©
1997 by Jean-François Revel, Matthieu Ricard, and NiL éditions. This
translation originally published in Great Britain by Thorsons,
an imprint of HarperCollins Publishers Ltd., London, in 1998.

Library of Congress Cataloging-in-Publication Data

Revel, Jean François.
[Moine et le philosophe. English]
The monk and the philosopher: a father and son discuss the meaning
of life / Jean-François Revel and Matthieu Ricard; translated from the
French by John Canti; foreword by Jack Miles.
p. cm.
ISBN 0-8052-4162-0
1. Buddhism – Doctrines. I. Ricard, Matthieu. II. Title.
BQ4165.R4813 1999 128 – dc21 98-36031 CIP

Random House Web Address: www.randomhouse.com

Printed in the United States of America
First American Edition
9 8 7 6 5 4 3 2 1

CONTENTS

CONTENTS

FOREWORD

by Jack Miles

C onversation is at once the most primitive and the most refined
expression of the human mind. We rightly cast even the experience of solitary insight in the dialogue form: "It occurred to
me," "It came to me," as if "it" had something to say and wanted me
to listen, as if "it" wanted to start something. The conversation that
fills this book is one that may well start something – especially as the
reader begins to talk back.

As in the Louis Malle film *My Dinner with André*, Matthieu
Ricard and Jean-François Revel talk of ideas, but the mood that lingers
throughout their talk is intimate. The two are in sharp disagreement
about issues that each considers of great moment, yet each cares about
the other as well as about the outcome of their debate.

Ricard, the younger man, a doctor of molecular biology, worked
for some time with Nobel Prize–winning French biologists François
Jacob and Jacques Monod at the renowned Institut Pasteur in Paris.
Then, still early in his career, he surprised family and friends by
leaving Paris for an apprenticeship with Tibetan spiritual masters in
Darjeeling, India, an apprenticeship that led before long to a true con-

version to Buddhism. Ricard now lives in Nepal and devotes much of his time to the translation (into French and English) of Tibetan literature, both ancient and modern.

Revel, the older man, Ricard's father, is a philosopher and political commentator influential on both sides of the Atlantic. Best known here for works like *Without Marx or Jesus* and *The Totalitarian Temptation*, he is also the author of works of philosophically informed cultural commentary like *The Flight from Truth: The Reign of Deceit in the Age of Information.*

In their dialogue, Ricard defends the validity of his own life-changing experience of enlightenment. His response to what he found in Darjeeling did not entail, as he saw it, any repudiation of what he knew as a scientist. Though admittedly a subjective experience, it was valid in its own way and as worthy of intellectual respect as objective science. Revel doubts the ultimate validity of Ricard's or any experience of which no objective, neutral account can be given. He maintains that any truth claim not accessible, at some level, to the methods of science must rest ultimately on religious faith, and the leap of faith is one he declines to make. The issue between them, in sum, is whether Tibetan Buddhist meditation may be understood as a humane secular practice uncomplicated by quasi-religious commitments – hostages to metaphysics, so to speak. Revel sees hostages. Ricard sees none – or no more than are surrendered by science itself.

The experience in question may be one that few Americans have had, but it is one of which most Americans have heard. The Zen Buddhism of Japan has had a substantial American following since the 1950s. In more recent years, the Dalai Lama has become an international celebrity. Within the past year, Buddhism (Tibetan rather than Japanese) has been on the cover of *Time* magazine.[1] By and large, however, the American frame of reference for the Buddhist experience has remained either historical, as in the college world-religions survey course, or therapeutic and quasi-religious, as in the wide variety of settings where meditation continues to be taught as a technique for stress reduction or inner peace. For American science and philosophy, Buddhism has generally not been an item on the agenda.

Whence the novelty and the interest in a debate about Buddhism conducted by a French scientist-turned-monk and a French philosopher. France, the mother country of Western secularism, has made a sharp turn toward Buddhism in recent years, a phenomenon that has been discussed at length in almost every major French magazine. According to some estimates, Buddhism – with some two million adherents – will soon become the third religion in France: after Catholicism and Islam but ahead of Protestantism and Judaism. Does Buddhism's growth in France stem from the revival of a latent French religiosity, or are its roots to be found rather in French secularism and its perennial hunger for a plausible secular alternative to religion? I suspect the latter, but something subtler is under way that would be captured in a line like "If not Jesus, Marx; and if neither Jesus nor Marx, then perhaps Buddha"; for though Christianity without Christ and Marxism without Marx are impossible, Buddhism – at least in some of its forms – actively encourages Buddhism without Buddha. *If you meet the Buddha on the road, kill him,* to quote one of Zen Buddhism's many paradoxical sayings. Revel and Ricard's book-length discussion of Buddhism became a bestseller in France in good measure, I suspect, because it subjects this emerging secular alternative to a relatively rigorous scientific and philosophical cross-examination. The combined effect of their credentials and the popular success of the book may well win a new scientific and philosophical hearing for their topic itself.

Will this be the effect of the book in the United States as well? I am thinking, as I ask this, of my experience in 1997–98 teaching a survey of world religions as a visiting professor at the California Institute of Technology. Caltech students, all young scientists in training, signed up for this course in unprecedented numbers, regarding it evidently as a welcome addition to the curriculum. The Caltech faculty, however, including notably the faculty in humanities and the social sciences, though without hostility to the course or to the students who were taking it, were themselves quite without curiosity about it. Were all these not settled questions? Why unsettle them?

Their intellectual tone of voice, as it were, is one I hear again in Jean-François Revel. If his own son had not gone so deeply into Buddhism, one wonders whether Revel would ever have looked into this tradition on his own. His assumption, broadly, seems to be that all the basic options were rehearsed long ago in the Hellenistic moral philosophy in which he is so well versed. But then Ricard is not just his son. Ricard has deeper formal training in the very science to which Revel has so large a philosophical commitment. Intellectual respect as well as paternal devotion requires that the father take the son seriously as the latter makes life commitments that call the scientific worldview into question.

Science as a worldview has a far broader constituency than does science as a profession. I venture to say that a majority of educated Americans will tend, as they follow this dialogue, to side first with Revel. This will be the case even for many who may retain a nominal affiliation with some form of Christianity or Judaism, for the truth of science and the adequacy of its methods are assumptions by now too widespread and habitual in the culture for even religious believers to escape them. I hasten to add, however, that the minority that will side with Ricard in this debate is not a group that rejects science as science, any more than Ricard does, but only one that has deep reservations about a Western philosophy of life assumed to be in accord with science.

Let me call this secular Western philosophy of life the philosophy of enlightened self-interest. Most of us assume that there is ultimately no alternative to enlightened self-interest as a moral code just as we assume that there is no alternative to the scientific cosmology as a picture of how the world has come to be physically. And yet a widespread weariness, a malaise, lingers about that assumption, and the measure of this malaise is the sense of liberation that a significant minority experiences at the suggestion that the self, the object of all this enlightened interest, may be itself an illusion. Many of us are bored with or burdened with the self, increasingly as little able to believe in it or serve it as to believe in or serve God.

Enlightened self-interest seems to hold as a necessary postulate that the world is real and the world's goods really worth acquiring. A stock portfolio, a law degree, a flat stomach, an art museum membership card, a foreign vacation, a sex life, a baby – the list is long, and each item on it seems to have generated an advertising campaign, a market strategy, an expert adviser. *Materialism* is too narrow a word for the army of cultural imperatives that both preserve and besiege the Western self. *Narcissism* might be better, or *solipsism*, or *cultural autism*. Whatever word or phrase is chosen, it is clear that a revulsion has begun to set in. The news that the self which is served by all this effort, this calculation, this cultivation, this from-birth-onward preparation – the news that this self may be an illusion is news that, for the affected minority, seems already to have arrived. They welcome it less as revelation than as confirmation.

This is the minority that, to repeat, will spontaneously take Ricard's side in this dialogue. But the majority, whatever it might begin by wishing, will eventually find it difficult to ignore Ricard if only because Revel has been unable to ignore his son, and Revel is right there on the page. As a formidable opponent of totalitarianism, Revel is *eo ipso* a formidable proponent of liberal Western individualism, of that enlightened self-interest which accords so well with Western science. But just this synthesis is "performatively" called into question when a pure-bred son of that tradition like Ricard converts to Buddhism. Revel is not stopped by Ricard's conversion, but he is slowed by it – he is given pause; and those pauses function here as intermissions during which latecomers may be shown to their seats. The latecomers are others who, skeptical as Revel is skeptical, can find through him their entry point into this emerging, extremely broad cultural debate.

The issue that neither Jean-François Revel nor Matthieu Ricard can be done talking about is a difficult scientific/philosophical issue; namely, the genesis of consciousness. The following exchange is typical of many:

JEAN-FRANÇOIS – According to traditional metaphysical ideas, whatever belongs to consciousness can only be born from what's conscious, and matter can only be born from matter. That's also something you'd find in Plato, in seventeenth-century philosophy and in Descartes' statement that there can't be more in the effect than in the cause. But then, on that very point, the whole of modern science shows the contrary, on the basis of experiment and observation that can't just be discounted or scorned. It's the thesis that your former boss Jacques Monod, in particular, set out in *Chance and Necessity:* that the biological world arises from the material world, and consciousness arises from the biological world. There's an evolution, therefore, along those lines – the birth of life from matter, then the evolution of species leading little by little to consciousness and language. This, we could say, is the scheme of things now generally accepted by contemporary science.

MATTHIEU – According to Buddhism, the conscious isn't just a more and more complex and perfect development of the inanimate. There has to be a qualitative change there, not just a quantitative one. There's nothing wrong with the observation that the gradually increasing complexity of the organization of the nervous system, as forms of life get higher, goes hand in hand with gradually increasing intelligence. But Buddhism holds that even very elementary forms of life are endowed with some form of consciousness – extremely primitive perhaps, but different from matter alone. As you progress up the evolutionary ladder, the faculty of consciousness becomes more and more effective, deep and developed, culminating in human intelligence. So consciousness is manifested to a varying extent in different supporting mechanisms and in different conditions.

. . .

J.F. – So where would that consciousness come from, even the very primitive one in some microscopic creature?

M – Buddhism answers that by saying that it can only come from a previous life, according to the law of 'conservation of consciousness' analogous to the conservation of energy in the world of matter.

J.F. – That's not, of course, what science would think at all.[2]

Jean-François is right, and Matthieu knows that he is right about "what science would think," but recall that it is Matthieu, not Jean-François, who is the doctor of biology. Revel might well have insisted even more than he does that the doctrine according to which consciousness can only come from consciousness is one that the West believes it has tried and found wanting. But does Ricard not know this as well, and does Revel not know he knows it?

Ricard, I believe, does indeed know about the turn toward materialism that has occurred in Western thought since the scientific revolution, but he regards this shift, the shift from pre-scientific metaphysics to science as we know it, to be, finally, just the shift from one metaphysics to another. As he puts it at another point in the conversation:

Buddhism has absolutely no objection to [scientists'] description of the functioning of the human nervous system on a physical level, but would maintain that to take consciousness as being limited to that physical mechanism was a metaphysical belief, rather than a scientifically proven fact.[3]

Ricard can speak as he does because the one thesis for which there can be in principle no scientific evidence is the thesis that only scientific evidence counts. And on this point, Ricard's old boss, Monod, is in perhaps surprising agreement with his student.

The decision "to take consciousness as being limited to ... physical mechanism" must come first, Monod has written. It is not the result of research. It is the premise that guides research. As we may read in *Chance and Necessity:*

> It is plain that to make the postulate of objectivity a condition for true knowledge constitutes an ethical choice and not a knowledge judgment inasmuch as according to the postulate itself, there can be no 'true' knowledge before this arbitrary choice. The postulate of objectivity, in order to establish a norm for knowledge, defines a value which is objective knowledge itself. To accept the postulate of objectivity then is to articulate the basic proposition of an ethics: the ethics of knowledge.[4]

Should Ricard wish to return to the Institut Pasteur, he need only put this arbitrary postulate of objectivity back in its methodological place and proceed accordingly. Though he may have left the game, there is no reason to believe that he has forgotten the rules. He has simply drawn a further lesson from the fact, admitted by his mentor, that scientific objectivity is located within and guaranteed by the scientists' subjectivity.

In a revealing moment in *Chance and Necessity,* Jacques Monod confesses that he has on occasion found himself identifying with a protein molecule. The remark betrays an asceticism, a sacrifice of normal selfhood to scientific inquiry, that is undeniably impressive, even heroic. But if there is a noble pathos about the method, there is an even greater pathos about the results. It was Monod's rare gift to be able to speak of this pathos with sacerdotal eloquence:

> If he is to accept this message [the accidental and purely physical character of human consciousness] in its full significance, man must at last awaken from his primeval dream to discover his total solitude, his radical strangeness. He knows now that, like a Gypsy, he must live at the edge of the universe, a universe deaf to his music, as indifferent to his hopes as to his sorrows and his crimes.[5]

Univers sourd à sa musique, indifférent à ses espoirs comme à ses souffrances ou à ses crimes. ... Monod puts all this with extraordinary eloquence. He makes it seem – as, classically, religious visions have always seemed – inevitable, inescapable, final. One may well guess that to escape the gravity field of this vision, Ricard might have had to flee halfway around the world. And yet what Monod as the Ecclesiastes of our time presents as the human condition, Monod as logician, as philosopher of science, traces unflinchingly to an "arbitrary choice." Ricard has simply seized the freedom he had – the freedom Monod knew he had – to make another equally "arbitrary choice." The question remains: Why did he make it?

The answer seems to me to have two parts, one expressed, one unexpressed. Ricard tells us, simply and affectingly, that he found a moral excellence in the émigré Tibetans – shaped, as he knew they were, by their practice of meditation – a spiritual depth that became, for him, an empirical fact as undeniable as anything in the laboratory. What he does not tell us so explicitly is that he needed what they had. They were different, unlike anyone he had known before, and he was drawn by the difference, drawn so strongly that he wanted to track it to its source.

Though the laboratory enforces a code of behavior for those behaviors which occur within the laboratory itself, the one general moral lesson that the scientific worldview has to impart is that the cosmos teaches no general moral lessons. The universe is not just deaf to our music, to use Monod's image; it is also playing no music to which we might hope to tune our own hearing, our own being. Tibetan Buddhism, I venture to say, disagrees, and at this point so does Ricard.

The Judeo-Christian tradition, believing in a God who transcended nature, has never been a tradition that taught submission to or harmony with nature, but the will of this God, his ten commandments, the example he gave when he revealed himself in human form as Jesus Christ – all this was for many centuries the music to which the West sang. Some still hear this music, but for a great many the music has died, whence the great dilemma of post-Christian, secular Western culture. For a good while now, it has had only science to turn to, and what science says is that there is no music but the noise that each hears autistically in his own head. This is less an answer than the refusal of the question. If life can only be lived in this way, then death begins to have a strange charm, or perhaps more exactly, all those expressions of enlightened self-interest that animate Western culture begin to seem a *danse macabre*. If you join the dance, then it is as if you have already died. No wonder that in some of the best fiction and poetry now being written, a recurrent subject is death within life, anaesthesia, numbness, acedia.

It is by no means my personal thesis that Tibetan Buddhism, or any form of Buddhism, is the one remedy for this sickness unto death. In fact, I confess a certain regret that in confronting these perennial issues, neither Revel nor Ricard shows any acquaintance with the resources of Christianity or Judaism. Ricard reports a late visit to a French monastery and finds many points of similarity between his own experience of meditation and that of these Catholic monks. But one might have expected a Frenchman to begin rather than end his spiritual quest with a visit to the Grande Chartreuse. "Christianity is an oriental religion," to quote the lapidary first sentence of Jean-Claude Barreau's preface to Olivier Clément's landmark study of the sources of Christian mysticism. The German theologian Dietrich Bonhoeffer spoke of "religionless Christianity," the American Mark C. Taylor of "a/theology." And there are no fewer points of contact between Tibetan mysticism and the ancient Torah mysticism of Judaism's Kabbalah, or between the paradoxes of Buddhism and those of Judaism as explored by a modern Jewish-French thinker like Emmanuel Lévinas.[6]

But in the post-Christian West, where the hope of salvation has disappeared almost without remainder into a craving for success, the appeal of Eastern detachment, as an escape from and a repudiation of this craving, may be larger than anything that can be synthesized from Western materials. To quote from an ancient Buddhist source:

> Now pleasant sensations, unpleasant sensations, indifferent sensations, Ananda, are transitory, are due to causes, originate by dependence, and are subject to decay, disappearance, effacement, and cessation. While one experiences the pleasant sensation, one thinks that 'I' am experiencing it. And after the cessation of this same pleasant sensation, one thinks that 'I' have ceased experiencing it.[7]

And similarly for unpleasant and indifferent sensations. So dependent is the self on sensations, that where there are no sensations there can be no "I." But from this it can be inferred that the self is as subject to "disappearance, effacement, and cessation" as the sensations. And it may be easier for a great many of our contemporaries to move from that perception to a calming and liberating disidentification with self than it is to move to the same point from any form of devotion to God, particularly to a God who loves the world, hears its music, and suffers with its suffering.

One way or another, the encounter that all of the world's pre-

scientific religious or mystical or spiritual or psychotherapeutic traditions will continue to have with world science, each separately in its
own unpredictable way, will prove more decisive for them than the
encounter that any one of them may have with any other one. When
Jean-François Revel speaks for science, what he does, in effect, is
demand that Matthieu Ricard confront the scientist still alive and well
in himself. Revel quite properly insists that Ricard, though a devotee
of Tibetan Buddhism, remains a man of the West.

We should not be surprised. At the turn of the millennium, all foreign relations are becoming domestic, and an "East-West" dialogue
may be conducted as easily by two Easterners or two Westerners as by
a mixed pair. By that token, the Ricard-Revel conversation is simultaneously a Ricard–Ricard and a Revel-Revel conversation along a fis-
sure which each opens in the other. Deep growth often entails in this
way a marring of surface integrity, a temporary alienation, a disorder
en route to an enlarged order. It can only be so in a conversation which,
taken as a whole, is a remarkable episode in one of the larger civiliza-
tional encounters of our time.

1. On this broad cultural phenomenon, particularly in its American manifestation,
   see Donald S. Lopez, Jr., *Prisoners of Shangri-La: Tibetan Buddhism and the West*
   (Chicago: University of Chicago Press, 1998).
2. From text, pp. 119–20.
3. From text, p. 54.
4. Jacques Monod, *Le hasard et la nécessité* (Paris: Editions du Seuil, 1970), p. 191
   (my translation).
5. Monod, pp. 187–88.
6. Olivier Clément, *The Roots of Christian Mysticism*, translated by Theodore
   Berkeley, O.C.S.O., and Jeremy Hummerstone from the original French edition
   Sources, copyright © 1982 Editions Stock, Paris, preface by Jean-Claude Barreau
   (New York: New City Press, 1995). Dietrich Bonhoeffer, *Letters and Papers from
   Prison* (New York: Macmillan, 1972). Mark C. Taylor, *Erring: A Postmodern
   A/Theology* (Chicago: University of Chicago Press, 1984). Emmanuel Lévinas,
   Nine Talmudic Readings, translated by Annette Aronwicz (Bloomington, Ind.:
   Indiana University Press, 1990).
7. Adapted from Henry Clarke Warren, *Buddhism in Translation* (Cambridge: Har-
   vard University Press, 1922), p. 136 (Maha-Nidana-Sutta of the Digha-Nikaya,
   25621).

INTRODUCTION

by Jean-François Revel

How did the idea of this book arise? What made us want to do it? Or made several people put friendly pressure on us – as they say in politics – to consider it in the first place? Of the two of us, I am writing this introduction on my own simply as a matter of convenience, to avoid the labored circumlocution we would have needed to cover, both together, the widely divergent motives that bring us to this shared interest of ours. Indeed, the complexities of our two approaches to the same subjects are exactly what the conversations in this book are intended to sort out and gradually distinguish.

It would be superfluous to say more here about what will be dealt with amply in the conversations that follow. Suffice it to describe briefly the meeting of lives and minds that created the initial spark.

My son Matthieu Ricard was born in 1946. After secondary school at the Lycée Janson-de-Sailly, he embarked on a brilliant university career in molecular biology which led him to a doctorate in 1972. The chairman of the board examining his thesis was François Jacob, eminent winner of a Nobel Prize for biology, in whose research team he had worked for several years at the Institut Pasteur. Suddenly, at this point, Matthieu announced to his boss and myself – to our great consternation – that he had decided to abandon scientific research, go to live in Asia, and follow the teachings of Tibetan Buddhist lamas. This was a total change in his life, which would later lead him to become a Buddhist monk.

My own university studies were essentially in literature and philosophy. I taught philosophy for several years, and then left academic life in 1963 to devote myself fully to a new career as a writer and newspaper editor. However, I never lost my enthusiasm for philosophy, and have written about it in several of my books.[1] Unlike many philosophers, I have always felt a keen interest in the evolution of science. Hence my satisfaction at having a son in first-rate scientific research, and my disappointment at seeing him abruptly put an end to a career whose beginnings had been more than promising. Moreover, my own points of view as a convinced atheist did not induce me to take Buddhism very seriously – not that I had anything against it, for its unadulterated and straightforward approach give it a distinctive position among religious doctrines and have earned it the respect of some of the most exacting Western philosophers.

Despite feeling momentarily upset about his decision, I never fell out with Matthieu, nor was I ever even on bad terms with him. I mention this because some recent articles in the French press claimed, without a shred of truth, that we had not seen each other for twenty years and that our plan to do a book together marked a reconciliation between us. In fact, over the years, we have continued to see each other as often as the distances permitted. As early as 1973, I visited him in Darjeeling, India, where he was living with his first spiritual teacher, Kangyur Rinpoche, and later on in Bhutan and Nepal. The only clouds that ever passed over our relationship were those of the Asian monsoon. As time went on, Matthieu had increasingly frequent opportunities to travel to Europe, on trips that led him to take part in the growing spread of Buddhism in the West. His role as interpreter for the Dalai Lama, especially after the latter was awarded the Nobel Peace Prize, brought him to France even more often.

The unforeseen phenomenon of the spread of Buddhism is indeed one of the things that suggested to us the idea of a conversation on 'Buddhism and the West'. Such was the title we had planned for our dialogue, in fact, until our publisher, Nicole Lattès, found a much better one: *The Monk and the Philosopher*.

What exactly is Buddhism? That is the overall question, the answers to which have been Matthieu's particular responsibility. Why does Buddhism today in the West attract such a large following and so much curiosity? Here, it has been more my task to suggest some hypotheses. Is it a consequence of recent changes, disappointing ones perhaps, undergone by Western religions and philosophies, as well as political systems? It goes without saying that the content of our exchanges derives a particular value from the fact that they took place not between a Western philosopher and an Eastern sage but between a Western philosopher and a Western monk trained in the East who, moreover, was originally a scientist and is capable, on his own and in himself, of comparing the two cultures at the highest level. Indeed, Matthieu has, in a way, transposed his scientific rigor to the study of the Tibetan language and tradition, and for twenty years has been helping to preserve and publish the fundamental sacred texts, ancient and modern, of Tibetan Buddhism, and translating them into French and English.

The texts that still exist, at least. For, as everyone now knows, the Chinese communists destroyed whole libraries full of them, at the same time as the six thousand or so monasteries in which they were housed. The massacres and destruction began with the invasion of Tibet by China in 1950 and its annexation in 1951, and grew more and more intense, first during the repression that followed the Tibetan uprising and subsequent crackdown in 1959, then during the Cultural Revolution. It was in 1959 that the Dalai Lama and over a hundred thousand Tibetans escaped into exile in India or the Himalayan kingdoms of Nepal, Bhutan, and Sikkim, before spreading out to many countries of the world. Communist colonialism tolerated no ideology other than its own, no intellectual, religious, or artistic freedom. With implacable ferocity, it set out not only to pillage Tibet's natural resources shamelessly but also to destroy Tibetan civilization – even the Tibetan language. Far from easing off as time went on, the Chinese extermination of the Tibetans and their culture intensified again in the eighties, despite the so-called 'liberalization' ushered in by Mao's successors. It is true that since 1980, while torture and summary executions have continued to take place, there has been no wholesale slaughter comparable to that of the sixties and early seventies, during which a million Tibetans – a sixth of the population – were annihilated. But destruction of Tibetan civilization has continued. Liberalization is confined to economic life, for pragmatic reasons and to bring material improvement. Beyond these domains, there is no freedom in China, even for the Chinese. And in Tibet Mao's successors have applied Stalin's old colonial method: populate the annexed region with your own nationals until they outnumber the native inhabitants.

There would be no point in denying that my indignation at the martyrdom of the Tibetan people was one of the things that reinforced my interest in Buddhism. Another, also of sentiment, came even more naturally – that it was the religion my son had adopted. I wanted to know more about what lay behind his decision and its consequences. As for Chinese politics, in 1983, I devoted several pages of my book *How Democracies Perish*,[2] mostly from information that Matthieu supplied, to a detailed description of the Tibetan genocide, which had lasted for almost three decades without world opinion being much affected or even much informed. That this small and isolated country – which posed no threat at all to its large neighbor – with its peaceful, pastoral people following a religion free of any proselytizing, should be the target of attempted annihilation by Stalinist-Maoist Marxism seemed to me a symbol of our century, skewered almost from beginning to end by the logic of totalitarianism.

For a long time after the Dalai Lama had been forced to flee into exile to escape enslavement or even death, news about Tibet remained difficult to obtain. The Tibetan question was buried for fifteen or twenty years by the self-censorship of a West wallowing in its idolatry of Maoism and reluctant to heed any criticism of communist China.

This evocation of the crimes of Chinese communist barbarity is not just a detour from the subject of these conversations between 'the monk and the philosopher'. It was the long stay of the Dalai Lama and numerous other Tibetan lamas, Buddhist teachers, and Rinpoches outside their own country that provided the circumstantial cause for the increased spread of Buddhism in the West. Their accessibility made it much easier, geographically speaking, for Westerners to discover the most authentic teaching of the doctrine – and not just a bookish, indirect, theoretical teaching, but a living one, at firsthand, flowing from the very source, its most qualified proponents. Another consequence of the tribulations inflicted by Chinese communism has been to reveal the Dalai Lama's political talent. All the solutions he has put forward to China to end the enslavement of his people have been realistic, moderate and nonviolent. They are also oriented toward the setting up of democracy in Tibet, which should please Westerners, if not Tibet's occupying forces. He has developed a subtle but cheerful way of dealing with the Western democracies' leaders, recognizing nevertheless how riddled with timorous servility they are before the irritable bureaucrats of Beijing.

For a long time, the conventional image that the West had of Buddhism was of a wisdom based on passivity and inaction, 'nirvana' defined as an inwardly turned indolence indifferent to the running of community and society. We now know that it is nothing of the sort. Like most Western philosophies, Buddhism too has its human, social, and political dimensions.

Such, in brief, were the circumstances and motives that finally led Matthieu and myself to take the decision one day to confront whatever questions we each had and to explore our mutual curiosity, in order to throw light on our similarities without hiding our differences. That is how and why, in May 1996, the conversations that follow took place in Hatiban, Nepal, a peaceful spot high up on a mountainside above Kathmandu.

1. Particularly *Histoire de la philosophie occidentale de Thalès à Kant* (*A History of Western Philosophy from Thales to Kant*), NiL éditions, Paris, 1994, and *Pourquoi des philosophes?* (*Why Philosophers?*), Laffont Bouquins, Paris, 1997.
2. Doubleday, New York, 1984.

THE MONK AND THE
PHILOSOPHER

~

~

ONE

FROM SCIENTIFIC RESEARCH
TO SPIRITUAL QUEST

JEAN-FRANÇOIS – I think the first thing we should emphasize is that the idea of this book was neither yours nor mine. It was suggested to us by some publishers who heard your story, knew that I was your father, and thought it would be interesting for us to compare points of view. So let me just begin by mentioning some details. You started out studying very successfully for a degree in biology, and then became a graduate student under François Jacob, working for several years in research at the Institut Pasteur. For your doctoral thesis, which you presented at the Paris Faculté des Sciences in front of an examining board that included François Jacob and other eminent biologists, you were awarded a highly commended Ph.D. What makes the series of conversations we're about to have so interesting, then, is the fact that you're someone steeped in European, Western scientific culture at the highest level who subsequently, or simultaneously, adopted this philosophy or religion rooted in the East, Buddhism. The reason you took to it, it should be said, wasn't that you were looking for some extra element in your life, or a religious adjunct to a career that would continue normally according to Western criteria. Rather, you abandoned your career in order to commit yourself completely to Buddhist practice. So my first question is this: when and why did that decision begin to ger-minate in you?

MATTHIEU – My scientific career was the result of a passion for dis-covery. Whatever I was able to do afterward was in no way a rejection of scientific research, which is in many respects a fascinating pursuit, but arose rather from the realization that such research was unable to solve the fundamental questions of life – and wasn't even meant to do so. In short, science, however interesting, wasn't enough to give mean-ing to my life. I came to see research, as I experienced it myself, as an endless dispersion into detail, and dedicating my whole life to it was something I could no longer envisage. At the same time I was becom-ing more and more interested in the spiritual life in terms of a 'con-templative science'.

At first my interest in the spiritual wasn't clearly formulated, as my education had been completely secular and I'd never practiced Christianity. Without knowing anything about religion itself, I'd always felt, from the outside, a sort of reverential fear when I went into a church or met a monk. Then, as a teenager, I started to read quite a few books on different religious traditions. On Christianity, Hin-duism, and Sufism, but, paradoxically, not much on Buddhism. At the time, in the sixties, few authentic translations of Buddhist texts existed. The small number of available essays and translations tended to reiterate, rather awkwardly, the distorted way in which the West perceived Buddhism in the nineteenth century as a nihilistic philoso-phy advocating indifference to the world. Thanks to my uncle Jacques-Yves Le Toumelin, who is quite famous as a solo yachtsman, I also discovered the writings of the French metaphysician René Guénon. All this stimulated and nourished my intellectual curiosity about religion, without leading to anything more concrete. For me, it all stayed quite intellectual.

J.F. – Intellectual in what sense?

M. – I found that reading these works full of meaning satisfied me deeply and opened my mind, but didn't really bring about any inner transformation.

J.F. – How old were you at this point?

M. – Oh, I suppose about fifteen. I'd also read some records of interviews with Ramana Maharshi, an Indian sage who was said to have attained knowledge of the ultimate nature of the mind, nondual-ity. But what triggered my interest in Buddhism was in 1966…

J.F. – You would have been twenty then.

M. – I was still at university, and just about to go to the Institut Pasteur, when I saw some films made by a friend, Arnaud Desjardins, as they were being edited. They were about the great Tibetan lamas who had fled the Chinese invasion and taken refuge on the southern side of the Himalayas, from Kashmir to Bhutan. Arnaud had spent several months on two trips with an excellent guide and interpreter, filming these masters at close quarters. The films were very striking. Around the same time, another friend, Dr. Leboyer, came back from Darjeeling where he'd met some of the same lamas. I'd just finished a course and had the chance of taking a six-month break before starting my research work. It was the time of the hippies, who'd set out to India overland hitchhiking or in a Citroën *deux-chevaux*, through Turkey, Iran, Afghanistan, and Pakistan. I was also drawn to the martial arts and had thought of going to Japan. But the sight of the pictures brought back by Arnaud and Frédérick Leboyer, what they told me and their descriptions of their encounters there, all helped me make up my mind to head for the Himalayas rather than anywhere else.

J.F. – So it was Arnaud Desjardins's film that started it all off.

M. – There were several films, *The Message of the Tibetans* and *Himalaya, Land of Serenity* (which included *The Children of Wisdom* and *The Lake of the Yogis*), four hours in all. They include long sequences of the great Buddhist teachers who'd just arrived from Tibet – what they looked like, how they spoke, what they taught. The films give a very alive and inspiring account of what it was like.

J.F. – Were they shown on television?

M. – Yes, several times from 1966 onward. They've recently been made available on videocassette.[1] They're extraordinary documentaries.

J.F. – At the time of the Cultural Revolution there was a renewed upsurge of Chinese repression in Tibet. Was that when those Tibetan lamas had fled the country?

M. – In fact, those who were able to escape at all had left long before, during the fifties. As the result of a disagreement, Tibet had practically broken off diplomatic relations with China between 1915 and 1945. It had a government and maintained relations with several foreign countries. Then, little by little, China began to infiltrate Tibet. Chinese officials came to visit the country. They said they felt an affinity for Tibetans and their culture. They went as far as making offerings in the monasteries. They promised to help the Tibetans modernize their country. But in 1949 they began a military invasion of Tibet, starting with the East, the region of Kham. The invaders showed no mercy, and as the years went by it became more and more obvious that they were going to conquer central Tibet, seize power, and capture the Dalai Lama. He therefore fled to India in 1959. Immediately afterward, the frontiers were sealed off and a period of savage repression began. Men, women, and children were thrown into prison or sent off to labor camps. Whether executed or succumbing to torture and famine in the camps and prisons, more than a million Tibetans – one in five of the population – died following the Chinese invasion. Enormous mass graves were filled up, one after the other. Even before the Cultural Revolution, six thousand monasteries, practically all of them, were destroyed. The libraries were burnt, the statues broken, the frescoes ravaged.

J.F. – What! Six thousand!

M. – Yes, there are six thousand one hundred and fifty monasteries on the list of those that were razed. And when you think that the monasteries in Tibet were the repositories of the culture! It reminds me of what Goering said: 'When I hear the word culture, I get out my revolver.' It's a fact probably unprecedented in human history that of Tibet's population up to twenty percent were ordained – monks, nuns, hermits in retreat in caves, learned lamas teaching in the monasteries. Spiritual practice was beyond any doubt the principal goal in life, and lay people too saw their daily activities, however necessary, as being of secondary importance compared to their spiritual life. The whole culture was centered around its religion. So in annihilating the monasteries, the centers of study and the hermitages, it was the soul – the very root of Tibetan culture – that was being destroyed. But the Tibetans' strength of mind proved impossible to destroy. Smiles, money, propaganda, torture, and extermination: the Chinese tried the whole gamut to change the Tibetans' minds. But nothing succeeded. The Tibetans' hopes of preserving their culture and regaining their independence is still intact.

J.F. – Let's come back to your story. We were talking about Arnaud Desjardins's films. You said they left a strong impression on you, personally. Why?

M. – I had the impression of seeing living beings who were the very image of what they taught. They had such a striking and remarkable feeling about them. I couldn't quite hit on the explicit reasons why, but what struck me most was that they matched the ideal of sainthood, the perfect being, the sage – a kind of person hardly to be found nowadays in the West. It was the image I had of St. Francis of Assisi, or the great wise men of ancient times, but which for me had become figures of the distant past. You can't go and meet Socrates, listen to Plato debating, or sit at St. Francis' feet. Yet suddenly, here were beings who seemed to be living examples of wisdom. I said to myself, 'If it's possible to reach perfection as a human being, that must be it.'

J.F. – I was about to say, about your definition – exactly, in fact it's almost as commonplace to emphasize that what characterized the philosophy of the classical period is that theory and practice went together. For the ancient philosopher, philosophy wasn't just an intellectual teaching, a theory, an interpretation of the world or of life. It was a way of being. His philosophy was something that he and his disciples would put into practice in their lives at least as much as they would theorize about it in their discourses. The first thing that impressed you when you came across Tibetan lamas is an approach that also lay at the very origins of Western philosophy. That, incidentally, is why philosophers had a role to play in listening, teaching, counseling, providing moral support and edifying company for a large number of important people up to the end of the Roman Empire, especially at the time of Marcus Aurelius, which Ernest Renan called 'the reign of the philosophers'. So here we're talking about an attitude that certainly used to exist in the West – not just to be content with teaching, but to be the reflection of what you teach, in your very way of life. That said, whether in practice it was really lived out as perfectly as one might have wished is another question. Such a notion of philosophy was also, in many cases, related to the religious side of things. Ancient-philosophy usually included that dimension, inasmuch as it was also a form of personal salvation. The Epicureans had that approach (although in modern usage the word 'epicure' implies indifference to any spiritual dimension). So there was always that double need, to develop a doctrine and at the same time to actually live and embody that doctrine. In the age of classical philosophy, therefore, there was no fundamental difference between West and East.

M. – That's right, except that Tibetan Buddhist masters are not trying to develop a doctrine but rather to be faithful and accomplished inheritors of a spiritual tradition thousands of years old. In any case, for me it was a great comfort to know that an authentic living tradition still existed, and was there for the asking, like a whole collection of beautiful things laid out on display.

J.F. – But what were those beautiful things – what did that doctrine bring you? It's not enough to live and embody just any old doctrine. It has to be a doctrine with some worth!

M. – At the time I had little idea what Buddhism was all about, but simply to see those wise men, even through what can be communicated in a film, gave me a sense of deeply inspiring perfection. It was a source of hope, by contrast with my experience hitherto. In the world I'd grown up in, thanks to you I'd met philosophers, thinkers, theater people; thanks to my mother (Yahne Le Toumelin, the painter), I knew artists and poets like André Breton, Maurice Béjart, Pierre Soulages; thanks to my uncle (Jacques-Yves Le Toumelin, the sailor), famous explorers; thanks to François Jacob, the eminent scientists who came to give lectures at the Institut Pasteur. I'd had the opportunity to make contact with people who in many respects were fascinating. But at the same time the genius they showed in their particular field was not necessarily accompanied by what you could call human perfection. All their talent, all their intellectual and artistic skills, didn't necessarily make them good human beings. A great poet might be a rogue, a great scientist unhappy with himself, an artist full of self-satisfied pride. All sorts of combinations, good or bad, were possible.

J.F. – I remember, by the way, that at the time you were also very keen on music, astronomy, photography, and ornithology. When you were twenty-five you wrote a book on animal migration,[2] and there was a whole period in your life that you spent deeply immersed in music.

M. – Yes, that's true. I met Igor Stravinsky and other great musicians. I was lucky enough to mix with many of the people much admired in the West, and to be able to make up my own mind and ask myself, 'Is that what I aspire to? Do I want to be like them?' But I had the feeling that something was still missing. Despite my admiration, I couldn't help noticing that the mastery such people possessed in their particular field was often not matched by even the simplest human perfections – like altruism, goodness, or sincerity. On the other hand, those films and photographs gave me a glimpse of something quite different, which drew me to those Tibetan masters. Their way of being seemed to reflect what they taught. So I set out to find them.

Another friend of mine, Christian Bruyat, had the same feeling of something suddenly clicking into place. He was preparing for his entrance exam to teachers' training college when he heard the last words of a radio broadcast in which Arnaud Desjardins was saying something like, 'I believe that the last great wise men, living examples of spiritual perfection, are now the Tibetan lamas who have taken refuge in the Himalayas of India.' At that very moment he, too, decided to set out on the journey to see them.

So I left on a cheap flight to India. I could hardly speak any English. You'd felt it was more important for me to learn German, Greek, and Latin, all more difficult than English which, you told me, I'd learn naturally anyway. It turned out you were right – but in the meantime I've forgotten all my German and the rest. I arrived in Delhi with a little pocket dictionary and had the greatest trouble managing to find my way, buy a railway ticket for Darjeeling, and get myself there, just across from the most beautiful Himalayan snow peaks. I had the address of a Jesuit father with whom Dr. Leboyer had left a sum of money to help support a great Tibetan Buddhist lama, Kangyur Rinpoche, who had arrived in India a few years earlier. He was then living in great simplicity with his family in a little wooden hut, together with all the books he'd saved from Tibet. It happened that the very day after I arrived, this master's son was to come to the mission. So it was Kangyur Rinpoche's son who took me to meet his father. I stayed there, simply in his presence, for the next three weeks. It left a deep and unforgettable impression on me. He was a man of seventy, radiating goodness and compassion, sitting with his back to a window that looked out over a sea of clouds, through which Kanchenjunga rose up sheer and majestic to an altitude of more than twenty-four thousand feet. I sat opposite him all day long, and had the impression that I was doing what people call 'meditating', in other words simply collecting myself in his presence. I received a few words of teaching, almost nothing. His son, Tulku Pema Wangyal, spoke English, but I could hardly understand a word. It was his person, his being, that made such an impression on me; the depth, strength, serenity, and love that emanated from him and opened my mind.

Thereupon, I continued my travels. I went to Kashmir. I fell ill in India, got typhoid, and set off back home. Stopping over in Damascus, I got off the plane, telling myself how stupid it would be not to see all those countries, and continued by rail and road. I saw the tomb of the great Sufi saint Ibn Arabi, the Krak des Chevaliers, the mosques of Istanbul. I ended my journey hitchhiking to the Abbaye de Tournus, where I meditated in the cool of the cloister, peaceful and deserted, while outside the traffic of August holidaymakers returning home was clogging up the main roads. Finally, worn out, I caught a train to Paris. So that journey was, for me, a huge physical upheaval and a great inner revelation. It was only after getting back from India, during my first year at the Institut Pasteur, that I realized how important that meeting with my teacher had been. That special quality of his kept coming back to my mind all the time. I became aware that I'd found a reality that could inspire my whole life and give it direction and meaning, even if I still couldn't say exactly how.

J.F. – So you could say that this major change you went through – to avoid using the word 'conversion' prematurely – was not brought about by any increase in intellectual, doctrinal, or philosophical knowledge about Buddhist texts as such, but mainly and initially through a personal encounter.

M. – Exactly. I only started studying quite a bit later.

J.F. – At the time, there were a lot of young Westerners, European and American, traveling in India, weren't there?

M. – Yes. It was a year before May 1968. All those people were looking for something different. Some were there to smoke marijuana, some were on a spiritual quest, visiting Hindu ashrams; others were exploring the Himalayas. Everyone was looking for something, here, there, and everywhere. Ideas and information were being exchanged all the time: 'I met such-and-such an extraordinary person there ... I saw this amazing landscape in Sikkim ... I met this or that master of music in Benares ... this or that yoga teacher in south India,' and so on. It was a time when everything was being questioned, everything was being explored – not only in books but in reality.

J.F. – And of the young Westerners who had gone looking for a new spiritual life, did a large number go to Darjeeling?

M. – At the time, very few. Perhaps a few dozen during the late sixties. Then, as time went on, interest in the Tibetan lamas and their teaching gathered pace. A few of the younger generation of Tibetan teachers had already settled in Europe and America during the sixties, and it was around 1971 that for the first time some of the great lamas of the older generation started to travel in the West too. Little by little, hundreds and then thousands of Westerners began to study Tibetan Buddhism. A number of those Westerners spent several years in the Himalayas with their Tibetan teachers, or went to visit them regularly.

To return to your earlier point, my interest wasn't based on any study of Buddhism, either on my first journey or on the two or three following trips. It was to meet my teacher again that I went back to India. For sure, I received some essential spiritual instructions from him, but never a continuous course on Buddhism. He told me, 'There are a lot of very interesting things in Buddhism, but it's important not to lose yourself in purely theoretical book study. It might distract you from practice, which is the very heart of Buddhism and all inner transformation.' In his presence, however, I'd intuitively discovered one of the basic things about the teacher-disciple relationship, putting one's mind in harmony with that of the teacher. It's called 'mixing your mind with the teacher's mind', the teacher's mind being wisdom and our mind being confusion. What happens is that by means of that 'spiritual union' you pass from confusion to wisdom. This purely contemplative process is one of the key points of Tibetan Buddhist practice.

J.F. – But to have what you call wisdom, then, means to have been initiated into a religious doctrine.

M. – No, it's the result of an inner transformation. What's called wisdom in Buddhism is the elucidation of the nature of the phenomenal world, of the nature of the mind. What are we? What is the world? In the end, and above all, it's the direct contemplation of absolute truth, beyond all concepts. That's wisdom in its most fundamental aspect.

J.F. – So it's the philosophical question *par excellence*!

M. – Exactly.

J.F. – Or at any rate, the philosophical question as it was up until the invention of science, in other words as long as philosophy thought it knew everything. Philosophies from classical times until the birth of modern physics in the seventeenth century covered knowledge of the material world, knowledge of the living world, morals, knowledge of man himself and knowledge of the beyond, of the divinity – whether the divinity was seen as personal, as by Aristotle, or as being Nature itself, as by the Stoics or Spinoza. From then onward, an overall doctrine of reality as a whole has no longer been considered seriously attainable. We'll come back to that.

What's more, the word 'wisdom' has another slant. I'll call it the Socratic outlook. For Socrates, wisdom is the consequence of science. For him, there can be no such thing as instinctive wisdom or morality. Everything comes from knowledge, so both must be derived from science. The classical philosophies were philosophies in which access to a certain form of wisdom and well-being, which they called the 'sovereign good' – meaning to reach a sort of full equilibrium by identifying yourself with virtue in relation to others and with well-being for yourself – flowed from scientific knowledge, or from what they considered to be scientific knowledge. Isn't that a bit what characterized Buddhism, too, at the time you discovered it? Your teacher told you that wisdom is to recognize the ultimate nature of things, but if I may say so wisdom in those terms is quite a vast program. It would include at the same time knowledge of all phenomena in the external world, in yourself, and perhaps in the supernatural world, too.

M. – Well, it's true that Buddhism includes the study of traditional sciences, such as medicine, language, grammar, poetics, astronomical or astrological calculation (especially of eclipses), handicrafts, and the arts. Tibetan medicine, which is based on a complex knowledge of healthy physiology and the many internal and external factors that can unbalance it, requires many years of study. Tibetan doctors even had considerable surgical skills, being capable, so it's said, of removing cataracts with the help of a golden scalpel. Although some of their more specialized expertise (including that particular skill) has now been lost, a very sophisticated knowledge of the pharmacology of natural substances remains a basic requirement for all Tibetan doctors. This is certainly one example of knowledge applied to the benefit of others.

But the most important science is knowledge of oneself and of reality, the essential question being, 'What is the nature of the phenomenal world, and of the mind,' and on a practical level, 'What are the keys to happiness and to suffering? Where does suffering come from? What is ignorance? What is spiritual realization? What is perfection?' Such discoveries are what can be called knowledge, or wisdom.

J.F. – And is the initial motivation to escape from suffering?

M. – Suffering is the result of ignorance, so it's ignorance that has to be dissipated. And ignorance, in essence, is belief in a truly existing self and in the solidity of phenomena. To ease the immediate sufferings of others is a duty, but it's not enough; suffering's very causes have to be put right. But, once again, none of this was clear to me at that time. I thought to myself, 'There's no smoke without fire. When I see my teacher, his physical appearance, the way he speaks, what he does, what he is – it all makes me feel utterly convinced that there's something essential here that I want to go deeper into. Here's a real source of inspiration and of certainty, a perfection I want to absorb myself.' Over the course of several journeys (I made five or six trips to India before going to live there), I realized that while I was with my teacher I could easily forget the Institut Pasteur and everything about my life in Europe – but while I was at the Institut Pasteur my thoughts would always be flying off to the Himalayas. So I took a decision that I've never regretted since: to go and live where I wanted to be!

By then I'd finished my thesis and Professor Jacob was thinking of sending me to the United States to work on a new subject of research. Like many researchers at the time, he'd switched from studying bacteria to animal cells, a much wider field of research, which was giving quite a boost to progress in biology. I said to myself that I'd concluded a chapter. I'd published papers about my five years of research. I hadn't wasted the investments of all kinds that had been made in me, by my family for my education and by François Jacob who'd taken me into his laboratory. Whatever happened, it was going to be a turning point in my research anyway. I was free to take another direction without breaking anything off, without disappointing all the people who'd helped me get as far as my doctoral thesis. I could now realize my own, personal wishes with a peaceful conscience. My teacher, Kangyur Rinpoche, too, had always insisted that I finish the study I'd started. So I didn't rush things; I waited several years, from 1967 to 1972, before going to live in the Himalayas.

So now was the moment, and I took the decision. I told François Jacob and yourself that I wanted to leave for the Himalayas, rather than for America. I knew that it was what I really wanted to do, and that it was better to do it while I was still young than to look back when I reached fifty and wish that I'd taken that path.

J.F. – But didn't the two things seem compatible to you?

M. – There's no fundamental incompatibility between science and the spiritual life; it's simply that one had become much more important to me than the other. In practice, you can't stay sitting in between two chairs, or sew with a two-pointed needle. I didn't want to divide my time between two things any longer, I wanted to spend all of it doing what seemed the most essential. Later on, I became aware that my scientific training, especially its emphasis on rigor, was perfectly compatible with Buddhist practice and the Buddhist approach to metaphysics. What's more, the contemplative life, for me, is truly a science of the mind, with its methods and its results. It's a matter of really transforming yourself, not just dreaming or twiddling your thumbs. And over the next twenty-five years I never once found myself at loggerheads with the scientific spirit as I understand it – that is, as the search for truth.

J.F. – OK, I understand that you applied the same rigor that you had used before to your research into the history and philosophy of Buddhism, the texts, and so on. But research in molecular biology over the last thirty years has been the field of some of the most important discoveries ever in scientific history. You could have taken part, but you didn't.

M. – Biology seems to have been doing fine without me! There's no shortage of researchers in the world. The real question for me was to establish an order of priorities in my life. Increasingly, I had the feeling that I wasn't using the potential of human life as well as I could, but that day by day I was letting my life slip away. For me, the mass of scientific knowledge had become 'a major contribution to minor needs'.

J.F. – What you did next allowed you to go deeper into a doctrine that dates back to several centuries before Christ, but not to bring up new knowledge, as taking part in molecular biology would have done. I'm not saying, by the way, that to discover something new is absolutely the only criterion of a successful life. I'm saying that at the stage you'd reached, your thesis was at the same time a successful conclusion and a starting point for more important research. You had within your grasp everything you needed to take part in one of the most extraordinary intellectual and scientific adventures in the history of mankind, as recent discoveries in molecular biology can witness.

M. – Wait a minute. With Buddhism, it's not a matter of blowing off the dust from some ancient, old-fashioned doctrine of the past. The spiritual search, when it brings true inner transformation, is an experience that's fully alive, an unceasingly renewed freshness. A metaphysical system like Buddhism can never 'grow old', because it tackles the most fundamental questions of existence. Over the course of history, scientific theories have far more often undergone a process of natural aging, being constantly replaced by new ones.

J.F. – Yes, but they're replaced by new ones for good reason – because knowledge evolves, because new facts are found, because experience sorts out one hypothesis from another.

M. – It's true that biology and theoretical physics have brought us some fascinating knowledge about the origins of life and the formation of the universe. But does knowing such things help us elucidate the basic mechanisms of happiness and suffering? It's important not to lose sight of the goals that we set ourselves. To know the exact shape and dimensions of the Earth is undeniably progress. But whether it's round or flat doesn't make a great deal of difference to the meaning of existence. Whatever progress is made in medicine, we can only temporarily treat sufferings that never stop coming back, and culminate in death. We can end a conflict, or a war, but there will always be more, unless people's minds change. But, on the other hand, isn't there a way of discovering an inner peace that doesn't depend on health, power, success, money, or the pleasures of the senses, an inner peace that's the source of outer peace?

J.F. – That I can easily understand. But I still don't see why the two approaches should be incompatible. Biology and science, in this case molecular biology, bring solutions to disease, and therefore help to reduce human suffering. And the intellectual satisfaction of discovering the fundamental mechanisms of life is a very unselfish kind of satisfaction. Didn't it occur to you that you could combine these two sides of what interested you most?

M. – Buddhism isn't against science. It looks on it as an important but incomplete way of knowing things. So I didn't feel any need to dedicate the same efforts to science and share out my life between them. I felt a bit like a bird in a cage, and had only one idea – to be free.

J.F. – Do you still keep up with science?

M. – Yes, I continue to follow new discoveries in biology – and with even more interest than if I was spending my days trying to map out genes on a bacterial chromosome, which is what I spent five years doing in my research days. Seen overall, the combined results of thousands of researchers over the decades are certainly fascinating, but the life of a researcher very often consists of studying one detailed aspect of that research for years and years. The result is one piece of a puzzle that, once put together, yields a clear image of some physical or biological phenomenon. Ordinary researchers sometimes feel frustrated when immense efforts only produce minor results. Of course, it does sometimes happen that a researcher makes some major discovery, like the structure of DNA...

J.F. – The double helix...

M. – ... which is more than ample reward for his efforts. But that's exceptional, and I for one could never compare the interest of scientific research with that of spiritual research, which brings such satisfaction and joy in every instant – you feel like an arrow flying straight toward the target. Each instant is so precious, used in the best possible way.

J.F. – What did you do next?

M. – I didn't move from Darjeeling for seven years. I lived with my teacher, Kangyur Rinpoche, until his death in 1975, and then continued to practice in a small hut just above the monastery. It was at that time that I first met my second teacher, Dilgo Khyentse Rinpoche, who had come to conduct Kangyur Rinpoche's funeral rites. I also spent a year in Delhi reproducing and printing about fifty volumes of very rare Tibetan manuscripts. When my friends were about to begin the traditional three-year retreat in Dordogne, I asked Khyentse Rinpoche whether I should join them. He replied, 'As long as I'm still alive, stay and study with me.' That's how I came to spend twelve years at his side, listening to his teachings, serving him, accompanying him on his travels. I was ordained as a monk in 1979. Those years that I spent in his company were the best retreat and the best teaching that I could ever have received, unforgettable years during which I developed an inner certainty that nothing and no one can ever take away from me.

J.F. – You also lived in Bhutan, but did you ever get to know Tibet?

M. – Bhutan is a mountainous kingdom that has always escaped invasion, ever since the ninth century when Buddhism was introduced. Buddhist culture has been able to blossom there without any hindrance, and its values are deeply anchored in the minds of the inhabitants. After fleeing the Chinese occupation of Tibet, Khyentse Rinpoche became the Buddhist teacher most revered by all Bhutanese, from the king to the humblest farmer. So for me it was a great privilege to be able to live there. I was also lucky enough to travel to Tibet with Khyentse Rinpoche three times. All that was left of his monastery in Eastern Tibet was ruins, but for those who'd survived, often spending fifteen or twenty years in prison, Khyentse Rinpoche's return was like the sun suddenly rising after a long, dark night. In spite of the ongoing tragedy by which it's plagued, Tibet is still an extraordinary country, highly suited to the contemplative life.[3]

Now I'm going to turn the tables and ask you some questions instead. You've made me describe and explain my story, and no doubt you'll bring me back to it. But what about your own life? What was it that made you want to undertake these conversations?

J.F. – It's only natural to feel curious about a story like yours, because of the radical break you made with what seemed to have been mapped out for you by your early life, your studies, and your cultural identity. My story's been much more classic, even though within my own culture and compared to my initial education I, too, made a sort of permanent break with the mainstream currents of my generation and rebelled against the conventional thinking that surrounded me. But, I'll say it again, within the framework of my own culture.

M. – But what made you want to discuss things with the representative of another culture, which is what I've now become?

J.F. – First of all, it's another culture and also the same one, both at once. The philosophies of the Far East belong to a universal heritage, however much one might deplore the inadequate degree to which we study them outside a small circle of specialists. Now, if I think back about the motives I had at nineteen, when I began my university studies, for choosing philosophy and not literature or history – which were just as much to my taste – I think it was because philosophy looked likely to bring me the key to a knowledge spanning all others, not only literature and history, but even science. And a knowledge that at the same time was wisdom, in other words an art of living linked to a system of ethics.

M. – And Western philosophy didn't bring you that key?

J.F. – I wouldn't exactly say that. I'd say, rather, that it seemed to me to have deliberately betrayed its mission, especially from the beginning of the nineteenth century onward. Of course, I only came to that conclusion after several years of familiarizing myself directly with the original texts, keeping my distance from the dictates of all the conformist commentators, even those who claimed to be reinterpreters. My feelings by the end led me to write my first book, *Pourquoi des Philosophes?* (*Why Philosophers?*), which was published in 1957. I was myself surprised at the success it met with – or at any rate the stir it caused. The noises it elicited were by no means all of approval, indeed far from it – I was deafened by outraged squawks from the philosophy establishment. But the extent of the controversy was such that I felt obliged to take it further and reply to my critics in a book called *Cabale des dévots* (*The Cabal of Bigots*), which appeared in 1962 and is the sequel to *Pourquoi des Philosophes?*

M. – Yet later on you were best known as a political commentator. How do you explain such a metamorphosis?

J.F. – It wasn't a metamorphosis; reflecting on politics has always been a branch of philosophy. This isn't the place to tell my whole life story, and anyway I've just published my autobiography.[4] But, as I was saying, not only has political theory always been part of philosophy but, since the eighteenth and especially the nineteenth centuries, it's also become the main axis of moral philosophy. The guiding notion of the Enlightenment, and later of Marx and Lenin's 'scientific' socialism, was that henceforth the alliance of happiness and justice would no longer come about through the individual quest for wisdom but through the rebuilding of society as a whole. And before building a new society, the old one first had to be completely destroyed. It was at the end of the eighteenth century that the idea of revolution took on its modern meaning. Personal salvation was from then on subordinate to collective salvation. I imagine that we'll have more to say about this crucially important subject later on in the course of these conversations. For the moment, suffice it to say that somewhere between 1965 and 1970 I thought I'd seen the irremediable bankruptcy of this illusion, the progenitor of the great totalitarian movements that have ravaged the twentieth century. To say so, in 1970 I wrote my first work on politics in general (I'd published two or three political books before that, but they were focused particularly on France). Its title, *Without*

Marx or Jesus,[5] implied a double refusal: of both political and religious totalitarianism. The book caused a certain amount of surprise, because in it I maintained that the true revolution of the twentieth century would end up being the revolution of liberalism rather than that of socialism, which was already dead, that is to say, a free-market economy and a political democracy; private ownership as opposed to collective ownership; freedom of trade as opposed to a centrally planned economy; freedom of speech as opposed to state-sponsored censorship; a representative government as opposed to an omnipotent oligarchy.[6] It was successful worldwide, and stayed on the United States bestseller list for a whole year (because it defended the American 'open society' against socialist and fascist 'closed societies'). It was translated into fifteen or more languages. I even have a copy of the Malagasy version!

M. – Wasn't it the impact those books had that pushed you into the role of political author – and political commentator in the national press – and therefore took you away from philosophy as such?

J.F. – No, I never left philosophy behind. Like *Without Marx or Jesus*, most of my later books were based on some question anchored in human nature itself. The fact that in some cases I dealt with such a question in terms of contemporary examples, though never exclusively so, doesn't make the question any less perennial. For example, the central question behind *The Totalitarian Temptation*[7] is whether mankind harbors a secret wish to be politically and intellectually enslaved – a wish all the more perverse for being disguised as a search for freedom. Another example is *The Flight from Truth*,[8] which starts from the enigma that as a species, not only nowadays but throughout history, we seem to deliberately ignore information that is available to us and that would allow us to avoid at least some catastrophes. Why do we so often plunge ourselves, as if intentionally, into failure, suffering, and death? Unless I'm mistaken, these are philosophical problems. But I'm not going to subject you to a lecture on my complete works. Most of these books have been well read worldwide, though with considerable variation between countries and regions. The mystery is that to have a large number of readers doesn't mean that you're truly understood, nor that you'll manage to influence what actually happens. Even if you're lucky enough, as I am, not only to have your books published but also to have platforms in the national and international press from which to broadcast and reexpose your ideas to an even wider public.

M. – How do you explain that mystery?

J.F. – If it could be properly explained, we'd be able to cure the sickness of the spirit that it comes from. And that brings us back to what's called 'first philosophy', focused on the personal attainment of perspicacity and wisdom – the very subject, in fact, of our conversations.

1. Alizée Diffusion, Chemin du Devois, 30700 St. Siffret, France (for Europe), or Edith Charest, 02-3330 Dumas, Quebec Qc, G1L 4S5, Canada (for North America). English versions are available.

2. *Les Migrations Animales,* Laffont, Paris, 1968; translated into English as *Animal Migrations,* Hill and Wang, New York, and Constable, London, 1970.

3. See *Journey to Enlightenment, the Life and World of Khyentse Rinpoche,* photographs and narrative by Matthieu Ricard, Aperture, New York, 1996. The video, *The Spirit of Tibet,* is available through the National Film Board of Canada, 250 Fifth Ave., Suite 4820, New York, NY 10118, (212) 629-8890.

4. *Le Voleur dans la maison vide (Thief in an Empty House),* Plon, Paris, 1997.

5. Doubleday, New York, 1971.

6. 'Liberalism' means in Europe almost the opposite of what it means in America. Thinkers considered liberal in Europe are John Locke, Adam Smith, Alexis de Tocqueville, and John Stuart Mill.

7. Doubleday, New York, 1977.

8. Random House, New York, 1991 (French edition 1988).

~

TWO

RELIGION OR PHILOSOPHY?

JEAN-FRANÇOIS – I've asked you about your story in relation to your vocation in Western scientific research. What I'd like to know now is how you made your particular choice in relation to other religions and spiritual doctrines. You turned to Buddhism not because you'd been disappointed by one or other of the religions of the West – you came from a culture that was basically not religious at all. Although both your parents came from Catholic families, neither was a practicing Christian; and your education was secular and rationalist, in a scientific milieu which, overall, wasn't particularly religious. A lot of Westerners turn to religions other than their own, like Islam and Buddhism, because they're disappointed by the religion they were born into. But in your case, you moved to Buddhism from a state of indifference to any religion, a kind of religious weightlessness. But we should be careful. I was just using the word 'religious', and here we're getting to one of the big problems in interpreting Buddhism. Is Buddhism a religion or a philosophy? Even today, that's still a much-discussed subject. You've mentioned the first contact you had, with the teacher who made such an enormous impression on you without even speaking, as you had practically no common language. That first experience reminds me of a young Greek approaching a wise man and being struck above all by the teacher's personality as a role model, long before being taught anything conceptual. In view of that first experience of yours, are we talking about a conversion in the religious sense of the term, or about some sort of purely philosophical breakthrough?

MATTHIEU – First of all, to answer the first part of your question, I think I was very lucky to come to Buddhism with an unencumbered mind. That meant I could approach it without any inner conflict or guilt about rejecting another religion or belief. Although I was brought up in a free-thinking environment, I'd never had a negative attitude toward religion. All the reading I'd done had given me a deep interest in the great spiritual traditions – Hinduism, Islam, Christianity – without actually leading to any personal commitment to practice any of them. So what finally inspired me to make a real commitment to the spiritual path was certainly that encounter with a great spiritual master, Kangyur Rinpoche. The perfection he embodied was obvious, even if at the time I was still unaware of many of its sides. It's hard to describe such a meeting. A Tibetan would say, 'as difficult as for a mute to describe the taste of molasses.' What gave it all its value was that it was nothing to do with any abstract speculation; it was a direct experience, something I just knew and could see with my own eyes, and that was worth more than a thousand descriptions.

Subsequently, what was I able to gradually discover and understand about Buddhism? Is it a religion? Is it a form of wisdom, a system of metaphysics? That's a question the Dalai Lama is frequently asked. His usual reply is to joke, 'Poor Buddhism! Rejected by religions as an atheistic philosophy, a science of the mind; and by philosophers as a religion – there's nowhere that Buddhism has citizen's rights. But perhaps that's an advantage that could allow Buddhism to build bridges between religions and philosophies.' In essence, I'd say that Buddhism is a metaphysical tradition, from which a wisdom applicable in every instant and in all circumstances is derived.

If religion means adhering to a dogma that you're supposed to accept by an act of blind faith, without it being necessary to rediscover the truth of that dogma by yourself, then Buddhism isn't a religion. However, Buddhism certainly doesn't exclude faith, neither in the sense of an intimate and unshakable conviction born from the discovery of an inner truth, nor in the sense of a feeling of wonderment at that discovery. On the other hand, what leads many Christians and others to think of Buddhism as not being a religion in the usual sense is the fact that it's not a theistic tradition. Moreover, Buddhism isn't dogma; the Buddha always made it clear that his teachings should be examined and meditated on, but never simply accepted as true simply out of respect for him. The truth of the teachings has to be discovered by progressing through the successive stages of the path that leads to spiritual realization. We should examine the teachings, said the Buddha, in the same way we'd examine a piece of gold. To check that it's really pure gold we'd rub it on a flat stone, pound it with a hammer, or melt it over a fire. The Buddha's teachings are like travel guides that show the way to enlightenment, to ultimate knowledge of the nature of the mind and of the phenomenal world.

J.F. – But Buddhists do venerate the Buddha, nevertheless.

M. – Yes, but not because they see him as a God or a saint, and worship him, but rather because he's the ultimate teacher, embodying enlightenment. The Sanskrit word *Buddha* means 'the awakened one', he who has realized the truth. In Tibetan, the word by which it's translated, *Sang-gyé*, has two syllables, *sang* meaning that he has 'dissipated' everything negative that obscures wisdom and 'awoken' from the dark night of ignorance, and *gyé* that he has 'developed' everything positive, all the spiritual and human qualities that there are.

J.F. – When you talk about the Buddha's teaching, what do you mean? There are, it seems, no original texts by the Buddha that remain.

M. – Far from it – in fact, Buddhism has more canonical scriptures than any other religious tradition. The Buddha never wrote down what he taught, but his collected sermons fill one hundred and three volumes of the Tibetan canon, the Kangyur.

J.F. – But are they really his words?

M. – Shortly after his death, a council was held at which his five hundred closest disciples met to compile a complete collection of his teachings. The sermons of the Buddha, the *sutras*, were recited from memory by one or other eminent disciple, while the others listened and corrected the speaker when necessary. You have to remember that the oral tradition has always played a primary role in the transmission of knowledge in the East, and does so even today. Trained Easterners often have an astonishing memory. This isn't just fiction. On numerous occasions I've myself heard Tibetan teachers, and students too, reciting texts several hundred pages long from memory, stopping from time to time to comment on the meaning, with an accuracy that always amazed me as I followed the text in a book.

Each *sutra*, therefore, begins with the formula, 'In such-and-such a place and in such-and-such circumstances, I heard the Buddha speak as follows...' When you think that the Buddha taught without a break from the age of thirty until his death at eighty, and that he dealt with the same subjects over and over again just like Buddhist teachers today, it's not unreasonable to think that his close disciples, after passing thirty or forty years with him, retained an accurate version of his teachings in their memory, even if not absolutely word for word. Those of us who have spent twenty or so years with a Tibetan teacher are capable, without being endowed with any exceptional intellectual capacities, of expressing the essence of his teaching with reasonable accuracy.

As well as the collected words of the Buddha, there are two hundred and thirteen volumes of commentary and exegesis written by eminent Indian teachers and scholars over the centuries following the Buddha's death, and thousands of volumes of texts written later by Tibetan authors. Tibetan classical literature is therefore one of the richest in any Eastern language, outdone only by Sanskrit and Chinese.

J.F. – You mean the richest in terms of Buddhist writing?

M. – Not only. It's true that Tibetan literature is entirely devoted to the Buddhist teachings and to the traditional sciences linked to them – medicine, grammar, language, and astronomy. But that doesn't prevent it from being the third-ranking body of Eastern literature in terms of richness and volume. Until a few years ago, there were no such things as Tibetan 'novels'. Reality provided enough material without having fiction, too.

J.F. – Yes – but all the same, when you apply the criteria of proper historical research to the study of Buddhism, the Buddha's successors seem to have used plenty of imagination.[1] They built up a whole hagiography about his miraculous birth from his mother's right side, his being fully formed in the womb ten months before birth, and so on. As in all hagiographies, oriental imagination has embroidered the story so much here that it's hard to get back to the underlying historical facts of the Buddha's teaching. You'd reply, no doubt, that the same applies to Socrates, whose ideas we only know of indirectly. In his disciples' accounts, we can't be sure exactly what comes from Socrates himself, and what was added by Plato or Xenophon. But at least both of them were his contemporaries. We also have Aristophanes' portrayal, which is useful evidence, as he was hostile to Socrates. But in the Buddha's case, that sense of the fabulous so characteristic of the Indian imagination seems to make any rigorous definition of his authentic doctrine very difficult.

M. – First of all, the actual content of the Buddha's teaching was, in fact, properly established by his contemporaries, as I explained just now. The supernatural accounts you mention have nothing to do with the body of teachings; they are the hagiographies that were written about him later, over the centuries. The teachings themselves are on philosophical or metaphysical subjects – the nature of being, ignorance, the causes of suffering, the nonexistence of either the self or phenomena as autonomous entities, the law of causality, and so forth. Such subjects hardly lend themselves to lots of supernatural embellishment.

J.F. – So let's come back to the question, philosophy or religion? Or philosophy and religion? What strikes me is this. Buddhism, on the whole, has a very positive image in the West. It's true that right now people's feelings toward Buddhism are reinforced by the sympathy they feel toward the Tibetans, with all the sufferings they are going through, and also by the impact the Dalai Lama's personality has had worldwide and the affection – and even veneration – that he arouses everywhere, even in parts of the world unfamiliar with Buddhism. But quite apart from that recent political limelight, Buddhism has been treated with considerable respect in the West for a long time. It's always been seen as a rather unadulterated and straightforward doctrine that can therefore be accepted by a critical mind. It fits with Western rationalism, to which it adds a moral and spiritual dimension – a dimension of wisdom, or even more, not incompatible with criteria that have been evolving in the West with the modern scientific outlook since the Enlightenment and eighteenth-century rationalism. But when you come to Asia, that ethereal vision of Buddhism is put to the severest of tests. Someone like me is struck, or perhaps I should say shocked, by many aspects of the way Buddhism is practiced that I can only qualify as superstitious. Prayer flags, prayer wheels, belief in reincarnation ... like that three-year old we met the other day who's supposed to be a reincarnated lama.

M. – Yes, the whole idea of reincarnation, especially, is something we'll need to talk about to clarify. But first, let's go through your points in order. I think the main reason Buddhism has been seen in the West as so intellectually acceptable is that it tackles the basic concerns of any living being. The core teachings of Buddhism are not at all exotic, nor are they influenced by cultural factors of the sort that caused you such surprise. They simply analyze and dismantle the mechanisms of happiness and suffering. Where does suffering come from? What are its causes? How can it be remedied? Gradually, through investigation and contemplation, Buddhism gets down to the deep causes of suffering. It's a search that concerns any human being, Buddhist or not.

J.F. – Can you define what you call suffering?

M. – A state of deep dissatisfaction, which may be combined with physical pain but is first and foremost a mental experience. As everyone knows, different people can perceive the same things in completely opposite ways, either as pleasant or as unpleasant. Suffering arises when the self, the 'me' that we cherish and protect, is threatened, or doesn't get what it wants. The most intense physical sufferings can be experienced in very different ways according to our state of mind. Moreover, ordinary goals in life, like power, possessions, the pleasures of the senses and fame, can procure temporary satisfaction but are never permanently satisfying. One day or another, they're bound to turn into sources of unhappiness. They can never bring lasting fulfillment, or an inner peace untouched by outer circumstances. Pursuing such worldly goals all our lives, we have no more chance of attaining true happiness than a fisherman has of catching fish by throwing his nets into a dry riverbed.

J.F. – The Epicureans and the Stoics both said the same thing, in exactly the same terms.

M. – That state of dissatisfaction is characteristic of the conditioned world, which, by its very nature, can only bring ephemeral satisfactions. In Buddhist terms, you'd say that the world or 'circle' of rebirths, *samsara*, is pervaded by suffering. But this isn't at all a pessimistic way of looking at the world, it's simply an observation. The next step is to look for remedies to that suffering, and for that you need to know what causes it. At the initial level of investigation, Buddhism concludes that suffering is born from desire, attachment, hatred, pride, jealousy, lack of discernment, and all the states of mind that are designated as 'negative' or 'obscuring' because they stir the mind up and plunge it into a state of confusion and insecurity. These negative emotions, in turn, arise from the notion of a self, a 'me' that we cherish and want to protect at all costs. Attachment to the self is a fact, but the self that is the object of that attachment has no true existence; it exists nowhere and in no way as an autonomous and permanent entity. It exists neither in the different physical and mental parts that constitute an individual, nor somewhere outside them, nor in their combination. If you object that the self corresponds to the meeting of those parts, that amounts to conceding that it's just a simple label that the intellect imposes on the temporary meeting of various interdependent elements. In fact, the self doesn't exist in any of those elements, and when they separate the very notion of it disappears. Not to unmask the imposture of the self is ignorance, the momentary inability to recognize the true nature of things. It's that ignorance, therefore, that is the ultimate cause of suffering. Once we manage to get rid of our erroneous understanding of the self and our belief in the true and solid existence of phenomena, once we recognize that this 'I' doesn't really exist, there's no more reason to be afraid of not getting what we want or being subjected to what we don't want.

J.F. – That part of the analysis is common to Buddhism and to numerous Western philosophies – to the wisdom of classical times, let's say. In France, it crops up again in Montaigne and then in Pascal, along with an intended apology for Christianity.

M. – It could be because of that initial simplicity of basic Buddhism that the Western world feels an affinity for its teaching and can easily get into it straight away.

J.F. – I myself feel that what's attracted certain Western philosophers in Buddhism is the idea of being able to attain a kind of serenity. I don't want to use the word 'apathy', because of its negative sense. It's more a question of what some psychological schools called 'ataraxia', to use a rather pedantic word. Ataraxia is an imperturbable state that the wise man has to attain, according to Stoicism; it's to no longer be exposed to the unpredictable effects of the good and bad that come up in daily life.

M. – It's very important not to confuse serenity and apathy. One of the characteristics of a stable spiritual practice is not to be vulnerable to outer circumstances, whether favorable or unfavorable. The practitioner's mind is likened to a mountain that the winds can't shake; he's neither tormented by the difficulties he may come across nor elated by his successes. But that inner equanimity is neither apathy nor indifference. It's accompanied by inner jubilation, and by an openness of mind expressed as unfailing altruism.

J.F. – That's the element common to all traditions of wisdom. You could easily be describing the Stoic sage. Nowadays, in our scientific age, philosophers have abandoned the ideal of wisdom, in which the philosopher would provide his readers or listeners with recipes to help them attain such wisdom. So it's perhaps not surprising that Buddhism has acquired a certain authority in the West these days. But the attraction of Buddhism seems to go a bit beyond this treasure shared by all wisdoms, to a fusion of the self in some sort of undetermined state.

M. – It's not at all a matter of a fusion or extinction of the self in some amorphous, undetermined state, but of lucidly recognizing that the self has no true existence and that it's the source of all your problems. Here, Buddhism offers a very abundant range of methods by which to attain the inner peace that flows from letting go of that belief in a self. It doesn't stop at just describing all the states that arise in the mind, but shows how to transform them, to 'liberate' them. Before we talk about those methods, I'd like to say a little about the ego, the attachment to the self as the basic expression of ignorance and cause of negative emotions. Buddhism recommends a very detailed investigation of the notion of ego, of the way we perceive ourselves as a 'person' and phenomena outside ourselves as solid 'entities'. The very root of all negative emotions is the perception we have of ourselves as a person, as an 'I' that is an entity existing in itself, autonomously, either in the stream of our thoughts, or in our bodies. But if this self really exists, where is it? In our bodies? In our hearts? In our brains? Could it be spread out over the whole body? It's not difficult to see that the self doesn't exist anywhere in the body.

J.F. – I feel as if we're going back to the time when Western philosophers wondered where in the body the soul could be housed. Descartes traced its localization to the pineal gland. Isn't that rather a puerile question? Consciousness of a self exists, without it having to reside in this or that part of the body!

M. – That's why the next step is to ask yourself if the self is somewhere in your mind, in the stream of your consciousness. That stream can be divided into past, present, and future thoughts. The self can't be the totality of all those moments, because such a totality doesn't exist at any one particular moment. The past thought is dead, it no longer exists. How could the self belong to what's only a memory? The future hasn't yet come about, so the self can't be in a nonexistent future either. Only the present is left. Now, to exist, this entity we call 'me' must have some definite characteristics. But it has neither color, nor form, nor localization. The more you look for it, the less you can find anything. So finally the self seems to be no more than a label attached to an apparent continuity.

Such analysis makes it possible to weaken the belief we have in an all-powerful entity, the self, which is what makes us want whatever is desirable and abhor whatever isn't. The feeling of being an autonomous 'me' normally sets up a break between 'myself' and 'others'. That alternation of attraction and repulsion gives rise to myriads of thoughts and negative emotions, which are expressed as words and actions and build up our suffering. To discover as a direct experience, through analysis and especially through contemplation, that the self has no true existence is a highly liberating process. I think many Westerners have found investigation along these lines very useful, and all the more so in that it comes along with an incredible variety of techniques with which to work on one's thoughts, so that one need no longer be enslaved by them. But that we'll come back to later.

J.F. – It would be interesting to hear some details of those techniques.

M. – In theory, there are said to be eighty-four thousand approaches, or entrance doors, in Buddhism. The large number is to indicate that, in fact, anyone can start wherever they are. To climb Mount Everest, you could set out from the traffic jams of a Parisian suburb or from the lush greenery of a Nepalese valley. The goal is the same, but the ways you might travel are different. In the same way, on the spiritual path we all have to start at the point where we find ourselves, each with a different character, set of dispositions, intellectual and belief structure. Everyone can find the particular means tailored to their needs, allowing them to work on their thoughts, gradually set themselves free from the yoke of the negative emotions, and finally perceive the ultimate nature of the mind.

J.F. – That point of view, although the methods aren't necessarily always the same, is also one aspect of a certain tradition of Western philosophy. How to impose some discipline on one's own thoughts is one of the major themes of classical philosophy. But modern philosophy is much more focused on understanding how the mind functions than on changing it.

M. – Buddhism combines knowledge of how the mind works – there are whole treatises on the subject – with knowledge of its ultimate nature. Such knowledge has a liberating effect on the belief in a self. The range of techniques used to that end are both effective and varied. One initial approach consists of applying antidotes to the negative emotions. You try to develop patience to combat anger, non-attachment to combat desire, and to analyze the mechanisms of cause and effect to combat confusion, or lack of discernment. Giving free rein to the emotions, hatred for example, can only give rise to more hatred. History, whether of individuals or nations, clearly shows that hatred has never resolved conflicts.

J.F. – Well, that depends for whom – unfortunately, in the never-ending story of human war, violence, and crime, there have also been winners. As for eradicating hatred, that's something you find in the Gospels.

M. – Of course! It's not surprising from a spiritual point of view to find such parallels with Western traditions. But let's come back to hatred for a moment. Take the example of someone who, in a fit of anger, hits you with a stick. No one would even think of feeling angry with the stick, that's obvious. But are you going to get angry with the person attacking you? If you think about it, the person is being consumed by a blaze of anger, of which the source is ignorance. They've lost all control over themselves. In fact, the most appropriate reaction would be compassion, just as you might feel for a sick person or a slave. You can't really blame it all on them. In the last analysis, the true enemy, without any right to your pity, is anger itself.

J.F. – Yes, but you're rather forgetting the practical side of things. It might well be that before you've had time to get through that brilliant bit of reasoning, the person's knocked the very life out of you! So...

M. – Of course, the best thing would be to avoid the confrontation by neutralizing your aggressor, or by running away. None of this excludes the use of whatever means might be appropriate, and any necessary force; but *never* with hatred. Deep within ourselves, it's important to maintain invincible compassion and inexhaustible patience. It's not a matter of either passively submitting to the mercy of anyone who attacks us, or trying to eliminate them by force (there'll always be more to come), but of discovering that our major adversary is the desire to harm others – something we'll need to combat mercilessly. That's what we have to understand and, as much as we can, get others to see, too.

J.F. – Wait a minute – you'll soon be taking me through the entire Buddhist teaching. But you haven't yet answered my objection about superstitions.

M. – We're coming to that, but first let me finish this overall picture. The use of antidotes is an effective method, but it has its limits. There are an infinite number of negative emotions, so to thwart them all would need an infinite number of antidotes. A second approach therefore consists of trying to grasp the nature of thoughts and trace them to their very source. A feeling of hatred, for example, can seem extremely solid and powerful, and can create a sort of knot somewhere in our chests and completely change the way we behave. But if we look at it, we see that it's not brandishing any weapon, it can't crush us like a boulder could, or burn us like fire. In reality, the whole thing began with a tiny thought, which has gradually grown and swollen up like a storm cloud. From far away, summer clouds can look very impressive and solid. You really feel you could sit on them. But when you get inside them, there's hardly anything there. They turn out to be completely intangible. In the same way, when we look at a thought and trace it back to its source, we can't find anything substantial. At that very moment, the thought evaporates. This is called 'liberating thoughts by looking at their nature,' meaning to recognize their 'emptiness'. Once we've liberated a thought, it won't set off a chain reaction. Instead, it'll dissolve without a trace, like a bird flying through the sky.

J.F. – That's an optimistic view of things, which belongs to a universal tradition of reassuring wisdom.

M. – Don't make any mistake about it – simple though it might seem at first glance, the liberation of thoughts is neither an optimistic view of things nor a collection of recipes without any basis or outcome. The techniques it uses are derived from a 'contemplative science' thousands of years old, built up at the cost of considerable effort by hermits practicing for many hours a day over twenty or thirty years of their lives. It's inevitable that, without taking some first steps in the context of their own experience to see what it's all about, some people will feel doubtful about any knowledge obtained using such unfamiliar methods. Every science has its own instruments. Without a telescope, you can't see the craters on the moon. Without contemplative practice, you can't see the nature of mind.

J.F. – Let's go back, then, to the inconsistencies I can't help seeing between Buddhism's purely philosophical aspects and the superstitious beliefs associated with it in practice, here in Asia. The day before yesterday, for example, we saw a three-year-old child being presented in your monastery in Kathmandu who's recently been recognized as the reincarnation of your late teacher, Khyentse Rinpoche. What was the process by which it was decided that the Rinpoche has reincarnated in that child?

M. – Continuing consciousness after death is, in most religions, a matter of revealed truth. In the case of Buddhism, the evidence comes from the contemplative experience of people who are certainly not ordinary but who are sufficiently numerous that what they say about it is worth taking seriously into account. Indeed, such testimonies begin with those of the Buddha himself. First of all, it's important to understand that what's called reincarnation in Buddhism has nothing to do with the transmigration of some 'entity' or other. It's not a process of metempsychosis because there is no 'soul'. As long as one thinks in terms of entities rather than function and continuity, it's impossible to understand the Buddhist concept of rebirth. As it's said, 'There is no thread passing through the beads of the necklace of rebirths.' Over successive rebirths, what is maintained is not the identity of a 'person', but the conditioning of a stream of consciousness.

J.F. – But doesn't metempsychosis exist in Buddhism? I thought the migration of souls was one of its most basic doctrines.

M. – Buddhism speaks of successive states of existence; in other words, everything isn't limited to just one lifetime. We've experienced other states of existence before our birth in this lifetime, and we'll experience others after death. This, of course, leads to a fundamental question: is there a nonmaterial consciousness distinct from the body? It would be impossible to talk about reincarnation without first examining the relationship between body and mind. Moreover, since Buddhism denies the existence of any individual self that could be seen as a separate entity capable of transmigrating from one existence to another by passing from one body to another, one might well wonder what it could be that links those successive states of existence together.

J.F. – That's pretty hard to understand.

M. – In fact, it's seen as a continuum, a stream of consciousness that continues to flow without there being any fixed or autonomous entity running through it.

J.F. – A series of reincarnations without any definite entity that reincarnates? More and more mysterious.

M. – It could be likened to a river without a boat descending along its course, or to a lamp flame that lights a second lamp, which in turn lights a third lamp, and so on; the flame at the end of the process is neither the same flame as at the outset, nor a completely different one.

J.F. – Those are just metaphors.

M. – We'd have to begin by studying the different ideas, ancient and modern, about the relationship between mind and body.

J.F. – Yes, that's certainly going to be one of our major subjects for discussion. But I'm still wondering about some other aspects. Prayer flags, for example. In the purest and most straightforward religions, or let's say those that keep the furthest away from any superstition, prayer is something very personal. The idea that some mechanical object that you cause to turn, like a prayer wheel, or a flag that gradually frays in the wind, could take the place of actually praying, looks to me like prayer at its most miserable, its very lowest point. I can't understand how a doctrine as subtle as Buddhism could encourage such beliefs!

M. – In fact, such customs are far from superstitious. They simply reflect the richness of the means employed by Buddhism to keep on reviving our presence of mind. All four of the natural elements are used as reminders – the wind to flutter prayer flags, the fire of a lamp flame from which the rising hot air turns prayer wheels, the rocks on which mantras are carved, and the water of a stream to turn the paddles of a water-driven prayer wheel – so that everything we do, every element of nature, whatever happens to be within our sight, can incite us to inner prayer, to altruistic thoughts. When a Tibetan prints those prayers and hangs them up to flutter in the wind, he thinks,

'Wherever the wind passing over these prayers may go, may all living beings there be freed from their suffering and the causes of suffering. May they experience happiness and the causes of happiness.' He renews his Bodhisattva vows...

J.F. – Bodhisattva?

M. – A Bodhisattva is someone who's set out on the path toward perfection, toward the state of Buddhahood, in order to be able to benefit others. The vow that Bodhisattvas have taken isn't centered on themselves. They don't think, 'May I be freed from suffering, from all the worries of ordinary life, and from the vicious circle of samsara.' Their vow is altruistic, born from their contemplation of the suffering that all living beings are going through. 'For the moment I'm powerless to relieve the many sufferings of living beings; may I attain the wisdom that will allow me to help them all free themselves from the causes of suffering.' You use the support of things outside yourself so that everything you see, everything you hear, brings back to mind this altruistic attitude and provides material for reflection. Nature itself thus becomes a book of teachings. Everything incites us to spiritual practice. It's also a very human way of not forgetting the Buddha's teachings.

J.F. – Are you sure that, for average Buddhists, that idea means anything? Don't they just think that the prayer wheel's doing the praying on their behalf?

M. – Perhaps not all Tibetans know the doctrine and its symbolism in detail, but I don't think they turn prayer wheels in the hope of achieving their ordinary wishes for prosperity or success. They have in mind the notion of accumulating merit. 'Merit' is a positive state arising for a while in the mind that helps to counteract negative states of mind. I think that the predominant idea for them is therefore that of purifying the stream of their consciousness by an 'accumulation of merit', to reinforce the positive stream that flows toward wisdom. That's why people do prostrations, walk respectfully around sacred monuments, and make offerings of light in the temples.

J.F. – In Catholicism, to light a candle in a church implies the very superstitious idea that the candle can earn us the grace either of a saint, of the Holy Virgin, or even of God himself, and grant our wishes. It's superstitious to the point that you often see people who are neither practicing Catholics nor even believers offering a candle when they visit a cathedral.

M. – Such customs are useful outer supports allowing believers to communicate with an inner truth. I know from experience that when ordinary Tibetans offer thousands of butter lamps (the equivalent of candles) they're well aware that the light they're offering symbolizes wisdom dispelling darkness. The prayer they'd be making as they offered lamps would go something like, 'May the light of wisdom arise in myself and all living beings, both in this life and in lives to come.' Even very simple people are aware of the symbolism. The same goes when they're reciting mantras.

J.F. – What exactly is meant by a mantra?

M. – Etymologically, 'mantra' means 'what protects the mind' – not from some calamity or other but from getting distracted and from mental confusion. A mantra is a short formula that's repeated numerous times, like the Prayer of the Heart in Orthodox Christianity, which is accompanied by constant repetition of the name of Jesus. Such techniques of repetition are found in all religious traditions.

J.F. – Yes, but they're hardly their spiritually most elevated aspect, are they!

M. – Why not? Reciting helps to calm the superficial movements of the mind and thus to see its underlying nature more clearly.

J.F. – I suppose it might. But let's get back to the question of reincarnation. You used the metaphor of a river without a boat. What I find hard to take in this whole idea is, on the one hand, this notion of an impersonal river, flowing from one individual to another – regardless, by the way, of whether those individuals are human beings or animals…

M. – Or yet other forms of life…

J.F. – Or other forms of life – and on the other hand the fact that the goal of Buddhist practice is to dissolve the self in *nirvana*, meaning, if I've understood it right, a complete depersonalization of any remaining spiritual element. Under such conditions, how could it possibly be announced that some particular individual – meaning someone with a high degree of personal specificity – has reincarnated in some other particular individual? Given that there are more than six thousand million human beings on earth, plus I don't know how many tens of billions of animals, etc., there must be that many rivers in circulation. And to pick out the concrete, individualized temporary form into which one or other particular river has flown after the death of the preceding incarnation seems to me a totally impossible undertaking.

Except, in fact, by resorting to methods of identification that are magical or subjective, of a supernatural order, which to me aren't terribly convincing.

M. – First of all, we can and do talk about an 'individual' consciousness, even if the individual doesn't exist as an isolated entity. The fact that there's no such discontinuous entity being transferred from one life to the next doesn't mean that there can't be a continuity of functioning. That the self has no true existence doesn't prevent one particular stream of consciousness from having qualities that distinguish it from another stream. The fact that there's no boat floating down the river doesn't prevent the water from being full of mud, polluted by a paper factory, or clean and clear. The state of the river at any given moment is the result of its history. In the same way, an individual stream of consciousness is loaded with all the traces left on it by positive and negative thoughts, as well as by actions and words arising from those thoughts. What we're trying to do by spiritual practice is to gradually purify the river. The ultimate state of complete clarity is what we call spiritual realization. All the negative emotions, all the obscurations that render the underlying wisdom invisible, have then been dissolved. It's not a question of annihilating the self, which has never really existed, but simply of uncovering its imposture. Indeed, if the self did have any intrinsic existence we'd never be able to bring it from existence into nonexistence.

J.F. – So you want to abolish something that, from the start, doesn't exist.

M. – A nonexistent self can't really be 'abolished', but its nonexistence can be recognized. What we want to abolish is the illusion, the mistake that has no inherent existence in the first place. The following analogy is often given. If, in dim light, you saw a piece of mottled rope and took it for a snake, you'd feel afraid and perhaps try to escape or drive the snake away with a stick. But if someone then switched a light on, you'd see immediately that it wasn't a snake at all. In fact, nothing has happened; you haven't 'destroyed' the snake, as it never existed in the first place. You've simply got rid of an illusion. As long as we perceive the self as a real entity, we'll tend to try and draw to us whatever we judge to be agreeable or beneficial, and to push away from us whatever we judge to be disagreeable or harmful. But as soon as we recognize that the self has no true existence, all these attracting and repelling impulses will vanish, just like the fear of that piece of rope mistaken for a snake. The self has neither beginning nor end, and therefore in the present it has no more existence than the mind attributes to it. So *nirvana* isn't the extinction of anything, but the final knowledge of the nature of things.

J.F. – If that's how it is, how and why does this illusion of a self build up?

M. – There's a natural feeling of self, of 'I', which makes you think 'I'm cold, I'm hungry, I'm walking', and so forth. By itself, that feeling is neutral. It doesn't specifically lead to either happiness or suffering. But then comes the idea that the self is a kind of constant that lasts all your life, regardless of all the physical and mental changes you go through. You get attached to the idea of being a self, 'myself', a 'person', and of 'my' body, 'my' name, 'my' mind, and so on. Buddhism accepts that there is a continuum of consciousness, but denies any existence of a solid, permanent, and autonomous self anywhere in that continuum. The essence of Buddhist practice is therefore to get rid of that illusion of a self which so falsifies our view of the world.

J.F. – But let me come back to my question. How can particular streams of consciousness be identified?

M. – Still with the analogy of the river, it's conceivable that a river could be recognized a hundred kilometers downstream from an initial sampling point by analyzing the pattern of the sediment of mineral and vegetable matter carried in it. In the same way, someone who has the ability to perceive beings' streams of consciousness directly could conceivably recognize the characteristics of a particular stream of consciousness. The question is, therefore, can the faculty of apprehending these streams of consciousness be developed or not?

J.F. – I must say that at the moment you're thickening the mystery for me more than explaining it.

M. – The problem here is one of methodology. From a scientific point of view, an experiment is said to be valid if it can be reproduced by other experimenters. It's presumed that the same means of investigation are available to all concerned. In sport, everyone agrees that athletes can develop exceptional capacities after intensive training. If you said to someone who'd never heard of the Olympic Games that a human being can jump a height of two meters forty, he'd say straight away that you were just joking. Nowadays, everyone, even the most ignorant person – including all those who, like me, can only jump one meter ten – can see, on television or in the flesh, a champion athlete capable of jumping two meters forty. It's acknowledged as being possible thanks to assiduous physical training. But when it's a question of training the mind, it's much more difficult to recognize any results and to acknowledge that it might be possible to attain a degree of mastery over the mind just as exceptional as the physical mastery of an athlete.

J.F. – Yes. But everyone can verify that an athlete can jump two meters forty or run a hundred meters in less than ten seconds.

M. – Why? Because they can see it happening.

J.F. – Yes.

M. – But if it wasn't visible to everyone, people could only verify it by themselves going into training, and jumping first one meter ten, then one meter eighty, and finally, if they're very exceptional, two meters forty.

J.F. – If it wasn't something visible, it would be the same as taking the athlete at his word.

M. – In the scientific world, we're constantly led to believe in the truth of lots of new discoveries, mathematical calculations or whatever, just on the experimenter's word, without having the slightest direct experience of them. We accept their validity because we know that a certain number of respected scientists have independently verified the procedures and obtained the same results, and that other scientists could reproduce those findings if they took the trouble to do so. To arrive at such conclusions by oneself, all alone, would necessitate a very long apprenticeship.

A statement can be accepted as valid when there are substantial reasons for believing the person making it. In certain cases, someone can be taken at their word without that being an act of blindness, because their integrity can be examined. If you really want to be sure of what we've been talking about here, the only way would be to commit yourself to the path of inner transformation. Besides personal experience, what other means are available to evaluate knowledge of the subtle aspects of consciousness? Consciousness has, by nature, no form, no substance, no color, and is not quantifiable. Not to rely on personal experience would be equivalent to denying *a priori* any possibility of training the mind to engender qualities beyond the average, and to limiting the domain of knowledge to the visible and measurable material world. That would also mean that, to exist, a phenomenon must necessarily be within everyone's reach, at any time, in any place, and exclusively in the material domain.

J.F. – There are two sides to your reasoning here. Going back to the comparison with the high jump, there's first the fact that if we couldn't see the athlete jump two meters forty, we wouldn't believe it to be possible. And secondly, the fact of believing that once the athlete was dead, his ability to jump two meters forty would be rediscovered in a new-born baby, identified by specific methods…

M. – *(Laughing)* No, of course that's not what I meant! The analogy of the high jumper is only to show that athletes' exceptional abilities are accepted because *everyone* can see them with their own eyes.

J.F. – But in the domain of the mind, that's also always been accepted. It's always been accepted that by hard work, training, and exercise it's possible to develop intellectual faculties or an intellectual mastery well above the average. That's something less acknowledged in modern teaching, which sees itself as being egalitarian – at the cost of considerable hypocrisy, incidentally, as we know very well that the facts are otherwise. We know very well that there are people who are exceptionally gifted intellectually. We also know very well that those exceptional gifts will yield nothing unless cultivated by intensive training and daily practice. And we know just as well that those gifts aren't something that can be transmitted from one individual to another, even by teaching.

M. – I'd apply the same reasoning, but in terms of contemplative science, not just of IQ. I want to come to the difficulty of judging from outside the testimony of those who've developed highly unusual spiritual qualities over a lifetime. To be able to appreciate those qualities directly, one would need to have developed them oneself, which requires a whole lifetime of work on the mind, at once analytic and contemplative. What's more, differences in physical capacity, as in the high jump analogy, are quantitative, whereas differences in spiritual capabilities are qualitative. For the last two centuries, the West has taken very little interest in contemplative science. I was struck by something in the writings of William James, one of the founders of modern psychology. He said (I'm quoting from memory), 'I tried to stop my thoughts for several moments. It's clearly impossible. They recur immediately.' Such an observation would amuse hundreds of

Tibetan hermits who, after spending years gaining mastery over their minds, are able to stay for a long time in a state of awareness free from any mental associations.

J.F. – William James is the American author who coined the term 'stream of consciousness'. And in fact, when you tell me that Buddhist hermits manage to stop the flow of their thoughts, who can prove it? Do we just take them at their word, too?

M. – Why not? It's not such an extraordinary skill. People don't need much talent to have that experience over some years of practice. You just need to take the trouble to try. It's not a matter of blocking thoughts, but simply of remaining in a clear state of awareness, in which discursive thoughts naturally calm down.

J.F. – What does calming down mean in this context?

M. – That the wheel of discursive thoughts stops turning – that the process of one thought leading to another in an endless chain is stopped.

J.F. – So there's nevertheless some thought, some representation left.

M. – There's an awareness, a clear state of consciousness, usually free of representations. It's no longer a linear pattern of thought, but direct knowledge. Here's how such a training is described. When you begin to try to master your thoughts, you find it very difficult. Your thoughts are like a waterfall tumbling down a cliff. It even seems that your thoughts are more numerous than usual – which doesn't mean there are really more of them, but just that you're beginning to be aware of how many there are. The next stage is like the flow of a river in a course which sometimes brings rapids, sometimes more tranquil stretches. This corresponds to a state in which the mind remains calm, unless it's stimulated by the perception of external events. Finally, the mind becomes like the sea in calm weather. Ripples of discursive thoughts occasionally run over its surface, but in the depths it is never disturbed. In this way you can reach a state of consciousness called 'clear consciousness' in which the mind is perfectly lucid, without constantly being caught up in discursive thoughts.

J.F. – William James wouldn't have disagreed. I think all psychologists and all philosophers have always acknowledged that there was a difference between the state of controlled, directed thought, concentrated on a specific object, and undisciplined thought, undirected associations of ideas, which are what a psychoanalyst specifically tries to elicit from his patient. But it's not a question of completely interrupting consciousness.

M. – No, that's right – it's not a question of consciousness being stopped, but of a temporary cessation of discursive thoughts, of associations of ideas.

J.F. – What are they replaced by?

M. – By a state of sheer consciousness.

J.F. – Yes, but does that consciousness have an object?

M. – No, it's a state of pure awareness without any object. Normally, that pure awareness is combined with the perception of an object, which is why we don't recognize it. It's very close to us, but we can't see it. We're only aware of consciousness inasmuch as it's qualified by an object. However, it's possible to experience that pure awareness directly by letting concepts, memories, and expectations dissolve as they form, in the empty clarity of the mind. To begin with, to calm and slow down the mind, you train it in what's called 'one-pointed concentration', focusing on an external object, an image of the Buddha for example, or an internal object, an idea like compassion or a visualized image. But you then reach a state of equanimity, transparent, clear, and aware all at the same time, in which the dichotomy of subject and object no longer exists. When, from time to time, a thought arises within that awareness, it unties itself without leaving any trace, just as a bird leaves no trace as it flies across the sky. But it's not enough just to try to stop the flow of thoughts for a few minutes, like William James. It requires personal training that may last for years.

Of the numerous lamas who dedicated their lives to contemplation, like my teacher Khyentse Rinpoche who spent seventeen years in retreat in caves and hermitages in the mountains, some attained exceptional mastery over their minds. How can we be sure of their accounts? By means of indirect evidence, and evaluating all sides of their character. There's no smoke without fire. I spent twenty years with some of these teachers who say that there is a nonmaterial consciousness and that it is possible to perceive another being's stream of consciousness. These are people I never heard lying, who never misled anyone, in whom I never detected the slightest harmful thought, word, or deed against anyone. To believe what they say therefore seems more reasonable to me than to come to the conclusion that they're telling tall stories. In the same way, the Buddha says that death is just one stage in life and that consciousness continues afterward. We don't have the power to see that consciousness ourselves, but given that all the Buddha's verifiable statements and teaching seem true and reasonable, it's much more likely that he's telling the truth than otherwise. The Buddha's goal was to enlighten beings, not to mislead them; to help them find the way out of their torments, not to plunge them into more.

J.F. – Despite what you say, it's a matter of confidence more than of proof.

M. – According to Buddhism, three criteria allow a statement to be considered valid: verification by direct experience, irrefutable deduction, and testimony worthy of confidence. Here, therefore, we're talking about the third category. But let's come back to those Tibetan teachers who can recognize the stream of consciousness of a lama like Khyentse Rinpoche after his death. That recognition, which is the fruit of meditation experiences, allows them to identify the person in whom the lama's stream of consciousness is now continuing. It's just as if it were possible to say – were there such a thing in Christianity – that the spiritual influence of Saint Francis of Assisi was continuing in this or that particular child.

J.F. – Yes, but I know some priests, and lay people, too, who have all the moral qualities you've just described and who believe in miracles at Lourdes or apparitions of Our Lady of Fatima in Portugal – phenomena that I myself consider fantasies, pure and simple. Someone can very well be perfectly sincere and have never tried to deceive anyone, and still be subject to illusions.

M. – In the case we're talking about, the events aren't miraculous, but inner experiences that many lamas have had over the centuries. It's different.

J.F. – Oh no, not at all. For someone who claims to have witnessed a miracle at Lourdes, it's not a matter of interpretation. He's quite sure he was in the presence of a fact. And he may also very well have the greatest sincerity, the greatest moral qualities, and not the slightest wish to deceive.

M. – Let's get back to the specific case of Khyentse Rinpoche. One of his close disciples and friends, a lama who lives up in the mountains two hundred kilometers from Kathmandu, sent us a letter saying that during dreams and visions that had arisen clearly in his mind he'd learnt the names of the father and mother of Khyentse Rinpoche's incarnation, his age, and the place we should look for him.

J.F. – And can you prove that he couldn't have known the names of the child's parents, and that he was nevertheless able to supply them with complete accuracy?

M. – He had no reason to know the personal names of either the father or the mother. In fact, the boy's father is himself a lama, who's only ever referred to by his title. In Tibetan society, no one would ever address him or his wife by their family names. As for the accuracy of the names, I was present when the letter was given to the abbot of our monastery and took part in the first reading. Finally, it's important to understand that the lama in question was looking for the reincarnation of his own teacher, the person he respected more than anyone else in the world. The goal was not to find some successor or other to occupy the monastery throne, nor to impress anyone with his mystical powers, but to identify the spiritual continuation of a great lama in the hope that he'll acquire all the qualities that will allow him to help people in the same way as his predecessor.

J.F. – Well at this point, to conclude this conversation on the question of whether Buddhism is a religion or a philosophy, I'd say that it's a bit of both. There's no doubt that there's an element of faith. Even if one subscribes to the explanations you've just given – and I for one am not convinced – it still wouldn't mean that there isn't an element of faith, of trust in certain individuals and what they say, which you'll surely admit is not of the same order as rational proof.

M. – I admit that, but it's not a matter of blind faith. I find dogmatic statements much more difficult to accept than evidence based on spiritual experience and realization.

J.F. – Oh yes, certainly.

M. – In fact, in everyday life we're continually being impregnated with ideas and beliefs that we take as true because we accept the competence of those who provide the information. They know what they're doing, it works, so it must be true. That's where confidence comes in. But most of us would be quite incapable of proving scientific truths by ourselves. Quite often, too, such beliefs – like that of the atom seen as tiny solid particles orbiting an atomic nucleus – continue to influence people's view of things long after they've been abandoned by the scientists themselves. We're ready to believe anything we're told as long as it corresponds to an accepted view of the world, and to be suspicious of anything that doesn't. In the case of the contemplative approach, the doubt that many of our contemporaries feel about spiritual values is due to the fact that they haven't put them into practice. Lots of things are seen as supernatural, until eventually we discover how they happen, or until the time comes for someone to have that experience themselves. As Cicero said, 'What cannot happen will never happen, and what can happen is not a miracle.'

J.F. – Nevertheless, I still think that in the events you've been talking about there's an element of irrational faith.

M. – It would be more accurate to call it an element of trust, which is itself based on a whole range of observable factors. One of the greatest lessons I've been able to distill from spending so many years with these lamas is that they live completely according to what they teach. You mentioned the mystical experience of certain priests. There have without doubt been some very great sages in Christianity, like St. Francis of Assisi. But I don't think that every priest, every monk, even practicing with great sincerity and integrity, attains spiritual perfection. In Tibet, twenty percent of the population were ordained monks and nuns, and of all those full-time practicing Buddhists, only about thirty people are said to have attained spiritual perfection during the present century. Only after evaluating their whole way of being, therefore, do I conclude that these teachers know what they're talking about when they supply the indications allowing a spiritual successor to be identified. Why would they want to fool anyone? Most of them live as hermits, and have no particular wish either to convince anyone of anything, or to promote themselves. What's more, just to show the point to which Buddhism condemns any imposture, I'd add that one of the four major breaches of the monastic rule is to pretend to have any high spiritual attainment at all. It happens that the lama who recognized Khyentse Rinpoche in the young child is one of the most exemplary holders of the monastic lineage. He's ordained thousands of monks, and would never allow himself to confer such ordination if he himself had broken his vows. So it seems only reasonable to suppose that it was in full knowledge of the facts and in complete sincerity that he spoke out about his visions in order to rediscover his own teacher.

J.F. – I'm casting absolutely no doubt on his sincerity. What I'm trying to shed light on is the phenomenon of self-conviction. It's a well-known phenomenon and one that exists in other domains, too. Lots of people convinced themselves of the validity of communism or Nazism, often without having anything to gain thereby. Purely and simply in terms of the capacity for self-conviction (I'm not at all comparing Buddhism with the great totalitarian systems, it's exactly the opposite) – if those great totalitarian systems had only been defended by fools and scoundrels, they wouldn't have lasted five minutes! The tragedy is that people of great intelligence, great scientists like Frédéric Joliot-Curie or even Albert Einstein, after the Second World War, became communists or communism's fellow travelers. Other people who devoted themselves to it sacrificed their lives or renounced their fortune, family, and friends for its sake. So the absolute sincerity of the person who believes in something has never constituted real proof. It doesn't change anything for this side of Buddhism which, for me, representing a Western rationalist tradition, is still of the order of an unverifiable religious belief rather than of the order of philosophy or rational wisdom.

M. – I think that in our next conversation, when we talk about the relationship between body and mind, there'll be a certain number of points that'll add to my argument.

J.F. – I could wish for nothing more.

1. See H.W. Schuman, *The Historical Buddha*, Arkana (Penguin), London, 1989. In *Old Path, White Clouds* (Parallax Press, Berkeley, 1991), Thich Nhat Hanh tells the story of the Buddha's life in a poetic and inspiring way pruned of its supernatural aspects.

~

THREE

The Ghost in
the Black Box

JEAN-FRANÇOIS – Looking at Buddhist psychology in relation to Western psychology, especially as developed since the nineteenth century,
leads us to examine the mind-body relationship. It's a classic problem. Is man a hybrid, Descartes' famous 'composite human'? In other
words, are we made up of a mind housed inside a body? Or is a psyche
separate from its material envelope in fact just an illusion, as all materialist philosophies and much of modern neurophysiology would
claim?

MATTHIEU – From the twenties until the sixties, psychology was
largely dominated by the idea that to study the workings of the mind it
was necessary to observe outward behavior, certainly not to look at the
mind itself. The mind, it was said, can't know itself in any objective
way. This, of course, excludes any contemplative approach. Study was
confined to outward manifestations of mental events, a position which
automatically leaves out all mental events that aren't translated into
behavior. Most experiments were, moreover, carried out in animals.
That approach has gradually been replaced by the cognitive sciences
(neuroscience, cognitive psychology, linguistics, artificial intelligence,

and so on) which accord much more importance to mental states, in terms either of cognitive activity that processes information from the outer world (perception, communication, movement), or of autonomous cognitive activity (dream, memory, mental imagery, language development, and so on). But even nowadays, introspection – the mind looking at itself – is still not accepted as a valid method of investigation, because for the moment we can't convert the results of introspection into physically detectable phenomena.

Moreover, most neurobiologists have come round to thinking that we can completely dispense with the 'ghost in the black box', the very notion of consciousness or mind as an element distinct from the nervous system. Their view is that the structure and function of the network of neurons, along with the chemical reactions and electrical phenomena produced within it, are enough to explain what we call thought. For them, the very idea of a mind, let alone that of a nonmaterial consciousness, has therefore become obsolete. The model they put forward is one of complex networks of neurons distributed over different regions of the brain, which determine the conscious and unconscious activity of the brain as a whole. We can call such attitudes 'reductionist,' because they reduce consciousness to chemical reactions and biological structures.

J.F. – In fact, the debate in the West goes back further than that. By the end of the nineteenth century, the schools of experimental psychology that were the precursors of behaviorism already held sway, some of them also practicing what was called at the time 'psychophysics'. They held that consciousness was no more than an epiphenomenon, a sort of gleam that was additional to the neurocerebral system. According to this view of things, a human being was indeed a set of physicochemical and biological reactions. Consciousness was a reflection of these processes, but couldn't actually influence them in any way. It was in reaction against this school of thought, which dominated the psychology of his time, that the distinguished philosopher Henri Bergson wrote and taught. Throughout his works, notably in his first book, his thesis, *Time and Free Will* in 1889, and later in 1900 in his bigger and more substantial work on this problem, *Matter and Memory*, Bergson aims to show that it's not true that consciousness is only the reflection of a set of neurophysiological processes. It has a reality which just can't be reduced to such mechanisms.

The same quarrel already existed in the eighteenth century. Some writers, like La Mettrie, author of a book called *Man the Machine*, developed the idea that man is just a set of mechanisms. Other eighteenth-century materialists, like Helvétius in his book *De l'Esprit (On the Mind)*, d'Holbach and Diderot, all tried to prove the same idea. So it's quite an old quarrel which, in the West, followed on from Descartes' view that the human body, the biological sphere, doesn't exist as such. It's all 'extended substance,' subject to the determinism of the external world, while the soul is something entirely distinct from the body, though nonetheless capable of acting on it. Descartes even went as far as tracing the location of the soul to a gland in the brain, the pineal gland. This was an idea that all the great post-Cartesians, Spinoza, Malebranche, and Leibniz, made fun of. They acknowledged that the soul was distinct from the body, but not that it could act on matter. And all of them invented highly subtle and complex theories, each more improbable than the last, to explain the spontaneity of will. If I decide to stretch out my arm, and manage to do so, it's not at all because my soul acts on my body, but because two parallel determinisms are operating – such, more or less, was Malebranche's thesis. And they all tried to find a solution that might explain the apparent simultaneity of our will and our actions. I've very briefly mentioned these writers as a reminder that the problem is by no means a new one. Then, as you said, the evolution of modern science and of neurophysiology has resulted in a much more detailed view of man as consisting of a set of neurophysiological mechanisms. The psyche is seen as comprising nothing more than those mechanisms themselves, or at the very most a sort of reflection, an epiphenomenon, which is additional to them but cannot influence them.

M. – Do you feel that the body-mind question has been resolved in that way?

J.F. – The developments of contemporary science have tended to confirm monist theories, and refute the idea that there could be two principles, mental and physical, that come together in man – and in mankind alone out of the whole of nature. Dualist theories hold that the universe itself consists of a mental substance as well as a material substance, which is a metaphysical postulate. Plato, Plotinus, the Christians, and many others all had versions of this idea. Among living creatures, this miraculous encounter, the union of the mental and material principles, occurred only in humans. The whole of Western philosophy exhausted itself trying on the one hand to explain the relationship of soul to body, in Greek the psyche and the soma, and on the other to prove that upon the death of the body the soul goes off to live out happier days elsewhere.

It was to counter such ideas that a whole wave of monist, materialist thought arose. Monist means that in the universe there cannot be two principles but only one, matter. It's also possible to maintain that mind is the only principle, but as it happens materialist monism has held sway for the last three centuries. Man is a material being, part of the biological sphere like other forms of life. The true distinction is between matter and life. Life, moreover, is derived chemically from matter. Consciousness arises from a set of neurocerebral factors, particularly language, evolution's latest development. It's principally language that is the matrix of consciousness – consciousness of things and of self – and the instrument of thought. And it's an illusion to think that it's a reality distinct from the body. Progress in modern neurophysiology, for a nonspecialist onlooker, has tended mainly to confirm this second point of view, the one you called reductionist. What position does Buddhism take in relation to that dominant tendency?

M. – I think that the different points of view reflect what are, in essence, metaphysical choices. Science rejects the idea of a nonmaterial consciousness, which by definition can't be detected by any physical means of measurement. That reflects the tendency to reify everything, to bring everything down to the material level, consciousness as well as phenomena.

According to the neurobiological model, and even more so in the case of any system of artificial intelligence, it's hard to see how it might be possible for consciousness to question its own nature. When the neurobiologists say that the brain doesn't really function like a computer, they mean that the brain is much more flexible, interactive and self-organizing than any currently available binary computer, but that any difference between the two is in the way they work, rather than being fundamental. Man and computer they say have one basic point in common: neither of them have a consciousness. In the case of a computer, it's obvious that it has no more consciousness than a heap of scrap. In the case of man, neurobiologists would say, what we call consciousness is neither an epiphenomenon of the nervous system nor an entity distinct from the system, but is nothing more or less than the functioning of the brain, than a set of chemical and electrical connections between neurons. There's no fundamental difference between such a model and a computer.

Now, it seems to me that the fact that artificial intelligence can win at chess doesn't mean that a computer has consciousness but simply that you don't need consciousness to carry out arithmetic calculations. It's more revealing to look at what artificial intelligence is not capable of doing. It can 'play' but knows nothing of the spirit of playfulness. It can calculate the future but could never worry about it; it can record the past but could never feel joy or sadness about it. It doesn't know how to laugh or cry, be sensitive to beauty or ugliness, or feel friendship or compassion. But above all, how could a system of artificial intelligence wonder what it itself might be, or what will happen to it after death – or, more accurately, when its batteries run out? Who am I? What is the nature of my mind? Neither a system of artificial intelligence nor a computer made of flesh and blood could even begin to ask such questions, let alone find any answers to them. How and why would a computer, or even a complex of neurons, spend years trying to puzzle out the ultimate nature of consciousness? It would seem that even the idea of a nonmaterial consciousness could never have arisen in a flesh-and-blood computer unless such a consciousness existed in some way or at some level. Isn't the very fact that consciousness is capable of wondering about its own existence some indication that consciousness cannot be exclusively a mechanism, however sophisticated?

Finally, the neurobiologist's model of man seems to deny that consciousness has any power to make decisions. Anything resembling a decision is supposed to be determined by a complex set of interactions between neurons, and free will has little part to play in such a scheme of things – indeed it's no more than an illusion.

J.F. – There are two questions here that shouldn't be confused. One is whether there's a mental principle that's metaphysically different from the material principle in man – or in other words whether man is the union of two different substances. The other is the question of human action and freedom. I personally believe that man exercises a certain degree of freedom. But I don't believe in the existence of the soul, nor in the soul's immortality. The two problems are quite distinct.

M. – But where could that freedom come from? The neurobiological model doesn't seem to be able to explain, for example, how a specific event can suddenly provoke a major change in the way we think or in the direction our lives take. There are criminals whose lives are dominated by hatred, and who even in prison kill each other, but who suddenly realize one day how monstrous their way of life has become. They say that the aberrant state they've been in until that moment was something akin to madness. There was also a lama just before the turn of the century who had lived, until he was thirty, as a hunter and bandit (in Tibet, hunters are viewed with no less disapproval than bandits). One day he was trailing a doe that he'd shot and mortally wounded. He caught up with the animal and found her collapsed on the ground. As she lay there, bleeding and exhausted, she'd been giving birth; and he saw that, to her very last breath, her only concern was the newborn fawn she was lovingly licking. The sight completely overwhelmed the hunter, and he decided there and then to give up hunting. Soon the preoccupations of ordinary life began to seem futile and deceptive to him, and he devoted himself from then on to meditating on love and compassion and studying the scriptures. He became a famous teacher.

If man is no more than his neurons, it's hard to understand how sudden events or deep reflection and the discovery of inner truths could lead us to completely change the way we see the world, how we live and our capacity for inner joy. Any such major upheaval would have to be accompanied by an equally deep and sudden major restructuring of the complex circuits of neurons that determine our habits and behavior. If, on the other hand, consciousness is a nonmaterial continuum, there's no reason why it shouldn't be able to undergo major changes quite easily, and much more flexibly than a network of physical connections formed during a slow and complex process.

From the point of view of the neurobiological model, what we take for a conscious decision is actually the result of an evaluation made by the nervous system of the optimal response to an external situation in terms of maximum contribution to the survival of the individual or the species. It could be an 'egocentric' response when it favors the survival of the individual, or an 'altruistic' response when it favors the survival of the species, sometimes to the individual's detriment. Let's not forget that all this is supposed to happen without any consciousness. According to this theory, we have the illusion of acting, but what we usually call consciousness is only a spectator, a passive witness that takes no active part in the workings of the brain and cannot influence the final result of any calculations made by the neurons. In short, consciousness has no power to make decisions.

According to such views, it's hard to understand, for instance, how the decision to renounce certain natural impulses, particularly those of desire, could contribute to the survival of the species. In Tibet, for example, before the Chinese invasion, close to twenty percent of the population were celibate, having taken up either monastic ordination or the life of a hermit. The country was one with a very low population density and abundant natural resources. Evolutionist anthropologists speak of competition between beliefs, the beliefs that win being those that confer a reproductive advantage on their adherents. But in the case of celibacy it's hard to see how such a choice could contribute to the propagation of the species!

J.F. – I think that what we call the psyche certainly does exist. It's the result of a neurophysiological evolution of the brain and the appearance of language. It's the fact that in our everyday experience we do choose between several possibilities, that what we do isn't completely determined by circumstances, appetites, desires, and aversions, like animal behavior. We're always conscious of having several possible courses of action to choose from. It's an existential reality, and I use that adjective deliberately, out of respect to a philosopher I don't, on the whole, much approve of – Jean-Paul Sartre. But the choice between several possibilities shouldn't be taken as an abstract principle. The choice is variable. It's set, as Sartre says, within a 'situation' that's not of your making. The range of choice may be restricted or enlarged. There are circumstances in which the environment, the context, leave very few possibilities available to you. When you find yourself plunged into a war, when hostile forces have invaded the country, when you have nothing left, the range of choice is very restricted, isn't it? You have only one choice, to escape or die. Under other circumstances – and that's why I'm explicitly in favor of peace and democracy – you have a much wider context, you live in a society that accepts different ways of life and morals and in which, in principle, the state ensures your security. Your range of choices is much wider. You yourself chose to become a Buddhist monk instead of staying a scientist at the Institut Pasteur. If it had been during the Second World War, you wouldn't have had that choice, would you? It's only the analysis of concrete situations that makes it possible to think that, in the best hypothesis, human action results from intelligence. So it can certainly be argued that, within limits, there is human freedom, adherence to certain values and rejection of others, together with the actions that arise from them. While the possibility of acting on the context is not unlimited, it does allow us to opt for this or that solution in practice. However, as I said, I don't see that any of this necessarily means that we have within us an immortal mind principle.

M. – Buddhism doesn't envisage any immortal entity, but a continuity that is constantly changing. An interdependence. But to come back to the notion of free will, a mechanical system is built to react to particular circumstances in a particular way, and even if it was capable of learning it would have no reason to 'want' anything in particular.

J.F. – I don't like the expression 'free will', because it's an old term that takes for granted the idea of a soul enjoying unlimited possibilities of decision-making. I don't think we know enough yet about the workings of the human machine, the human being, the brain, to know for sure where the power to make decisions could come from, but there has been progress. The network of neurons investigates the different possibilities and the 'choice' it ends up with is the one that affords the best chance of adaptation to the environment. I don't see why it shouldn't be possible to accept that the faculty of choice appeared at the end of that period in the evolution of the nervous system that led to the human brain as it appeared relatively recently, more or less with Neanderthal man and *Homo sapiens*, along with the faculty of language. We know that this faculty is the extension of a development of the brain and nervous system. And we know that this phase implies, includes, and allows the possibility of choice, albeit within a certain degree of determinism, of course – nature's determinism, to which as biological organisms we're inevitably subject, and the determinism imposed by history and society. I think that any analysis of individual human lives or of the history of societies shows that the possibility of choosing between several types of action at any given moment has always existed – except, once again, in extreme cases of total restriction. That's what thought is for. That's what reason's for. That's what information's for. Action is suspended to allow several hypotheses and conjectures to be envisaged, like a chess player trying to take account of several future moves and foresee the consequences of making one particular choice rather than another.

M. – What do you mean when you say that's what thought is for, when all there's supposed to be is a computer made of meat?

J.F. – The possibility of choice is an experiential fact. Besides, if it wasn't true, if for example the sequence of events only obeyed the determinism imposed by historical materialism, as Marxists would have us believe, it's hard to see what the point of governments, international institutions, or institutes of political science would be. If everything that happens had to happen, no court should find anyone guilty, not even those who perpetrate crimes against humanity.

M. – That's true. If all the people who suddenly decided overnight to kill their neighbors, as in Bosnia, were just suffering from poor connections between neurons, the only thing to do would be to grant them a pension for life. To sentence them would be the equivalent of eugenics. But in fact it's motivation that determines whether actions are negative or positive, and motivation is part of the stream of consciousness. Some people explain that we believe ourselves to have free will because it's an illusion that has given our species an evolutionary advantage. As Christian de Duve, winner of a Nobel Prize for medicine, says in *Vital Dust*,[1] such arguments leave unanswered the problem of who or what it might be that experiences that illusory feeling of freedom. He adds: 'But if free will does not exist, there can be no responsibility, and the structure of human societies must be revised. Very few among even the most uncompromising materialists are willing to drive this argument to its logical conclusion.'

J.F. – Therefore, to return to the crux of our discussion, I think that it's absolutely possible not to deny the existence of individual freedom, and more generally of human freedom – without necessarily accepting in metaphysical terms that there are two principles combined in man, one mental and one material.

M. – Fine, but let's go back to look at the initial moment in a decision. If what we call consciousness is just an impotent and useless puppet witness, we're in the most complete determinism possible. Neurology tells us that around ninety percent of activity in the brain is unconscious. Why not one hundred percent, if consciousness is just a passive witness that can't have any influence on the workings of the brain? When the nervous system is in a state of equilibrium, it carries within it a number of possibilities related to connections between neurons that are the result of our genetic inheritance and our learned experience. It must be possible for that equilibrium to be broken in one direction or the other.

J.F. – But that's assuming that the system's liable to take one or the other of two directions.

M. – Apart from will or thought, what else could determine the direction that the system takes? Chance? In that case everything is chaotic, inconsistent, and arbitrary. Necessity? Then we're back in complete and total determinism.

Experience shows that you might, for example, decide to renounce all passions, even though they're natural biological tendencies, to become a monk. Or decide to spend hours on end looking into the nature of the mind. Or decide to make an anonymous and disinterested act of generosity.

J.F. – Yes, but will is never something absolute. It's subject to certain restrictions. Wisdom consists of taking account of those limitations, and of reminding oneself that neither freedom nor slavery are ever total. The expression 'free will' implies that a human being could have total freedom, like a sovereign god who could impose his will on reality. But that's not at all the case.

M. – I'm not talking about total freedom, but of the very existence of a faculty to decide things, which already goes a long way in fact, as we do have power over our lives.

J.F. – That's all very well, but to me such arguments seem quite inadequate as an answer to the neurophysiologists who think that everything can be explained without recourse to the idea of a mind distinct from the body.

M. – Buddhism has absolutely no objection to their description of the functioning of the human nervous system on a physical level, but would maintain that to take consciousness as being limited to that physical mechanism was a metaphysical belief, rather than a scientifically proven fact. For example, look at the effect on the brain of crack cocaine. Crack blocks the reabsorption of dopamine by nerve endings, which induces a state of euphoria. As long as the effects of the drug last, crack takers neglect any other activity and no longer eat, work, or sleep, but stay in that artificial euphoria. In fact, dopamine is involved in most pleasurable sensations, whether arising from drugs, tobacco, sex, or even eating chocolate. The quality and intensity of our sensory experiences, feelings, and perception of the world, like pleasure and displeasure, would therefore seem to depend entirely on chemical processes in the brain. Who knows – perhaps the monk who renounces alcohol and drugs and takes a vow of chastity, but is still perfectly happy and indomitably cheerful, could just be someone with natural dopamine levels somewhat above the average! At first sight, it seems to me that the euphoria caused by a drug is no more than a pitiful sham of true well-being, of the bliss of the wise man, for example. Such euphoria is suffering in disguise. It brings alienation and insatiability and ends in agony, in an intractable feeling of there being something missing. It ruins the person psychologically, which then brings physical ruin in its wake. On the other hand, the serenity and happiness of the wise man doesn't need any outer agent to bring it about, and is invulnerable to life's circumstances, whether favorable or unfavorable. Far from being ephemeral, it grows and strengthens over time. It doesn't lead the person to an artificial paradise (or, more accurately, hell) to retreat into. Instead, it makes them more and more open to others. It's a serenity that can be communicated and transmitted.

But according to the neurobiologists, there are two unavoidable conclusions to be drawn from the effects of drugs on our experience. The first is that while a simple substance can have a considerable effect on the mind, it's hard to see how it could interfere with a nonmaterial consciousness. The second is that while consciousness could, at the very most, in some way be reading whatever happens in the brain, it certainly couldn't take part in any decisions. David Potter, Professor of Neurobiology at Harvard Medical School, who took part in a conference on the subject with the Dalai Lama, concluded: 'One is led to wonder whether decisions are ever made in consciousness, or whether the consciousness in which we take so much pride is simply a reporter function in the brain. Are decisions and emotions calculated by nerve cells whose behavior we cannot bring into consciousness and cannot control by conscious mechanisms?'[2] So this is the extreme point of view we've reached. This is the opinion held by a majority of scientists, but it's nevertheless not unanimously accepted. For example, Christian de Duve writes, 'We still know too little about the human mind to affirm categorically that it is a mere emanation of neuronal activity lacking the power to affect this activity.' And my former boss, François Jacob, concluded in his inaugural lecture at the Collège de France: 'Can knowledge of the relevant structures and the intelligence of the mechanisms involved ever be enough to describe processes as complex as those of the mind? Is there any chance that one day we'll be able to specify in terms of physics and chemistry the sum total of all the interactions giving rise to a thought, a feeling, or a decision? Some doubt is surely permissible.'

J.F. – So, what would you finally argue against those who think that the word 'consciousness' doesn't really mean anything?

M. – Once again, consciousness has the faculty of knowing itself. It's an experiential fact that can't be denied. If consciousness took no part in decisions, what on earth would it be for? Why does it observe us, and who does the observing? A bunch of robots would manage just as well and the existence of consciousness would just be a completely free luxury, a bonus granted to man so that he can enjoy the show. That's not a conscious act, it's voyeurism.

J.F. – What you're talking about is the metaphor of the 'ghost in the machine'. It's also Bergson's theory; consciousness goes beyond the brain.

M. – There's certainly a ghost in the machine, and it's the stream of our consciousness. That stream, I can't repeat too often, doesn't imply that there is some truly existing entity that is carried over from one life to the next. Nonetheless, it does retain the marks of its own past. That consciousness allows the will to influence the body within the physiological limits that the body permits.

J.F. – How could consciousness and the brain interact?

M. – According to Buddhism, the conflict between materialist and idealist points of view, between mind and matter, is a false problem. In fact, in the mind of most philosophers and scientists, it's a question of 'solid' matter and 'nonmaterial' mind being in opposition to each other. But the dominant idea today among scientists is that such dualism infringes the laws of conservation of energy by supposing that a nonmaterial object can influence a material system. Such a view of things does indeed raise insoluble problems. So it might be useful instead to investigate the 'reality' of matter itself, for it's actually in reifying matter that materialism comes up against its failure to understand the nature of mind. According to Buddhism, atomic particles can neither be 'solid' nor even exist intrinsically at all. No collection of such entities, however numerous, is any more real than its constituent parts. Without making too much of the parallels with modern physics, it's hard not to be reminded of Heisenberg, who wrote, 'Neither atoms, nor even sub-atomic particles, are real. They form a world of potentialities or possibilities rather than of objects or facts.' We'll come back to the Buddhist analysis of the reality of phenomena later. For the purposes of the present argument, suffice it to say that according to this view, the opposition of mind and matter is not irreducible because neither one nor the other exists in an autonomous and permanent manner. There's nothing, therefore, to stop consciousness being able to manifest in the brain through chemical reactions, leading to physiological processes that act on the body; nor anything to prevent such processes exerting an influence in return on consciousness. This interaction lasts as long as the consciousness is associated with the body. But Buddhists add that what guides the workings of the brain and its decisions is the nonmaterial consciousness. To deny that is a metaphysical choice made by neurobiologists, just as asserting it is a metaphysical choice made by Buddhists. By its very nature, consciousness escapes the methods of investigation used by physical scientists. But not to be able to find something is no proof of its nonexistence. Buddhism's choice is based on experience acquired through contemplation. So finally the only way to settle the debate is to investigate any indirect indications there might be that a consciousness separate from the body could exist. In Buddhist terminology, the subtle or nonmaterial consciousness is 'without form', but it's not 'nonexistent' because it's capable of fulfilling a function. Consciousness carries within it the capacity to interact with the body, which itself has no ultimate reality.

J.F. – Wait a minute. As a professional philosopher, I've always been very wary of the various trends that come and go whereby people try to justify metaphysical theories by exploiting certain scientific developments. That's not what science is meant for. Take Heisenberg's uncertainty principle, for example. Indeterminacy in particle physics, at the time I trained in philosophy – just at the beginning of the Second World War – was the major scientific phenomenon of the time. All the nonmaterialist philosophies jumped on the indeterminacy bandwagon, saying, 'Ah, you see? Free will is perfectly possible, because matter's not completely determined.' I don't think much of that sort of reasoning. It's hard to see how indeterminacy in particle physics could make it any more possible for human action to determine natural phenomena. Later on, other ways of using what I call 'support disciplines' appeared. Michel Foucault used linguistics – in an extremely unrigorous way – to write *The Order of Things*. Such parasitizing of science by metaphysics recurs periodically, and in fact it's existed since the eighth century. It seems to me to lack rigor.

M. – I agree that such comparisons are rather artificial. Buddhist philosophy is consistent enough by itself to do without them. Nevertheless, they sometimes help to throw a bridge, or at least a gangway, between Buddhist ideas and those of Western philosophy, and make for greater openness of mind. According to Buddhism, there is an interaction between consciousness and a body with which it's temporarily associated. The stream of consciousness continues after death and experiences different states of existence between each birth and each death. The 'embodied mind', to use an expression of Francisco Varela's, is what defines the relationship between the stream of consciousness and the nervous system. That embodied mind could also be called the gross aspect of consciousness, as it's associated with the physical body. The subtle aspect constitutes the continuum of consciousness, which carries on from one life to another. It's a continuum without beginning or end, because consciousness could never arise from nothing, nor from inanimate matter – each instant of consciousness can only be born from the preceding instant of consciousness and result in the following instant of consciousness. In physics there's the principle of the conservation of energy: mass energy can neither be created nor disappear, but only be transformed. In just the same way, we could speak here in terms of a principle of the conservation of consciousness. So there's a continuum, a current of consciousness for each being, which can be changed, just as the water of a river can be either polluted or purified. That's how, through such transformation, it's possible for the confused state of ordinary beings to become the enlightened state of a Buddha.

J.F. – The suggestion that there's a mind principle that can be hung on the brain is exactly what Bergson put forward in *Matter and Memory*, as I've already mentioned. He wrote the book at the end of a period during which neurophysiologists were particularly interested in the study of aphasia. By showing that aphasia, the total loss of language, was associated with highly localized brain lesions, neurophysiologists thought they'd proved that destroying such parts of the brain also destroyed consciousness. Therefore, consciousness is nothing more than the brain. In an attempt to refute that conclusion, Bergson spent six years studying the literature on aphasia. He claims to show in his book that memory, that's to say consciousness, 'goes beyond' the brain. It hangs on the brain 'like a coat on a coathanger', he says, but can't be reduced to just the brain any more than a coat can be reduced to a coathanger, or the supernatural to the natural.

M. – The fact that drugs or lesions in certain parts of the brain can have such a powerful influence on our thoughts and faculties doesn't in the end prove anything. If there is a nonmaterial consciousness, it's obvious that it wouldn't be able to express itself normally through a faulty brain – just as a pilot at the controls of a damaged aircraft might be unable to maintain its proper flight path.

J.F. – Would it be true to say that the existence of a nonmaterial consciousness is indispensable for Buddhism, because of the fundamental doctrinal point of reincarnation?

M. – Yes, in fact the only definite proof of the reality of a nonmaterial consciousness would be the existence of reincarnation, or more accurately the continuity of consciousness. But I'd first like to say a few words about the transmission of thoughts, which also presupposes a nonmaterial consciousness. There are so many examples of the transmission of thoughts, not only accounts in the texts but also in everyday life around the great teachers, that it's almost commonplace for Tibetans. It's seen as a manifestation of the interdependence of phenomena. Since there's nothing quite like personal experience, I'll tell you about my own. During the twenty-five years I spent with great Tibetan teachers, I was able to see for myself that they were aware of exactly what I or some of my friends had just been thinking. I'll limit myself to a single example, the one that I found most striking. While I was meditating in a small hut near my first teacher, Kangyur Rinpoche, I started to think about the animals I'd killed when I was young. I used to go fishing, until suddenly when I was fifteen I realized that I was bringing suffering to and killing living creatures. Once, I'd also shot at a rat with a rifle. Thinking about it, I felt a mixture of profound regret and incredulity that I could have been so blind to the suffering of others and have cared so little about it. So I decided to go and see Kangyur Rinpoche and tell him what I'd done – to confess, in a way. I went in to see him; I didn't speak Tibetan at that stage, but his son was there…

J.F. – To interpret for you...

M. – As soon as he saw me, Kangyur Rinpoche looked at me and laughed. Before I could utter a word of my confession, he said a few words to his son, who translated, 'How many animals have you killed in your life?'

J.F. – That's interesting.

M. – At the time, this event seemed completely natural to me. I just smiled. It wasn't at all a feeling of being plunged into something strange and supernatural. But, at the same time, one such experience is enough to open the mind. As they say, it's enough to taste one drop of the sea to know that it's salty.

J.F. – I agree. But the fact that certain psyches can communicate with other psyches – something that is only very rarely observed but which some people have nevertheless experienced, including yourself – doesn't completely prove that there's a purely mental principle in man.

M. – It doesn't prove it, but it makes it a pretty strong presumption. I should add, too, that the attitude of these Tibetan teachers is always very humble. They might be having this kind of experience all the time, but they only very rarely let anyone know. They don't like putting their powers on display and are certainly not trying to impress anybody. It's a faculty that's relatively common in great Tibetan teachers and always goes hand in hand with a high degree of spiritual realization. I've never seen or heard of it in ordinary practitioners.

These are the same great teachers who speak from their own experience of a state of consciousness after death. In view of the capacities that can be observed in them and of all the other signs of perfection they show in daily life, it seems more likely that they're telling the truth than otherwise; that's all I can say.

J.F. – That kind of reasoning, the very considerations you've just brought up, are found in many of Plato's dialogues. People who've attained a high degree of spiritual development, whose exceptional character is revealed by this or that sign of selflessness, humility, and nobility altogether, seem to be able to perceive supernatural phenomena. All these things come together to allow those who are open to such arguments to accept the hypothesis of a mental principle and the immortality of the soul. But stringent evidence alone, if there was no act of faith added on, wouldn't allow them to reach that conclusion.

M. – If you define faith as conviction born from experience, why shouldn't such an act of faith be valid? Of course, it's always difficult to get anyone else to share that conviction if they haven't had the same experience.

J.F. – That's just the point. That's why the only real evidence is evidence independent of any subjective experience.

M. – Why the only real evidence? Faith in Buddhism isn't blind, irrational belief in particular points of dogma. André Migot said in his book on the Buddha:[3] 'Faith becomes superstition when it parts from reason, and even more so when it goes against reason. But when it is combined with reason, it prevents reason from remaining just an intellectual game.' What we're talking about here isn't just an act of trust, it's the most likely and credible explanation.

J.F. – Here, we're back to the everlasting great attempt – and I do mean attempt – the effort to rationalize what is in fact irrational. Here again the basic reference is Plato, or Pascal. It's to try to use a dialectic (in Plato's sense, not Hegel's), a very tight argument, very rational in its word-for-word structure, to end up with proof, through reason, of something that just doesn't depend on reason. So you always come up against a final limit, because there's always a step to be surmounted that no longer depends on evidence.

M. – There are some steps that it would be well worth surmounting. The way those teachers conduct their lives seems perfectly consistent, without the slightest false note. Why would such remarkable people with so many admirable qualities, those still alive and all those who've appeared throughout the history of Buddhism, suddenly start inventing false truths when it comes to their experience of a stream of nonmaterial consciousness continuing after death?

J.F. – That's not what I'm saying. An act of faith doesn't have to be fraudulent. But it's not absolute proof; it's testimony, like historical knowledge.

M. – Wait a minute, let's be careful here. The act of faith is something *we* make. It's not the same for those who, like the Buddha, assert that consciousness is nonmaterial, that its stream continues after death, and that one stream of consciousness among others is identifiable. For them it's a matter of direct experience, not faith.

J.F. – It's a bit the same situation as for the mystics of Western tradition. Take St. John of the Cross, St. Catherine of Siena, and others who saw God within their own lifetime, in states of transport or ecstasy. They were quite sure they'd had experience of the divine. But the mass of Christians take them at their word – or not, as the case may be – without casting any doubt on their honesty or their humility. All the same, their testimony isn't the same as rational proof. What I've noticed about this sort of reasoning is that it uses two different pathways together. One is to use bits and pieces of science to try to show, through rational demonstration, that an immortal, mental principle exists. The other is to call on the suprasensory and supernatural experiences of people who may well have lived those experiences in complete sincerity and, being perfectly respectable and honorable, may well have no intention of deceiving anyone. But that's not enough. History is full of people of perfectly good faith who were wrong.

M. – But how could someone be wrong about that kind of experience?

J.F. – They could have an experience that they feel proves the existence of a principle that continues in the hereafter, when in fact it's just an impression. Couldn't they be wrong? It's no real evidence for anyone who hasn't had that experience himself. It remains something of the order of probability or possibility only.

M. – It could only be proved if you had the experience yourself.

J.F. – That's just the problem. As for attempts to demonstrate the existence of God or the immortality of the soul rationally, libraries of philosophy and theology are full of them. There have been tons, over the centuries. The only trouble is that none of them have ever managed to demonstrate the existence of God or the immortality of the soul rationally! That's why Kant resorted to indirect proof via morals and the idea of good. But especially not via reason.

M. – It's really an indirect proof that I've been proposing here, that of the validity of testimony. But we still have a second point to tackle – people who remember their previous lives. That's something that, in the end, could clarify the question of reincarnation.

J.F. – Well, yes, it could, as long as such people could convince us that they're remembering real events, and that it's not just a novel. Pythagoras also claimed to remember all his previous lives.

M. – There have been several studies of case histories of this kind. Sogyal Rinpoche mentions in his book[4] two of the most interesting cases. One was a little girl in the Punjab, in India, who remembered a whole mass of details about the circumstances of her death, her former family, her home and so on. The facts of the case were also described by observers sent by the Dalai Lama. I myself don't have any direct experiences of the kind to relate, and we won't get anywhere by trying to reach any sort of conclusion about the validity of such testimonies. The only side of it that I can speak about with any familiarity is the particular case in the Tibetan world of these young children considered to be the spiritual continuation of lamas who've recently died. There are numerous cases in which such children have recognized people who'd been disciples of the former teacher, and who've also recognized things that belonged to them, and places where they lived.

J.F. – Has all that ever really been proved?

M. – Hundreds of cases have been reported in the history of Tibet. I personally have heard several firsthand accounts whose validity I had little reason to doubt, and I can cite one case whose validity I have no reason to doubt at all, as I myself witnessed it.

J.F. – But when you say that a child of three recognizes someone, what do you mean? He smiles at them, or waves?

M. – Sometimes such children have called some of the former lama's attendants by name.

J.F. – Without having been told what it was? Well, that's really something.

M. – I'll give you two examples. The first is not something I witnessed myself, but I heard the account from someone I trust completely. A great teacher called Dudjom Lingpa died in 1903. He'd lived in Amdo, in the northeast of Tibet. Just before dying, he told his disciples that he had to leave for the region of Pemakö in southern Tibet, near the Indian border, two months' walk from Amdo. After his death, faithful to his dying words, a hundred or so of his disciples set out for Pemakö with the idea of finding his reincarnation there. They searched in vain for almost five years, and gradually, one after the other, gave up and made their way home. Only about fifteen really stubborn ones remained and continued looking. One day, they arrived at the edge of a village where they saw a group of children. Running around among them was a young boy who'd said to his parents that morning, 'Some friends are coming today, we'll need to get a meal ready for them.' The children were playing by jumping over a low stone wall.

J.F. – How old was the child?

M. – Five or six. Just as the monks were passing close by, the boy in question stumbled over a stone and, on the point of falling, reached out his hand to the lama who was just next to him, calling, 'Yeshé, give me a hand!' Yeshé was indeed the lama's name. He was quite shocked, but for the moment kept quiet. The travelers were then invited to share the household meal. Now, it happened that this lama Yeshé was wearing round his neck a reliquary containing a lock of hair. Seeing the reliquary, the child exclaimed, 'Hey! But that's the hair I gave you!' It was indeed a lock of hair that his former teacher had given him. That child became Dudjom Rinpoche, who died in 1987 and was one of my own main teachers.

Secondly, here's the story I witnessed myself, the reincarnation of Khyentse Rinpoche, the teacher I lived with for fifteen years.

J.F. – The one I met in Darjeeling in 1973?

M. – No, the one you met in Bhutan in 1986. He was identified by one of his closest disciples, a great teacher in his own right called Trulshik Rinpoche, who is now seventy-two and lives in the mountains in Nepal. He was the one who had the dreams and visions we were talking about yesterday that made it possible to find the child. I took part in the search myself. Once the child was found, it was decided that a ceremony for his longevity should be performed in a sacred cave in the east of Nepal. So we went off to the cave, near which Trulshik Rinpoche had been in retreat. A hundred or so former disciples of Khyentse Rinpoche's assembled there for the occasion. During the ceremony, Trulshik Rinpoche read to the child the name that had been given to him and sent by the Dalai Lama, offered him some ceremonial robes and performed a long life ritual in his honor. On the last day, there was a celebration during which the officiating lama would normally give each participant a little bit of a consecrated liquid to drink. Trulshik Rinpoche, who was presiding over the ceremony, was expected to be the one who distributed this substance. But the child, seeing Trulshik Rinpoche beginning to do so, decided that he'd do it himself, although only two-and-a-half years old. With great calm – the scene lasted a good five minutes – he got his mother to come over to him and gave her a drop of the liquid, then Khyentse Rinpoche's grandson, whom he knew, and about twenty other people whose name he'd heard only once or twice. As he called them, he distinctly spoke the names of several of these people who'd only been introduced to him the day before.

J.F. – At two-and-a-half! But at that age children can hardly talk!

M. – Hardly, but just enough to call people by name.

J.F. – This particular child would have needed a phenomenal memory to do that.

M. – The day before, for example, I was holding the boy in my arms and pointed out to him a friend of mine, Luc, a French engineer, who's building one of our monasteries in India. A little bit jokingly, I said, 'There, that's Luc, who's building your monastery in Bodhgaya.' The next day, he called Luc by name and gave him the blessing. So this is certainly an especially bright child, with an astonishing memory. But that wasn't the most astonishing thing that happened.

Among the participants, of whom there were about a hundred, were a group of Bhutanese who had just arrived after three days' walk from the Nepalese border. One of them had been an old servant of the former Khyentse Rinpoche. When the child had blessed all the people sitting nearby, one of the monks asked him 'So, now, is that all?' 'No, no,' he replied, and pointed at someone in the small crowd. Another monk went over to indicate different people sitting in the direction the boy was pointing at – 'This one? That one there?' and so on, until he reached the old Bhutanese servant, whereupon the boy said, 'Yes! That one!' So the old man was brought over and the boy, perched on his throne, gave him the blessing. The man burst into tears.

J.F. – It's very striking. Nevertheless, I'd still say, once again, that events of this kind can only be taken as proof if you experience them yourself. Even if you believe that accounts of them are given in absolute sincerity.

M. – Yes, I do understand that. I'm only telling this story because it was something I saw with my own eyes. For me, it has a greater weight of truth than something I've heard someone else recounting. But I should add that I've heard descriptions of dozens of similar events. When people ask the Dalai Lama – surely the very personification of sincerity and honesty – if he had these kind of memories, he says, 'As soon as I arrived in Lhasa, I told my attendants that my teeth were in a box in a particular room of the Norbulingka, the Summer Palace. When they opened the box, they found the thirteenth Dalai Lama's false teeth. I pointed at the box and told them my teeth were inside. But now, I don't remember anything!'

J.F. – Well, let's say all that belongs to Buddhism's metaphysical beliefs. And I do think it has all the features of metaphysical (not to say religious) conviction. What characterizes rational thought is that all the evidence can be communicated to anyone, and they can even be obliged to admit its validity – even those who haven't themselves observed the experiment being carried out and who wouldn't be able to carry it out themselves, but who are bound to accept that it could always be reconstituted. The kind of experience you're talking about, on the other hand, is only completely convincing at firsthand. It's a unique testimony, of the same order as those of the mystics and other sorts of specific experience, whether religious or otherwise.

M. – I know very well what the criteria of rational thought are, and that its evidence has to be communicable to everyone or to be such as to oblige them to accept its validity. For example, conviction of the truth of a mathematical demonstration arises in the mind, doesn't it? If it has a physical application, it can also be verified experimentally. Contemplative thought leads to a conviction which arises in the mind, too. The certainty arising from a life of contemplative practice, or a life lived with a spiritual teacher, is just as powerful as that arising from the demonstration of a theorem. As for its experimental verification, the only difference is that it's usually inner, which removes none of its authenticity. Its outer aspects – goodness, tolerance, compassion, wisdom – are only 'signs' of inner realization.

J.F. – I'm not arguing against its authenticity for those who experience it at firsthand. But in the context of our dialogue, which is supposed to be getting at the details of what Buddhism means for a Westerner, I'm just emphasizing that as well as the dimension of practical, purely psychological wisdom there's also an additional dimension that's metaphysical or supernatural.

M. – The events I was telling you about just now have absolutely nothing to do with mystical experience, and my own testimony is not in the slightest bit metaphysical. These are events that I saw with my own eyes, and not in some exalted state of mind, but in the calmest – I'd almost go so far as to say the most ordinary – circumstances possible. And since you mention mystical accounts, I'd like to add, by way of a parenthesis, that people sometimes try hard to belittle such accounts using what could be called 'medical materialism', which consists of saying that St. Teresa of Avila was an hysteric, that St. Francis of Assisi had some hereditary psychological problem, that St. Paul had an epileptic fit on the road to Damascus, that Joan of Arc was schizo-phrenic, and so forth. It's true that stimulating certain parts of the brain can give rise to hallucinations and other disturbances of experi-ence, as can the various lesions and malfunctions that the brain is sub-ject to through disease. But such explanations can't possibly cover the spiritual experiences of thousands of perfectly sane and healthy con-templatives. Anyway, concerning the facts about the young reincarna-tion of my teacher, I can assure you that neither I nor anyone else present was in any kind of mystical state. And without having the slightest wish to impose my inner conviction on anyone, I cannot but trust my own senses.

J.F. – Even if one doesn't resort to the degrading or even contemp-tuous sort of explanations you mention, nevertheless one can – and must, in good methodology – distinguish between the type of proof that can be communicated to the whole of mankind, such that everyone's obliged to accept its validity, and the type of proof that's only proof for those who've had that particular firsthand experience.

M. – You're right that it's a problem of methodology. If you dis-miss one particular phenomenon because it's an exception and can't be reproduced, how could you ever recognize that it corresponds to real-ity, should that in fact be the case?

J.F. – I think it has to be dismissed as long as it isn't part of your own experience.

M. – But in that case the only truths we could accept would be those that everyone can see or experience at the same time.

J.F. – My opinion is that the events you've recounted are of the order of historical testimony rather than scientific proof. Now, histori-cal testimony, meaning, 'So-and-so said this or that, I was there, I heard him say so,' is very valuable evidence. Without it, there'd be no history. But it's never final proof. Any historian can contradict another historian and say, 'I've found another source which proves that this or that testimony is false or incomplete.' That's why history, although it's a science, is not an exact science. It's based exclusively on the testi-mony of a limited number of individuals about an experience which can't be reproduced. Yet history is more scientific than the accounts you've been talking about, because it relies not only on personal testi-mony but also on nonpersonal documents and monuments, even if they're subject to various interpretations too. For supernatural experiences, it can only be one mind against another. I don't think we'll get any further on that theme. The idea we should stay with is this: unless you're within a certain system of faith – and I do mean that in the noblest sense of the term – there'll always be something missing that will prevent a viewpoint that is metaphysical by definition being proved. A metaphysical viewpoint can never be completely proved. We've been trying for two thousand five hundred years to build a rational system of metaphysics, to make metaphysics as rigorous as mathematics. But it's never worked – because metaphysics, intrinsically, is outside the scope of that system of reasoning.

M. – But it's not outside the scope of spiritual realization, which is an undeniable reality and takes place on another level, that of contemplative experience – the direct vision of a truth that the mind is obliged to accept because it corresponds, in that domain, to the nature of things. That doesn't make such a point of view irrational, either. It simply goes beyond conceptual reasoning.

J.F. – So we have to sort it out. There are two different approaches. In a tradition of wisdom like this, the importance of which no one's denying, it's crucial to distinguish what depends on that system of metaphysics from what doesn't. What teaching can be drawn from Buddhism by those who don't adhere to its metaphysical dimension, to help them enhance the way they lead their lives? In my opinion, that's the most interesting problem. In fact, it's a problem that's pertinent to any religion or philosophy, but one that's all the more fascinating in Buddhism which is both at once and neither one nor the other. Don't you think so?

M. – Let's tackle our problem from the other end. Just suppose for a moment that such unusual phenomena as memories of previous lives really did exist. How could they be proved if the very fact of being the exception makes them unacceptable?

J.F. – For that, you'd need an impartial observer who spoke the language fluently and was accepted within the Tibetan community, to observe these matters with skepticism and rigor.

M. – If that's all you need, Yours Truly could perhaps be considered a candidate. Personally, I always try to adopt the most objective possible attitude, knowing that otherwise I'd be an easy target for those who denounce anything asserted on the basis of blind credulity. In discussions with my Tibetan friends, I always try to be the devil's advocate, and to add spice to the argument I always adopt a materialist point of view. There's no doubt that I couldn't believe fully in the transmission of thoughts until I experienced it myself. In the case of the child who made the old man come over to him, I'm happy to have seen it with my own eyes. But my deepest conviction in the spiritual path doesn't just arise from a few outer events of the sort. It's rooted in confirmation of certain metaphysical and contemplative truths, moment by moment.

J.F. – My own conclusion, then, which is not definitive, is that your testimony carries more weight than that of some drugged hippie who'd approached Buddhism in a much less authentic way. Any scrupulous historian would say the same. That's exactly how one proceeds in history: the testimony of such-and-such a witness carries great weight, but it's still only a testimony. Once again, we have to distinguish between the historical sciences, mind sciences and human sciences on the one hand, and the 'hard' sciences on the other. The latter entail proofs that everyone, whatever their opinion might be, would be bound to accept; whereas in the former, the gathering of testimonies helps to get to ever higher and higher probabilities of truth, but there's nevertheless a threshold of absolute certainty that can never be completely reached.

M. – I can guarantee that you'd have no chance at all of getting an inhabitant of the tropical forests of New Guinea to accept even a hundredth of the discoveries of science. The other person has to have some comparable mental framework. You'd have to educate him in a particular way for many years. Similarly, people who haven't opened their minds to it could never be made to accept the results of contemplative research. There too, some education is necessary. The goal of the sciences of what is reproducible, the hard sciences, is actually not to solve metaphysical problems, nor to give meaning to life, but to describe the material world as exactly as possible. To say that reality can be reduced simply to matter and that consciousness is just a property of the nervous system is no more than a definition of the context in which science operates. Contemplative life, too, has its own rules, and the deep conviction that comes from practicing it has, on the mind, as much impact as any experiment whatsoever that can be carried out in the material world. Observation of the nature of the mind, from a purely contemplative point of view, can bring about a certainty just as complete as observing a body falling under the effect of gravity.

1. Christian de Duve, *Vital Dust, Life as Cosmic Imperative,* Basic Books, New York, 1995.
2. From *Mind Science: An East–West Dialogue,* the Dalai Lama and participants in the Harvard Mind Science Symposium; edited by Daniel Goleman and Robert A.F. Thurman, Wisdom Publications, Boston, 1991.
3. *Le Bouddha (The Buddha),* Club Français du Livre, 1960, Complexe, 1990.
4. *The Tibetan Book of Living and Dying,* HarperSanFrancisco, San Francisco, and Rider, London, 1992.

❧

FOUR

A SCIENCE

OF THE MIND

JEAN-FRANÇOIS – We now come to what could be called Buddhist psychology, the study of the mind and how we can gain control of it. This is the aspect of Buddhism that has recently been the particular focus of Westerners' interest. In the nineteenth century, it was above all Buddhist wisdom as a method for finding some sort of serenity through self-effacement that attracted some philosophers, like Schopenhauer. But more recently it's been the techniques for mastering the mind that have aroused more attention. In 1991, for example, a symposium was held at Harvard Medical School during which several scientists met the Dalai Lama.[1] The account of these Western scientists familiar with what's called scientific psychology in the West, exchanging and comparing views with the Dalai Lama, is very interesting. Some of the scientists had been to the East themselves to study practices there at firsthand. During the symposium one of them, Daniel Goleman, who's also on the behavioral science team of the *New York Times,* read a paper on Tibetan and Western models of mental health. What, then, can we say about Buddhist psychology?

MATTHIEU – One of the characteristics of Buddhism as a 'science of the mind' is that it's not enough just to recognize and identify a conscious emotion or a latent tendency and bring it back to the surface. We need to know how to 'liberate' such thoughts and feelings. Liberating thoughts is to stop them leaving any traces on the mind, to stop them keeping it bound in confusion. Otherwise, they all too easily give rise to a chain reaction. A thought of dislike, for example, becomes one of animosity, then of hatred, and ends up completely taking over the mind, until we finally express it in the form of words or deeds. We do something negative to someone, and our inner peace is destroyed as well. The same goes for desire, arrogance, jealousy, fear, and the rest. We can give free reign to our impulses to destroy, possess, or dominate, but any satisfaction we so obtain is ephemeral. It'll never bring us the kind of joy that's deep, stable, and long lasting.

J.F. – But surely not all moral suffering's caused by hatred or desire?

M. – No, it can come from a whole multitude of negative emotions. The key to working on the mind is not only to identify your thoughts and feelings but also to dissolve them, to let them vanish in the mind's own spaciousness. There are a number of techniques that can be applied to this end. The most important is not to concentrate on the content of the emotions, on the causes and circumstances that trigger them, but to trace them to their very source. There are two ways of meditating, like a dog and like a lion. You might try to tackle your thoughts in the same way that a dog runs after every stone thrown at it, one after another. That's just what human beings do most of the time, in fact. Whenever a thought arises, we let ourselves be carried away by it. That first thought gives rise to a second, then to a third, and to a whole endless chain of thoughts that only sustain our mental confusion. But the other way to react is like a lion. You can only throw one stone at a lion – because he turns on the thrower and jumps on him. This second analogy describes the kind of meditation in which you turn to the very source of thoughts, and examine the primary mechanism by which they arise in the mind.

J.F. – Going a bit beyond the metaphors, what actually is that mechanism?

M. – To start seeing it, you have to try to break the flow of thoughts for a few instants. Without prolonging past thoughts, and without inviting future thoughts, you just remain, however briefly, in awareness of the present moment, free of any discursive thoughts. Little by little you get better at staying for longer in that state of awareness. As long as there are waves stirring up a lake, its waters stay cloudy. But if the waves die down, the mud sinks to the bottom and the crystal clarity of the water returns. In the same way, when discursive thoughts calm down, the mind becomes clearer and it's then easier to discover its true nature.

You then have to examine the nature of discursive thoughts. To do that, you might even deliberately stir up some strong emotion in yourself, perhaps by thinking of someone who's harmed you, or conversely by thinking of something that arouses your desire. You let that emotion appear in the field of your consciousness, and then you fix it with your inner perception, alternating analytic investigation with sheer contemplation. At first, that feeling dominates and obsesses you. It returns constantly. But you continue to examine it carefully. Where does it get its apparent strength from? It doesn't have any intrinsic capacity to harm, like some living creature of flesh and blood. Where was it before it arose? When it appears in your mind, does it have any characteristics – a location, a shape, a color? When it leaves the field of your consciousness, does it go anywhere? The more you investigate it, the more that powerful-seeming thought escapes you; it's impossible to catch it or point it out. You reach a state of 'not found,' in which you stay for a few moments in contemplation. This is what's technically called 'recognizing the emptiness of thoughts'. It's a state of inner simplicity, of clear mindfulness and awareness, stripped bare of any concepts. When you understand that thoughts are just a manifestation of that aware consciousness, they lose their confining solidity. Eventually, after a great deal of persistent practice, the process of liberation becomes natural and as soon as new thoughts arise they release themselves, no longer disturbing and dominating your mind. No sooner do they take form than they disappear, like drawings made on the surface of water with your finger.

J.F. – What strikes me in that whole way of reasoning is that everything's described as if the reality of the world outside, things you do, other human beings and the weight of circumstances didn't exist at all. Surely there are moments when real dangers might actually threaten you. Being afraid of that danger, or wanting to be rid of it, and thus taking an actively hostile attitude toward the threat, when your life is in danger for instance, isn't just something to be solved by working on your thoughts! The right response is to take some particular outward action.

M. – In a given situation, we can react in several different ways, according to our inner state of mind. Actions are born from thoughts. Without mastering your thoughts, you can't master your actions. So you need to learn how to liberate your emotions...

J.F. – Yes, but those are only very marginal cases...

M. – ... in order to then use that mastery in the heat of the action. In everyday parlance we say someone 'stayed in control of himself' or 'completely lost control of himself'. Here, it's a matter of making that control more total, more stable, with the help of knowledge of the nature of the mind. It absolutely doesn't mean looking on helplessly, apathetic and indifferent, while a murderer kills your family in front of you. It means doing the minimum necessary to neutralize your adversary without letting yourself be invaded by hatred, or killing your aggressor in a vengeful state of mind. Mastery of the mind is therefore fundamental.

J.F. – But human life isn't just thought. It's action.

M. – Aren't your body and speech at the bidding of your thoughts? The body does only what the mind tells it to, and speech too – they don't just work through unconscious reflexes.

J.F. – It seems rather optimistic to me to say that the body only does what the mind tells it to.

M. – Optimistic? I'm not talking about the body's physiological functions, only about voluntary actions. If we were capable of mastering our words and deeds, most conflicts between people would be resolved. But that's impossible without mastery over the mind. What's more, it's your mind that colors your actions, because according to your motivation two apparently identical actions can have completely opposite effects, positive or negative. For example, giving money to someone can be either to help him or to corrupt him. But to come back to the use of mastery over the mind in concrete situations, true patience isn't a sign of weakness, but of strength. It doesn't just mean to let everything happen completely passively. Patience gives you the strength to act correctly without being blinded by hatred and a thirst for revenge, which deprive you of any capacity for judgment. As the Dalai Lama often says, true tolerance isn't a question of saying, 'Come on, do me some harm!' It's neither submission nor resignation – it's accompanied by the courage, strength of mind and intelligence that keep us from needless mental suffering and hold us back from falling into ill will.

True patience and nonviolence consist of choosing the most altruistic solution. Sweet words, if spoken with the intention to deceive, look like kindness but are actually violent. Conversely, for a mother to tell off or slap her child, with love and for the child's own good, looks like violence but is really kindness. What counts is the motivation behind our actions and the final result of those actions. The choice of methods comes from exercising our intelligence. In theory, therefore, the use of violence for beneficial ends might be acceptable. But, in practice, it's very difficult to use it successfully. Violence encourages violence, and usually has disastrous effects. So it's best to avoid conflict or, whenever it's inevitable, to try to neutralize anyone who's about to commit a violent action, without ever going beyond what's strictly necessary and without adding any negative emotions to the situation.

J.F. – There's something very true about what you're saying, but to me it all seems to apply mainly to what I'd call useless or superfluous emotions – excessive annoyance, or the sort of ambition that comes more from megalomania than anything else. Or to overkill, like displaying a spirit of vengeance and retaliation that goes far beyond what's necessary to neutralize any real danger. As an examination of superfluous emotions and excesses of all kinds, it seems rather humdrum to me. I don't mean that it's easy to put into practice, but it's hardly a sensational discovery. It's simply that the vast majority of our emotions, desires, and ambitions operate in the context of what we do or how we react in the face of reality. That implies that most of our underlying feelings, wants, ambitions, wariness, and precautions are by no means superfluous, nor are they contemptible or pointless, because they're related to our actual circumstances. If I want to build a house or do some work or some scientific research, I must have some sort of ambition, you could say. That's perfectly legitimate, is due neither to hatred nor covetousness, and is going to do no one any harm. But it might give rise to some negative feelings of disappointment if what I'm doing runs into obstacles, or if someone interferes and sabotages my project. None of these are emotions I can just dismiss, because they don't just come up in my mind, they're related to my real situation and are part of how I deal with it.

M. – It's true that they're triggered by the external situation, but they don't belong exclusively to it. A particular individual might seem desirable to one person and detestable to another. A politician works hard to exercise power, a hermit to be rid of it. So the pattern of our emotions is determined by the way we perceive reality. Once again, it's not at all a matter of cutting ourselves off from all human feelings, but of attaining a vast and serene mind which is no longer the plaything of our emotions, which is no longer shaken by adversity or intoxicated by success. If a handful of salt falls into a glass of water, it makes that water undrinkable; but if it falls into a lake it makes hardly any detectable difference. Because of the narrowness of their minds, most people suffer pointlessly all the time from not getting what they want and having to face what they don't want. Another source of suffering is self-centeredness. If you're completely centered on yourself, the difficulties you encounter and the disquiet they cause you work directly against your well-being. You feel depressed and can't accept such problems. On the other hand, if your main concern is others' good, you'll cheerfully accept whatever personal difficulties might be entailed in bringing about their good, because you know that others' well-being counts for more than your own.

J.F. – But there are numerous instances when people feel dissatisfied at not obtaining what they want – not for artificial reasons, not because they haven't mastered their inner thoughts, and not because what they want isn't legitimate or is motivated only by pride, but for reasons based in objective reality, even in altruism. A doctor who wants to cure his patient experiences feelings and emotions that are admirable. If he fails, the disappointment he feels is also admirable. He's dissatisfied, but for excellent reasons.

M. – Yes, that sort of ambition is more than just legitimate, it's necessary.

J.F. – So is there any place for classifying ambitions into admirable and not so admirable?

M. – Yes, there certainly is. The undesirable emotions are those that falsify or paralyze our judgment, not those that encourage us to accomplish great tasks. The wish to allay others' suffering, which may inspire a whole lifetime's work, is an admirable ambition. It's important to distinguish between negative emotions, like desire, hatred, and pride, that solidify still further our self-centered outlook, and positive ones, like altruistic love, compassion, and faith, that allow us to free ourselves little by little from those negative and self-centered tendencies. Positive emotions don't disturb our mind, they reinforce it and make it more stable and more courageous.

J.F. – So are we back to the Epicurean distinction between necessary and unnecessary desires?

M. – Positive ambition – the pursuit of others' well-being by all possible means, the fervent wish to transform oneself – is one of the cardinal virtues in Buddhism. In fact, Buddhists nurture one main ambition without any limits, that of removing the suffering of all living beings throughout the whole universe. That sort of ambition stops you succumbing to inertia and makes you strong-minded and determined. So the distinction between the positive and negative, selfless and self-centered sides of ambition is important. You could say that ambition is positive if its aim is to help others. That's the simplest definition. Conversely, ambition is negative if achieving it is detrimental to others, and an emotion is negative if it destroys your own and others' inner peace.

J.F. – Do you exclude from positive ambitions all those aimed at improving our own lot?

M. – Absolutely not. Our own well-being is important, but it should never be to the detriment of others. Curiously enough, the best way to improve our own lot is to be concerned above all by that of others. As Shantideva, an eighth-century Buddhist teacher, said:

> All the joy the world contains
> Has come through wishing happiness for others.
> All the misery the world contains
> Has come through wanting pleasure for oneself.
> Is there need for lengthy explanation?
> Childish beings look out for themselves,
> While Buddhas labor for the good of others:
> See the difference that divides them![2]

To conclude our previous discussion, it may be commonplace to say that power and money don't bring happiness, that jealousy and pride destroy all the joy in life, and so on. But the fact that it's commonplace absolutely doesn't stop us falling all the time into the trap of our usual preoccupations – gain and loss, pleasure and pain, praise and blame, fame and obscurity – and feeling totally vulnerable to them. It's not every day that someone tries to stab us in the back, but it's in every moment that we're the prey of our negative emotions. How many unhappy people find their lives wrecked by jealousy! If only they were able to recognize how insubstantial that jealousy really was and let it dissolve in their minds like a cloud vanishing in the sky, not only would jealousy leave them in peace but it would certainly never develop to the point of pushing them to commit a crime, as so often happens. Small clouds, as they say, don't bring rain. It's when a thought first arises that you have to do something about it, not when the emotions it engenders get completely out of control. If you don't deal with the spark, what hope do you have of doing something when the whole forest's on fire?

J.F. – Here again, all philosophies agree. There's a sort of shared foundation of practical wisdom, both Eastern and Western, the art of managing our set of psychological dispositions in their relationships with reality, so as to avoid all the excesses that in the final analysis make us miserable and dissatisfied. However, what we now call psychology, the science of the mind, isn't only that sort of practical advice, like Epictetus' manual in Stoicism, designed to help us lessen as much as possible our vulnerability, not only to outer circumstances and life's mishaps but also to our own passions. Psychology nowadays, before any idea of practical application or of recipes for inner serenity, is simply the study of cognitive phenomena. And there, in that symposium at Harvard that I referred to earlier, several of the American participants said that they'd discovered in Buddhism a science of the mind that they felt was of an exceptional richness.

M. – Don't let's forget, though, that scientists interested in that kind of dialogue with Buddhism are far from numerous.

J.F. – So what does this science of the mind consist of?

M. – Buddhist psychology has many facets. For example, it investigates how mental factors arise when the mind gets attached to the innate feeling of 'me' and takes that self for an independent, truly existing entity. A whole cascade of mental events are engendered by that belief in a self.

J.F. – Just a minute. Did you say the self was innate?

M. – I mean that we all naturally have that idea of 'me' – we reply when we're called, we think 'I'm hot' when it's hot, we're aware of our own existence, and so on. That's what Buddhism means by the innate feeling of a self. But we then superimpose, on top of that feeling, an idea that the self is a separate entity that constitutes our identity as an individual. That idea's just the mind's own fabrication, a simple mental designation, as I've already said. If you look for that 'me' somewhere in the stream of consciousness or in the body, or even in the combination of the two, whether using analysis or contemplation, you'll never succeed in identifying any entity, mental or physical, that corresponds to an individual self.

J.F. – Yes, but even if the self, the personality, and the ego are without any real location, the feeling we have of them is perhaps not completely innate, because it varies according to culture and individual. There are cultures and individuals in which it's particularly elevated. Hypertrophy of the self is a cultural and individual factor. The feeling of personal identity is at least as much a product of society and our own individual story as it's innate.

M. – That's just what I meant. The most basic feeling of 'me' is innate, and everything superimposed on it is fabricated by the individual under the influence of society and his or her own personality. The basic feeling, the one that makes us feel we exist, is common to all beings. The difference is in the different magnitudes this feeling of a self takes on, the different degrees of belief we have in it as an entity that exists in itself.

J.F. – What is it that's so harmful and wrong – the self as such, or its egomaniac excesses?

M. – It's not the self as such. Even someone free of any attachment to the idea of a self still answers when called. What's so harmful is, of course, the ego's excesses. But there are also more benign forms of attachment to a self, which may be less visible but are no less the source of many of our torments. In this context, we find in Buddhism a whole catalogue of mental events which result from attachment or nonattachment to a self. Fifty-eight of them are described in the first instance, followed by many more variations. They range from positive factors like impartiality, self-respect, consideration for others, trust, nonattachment, vigilance, and so on, to negative ones like arrogance, torpor, overexcitement, secretiveness, dogmatism, indifference, and many more.

J.F. – But what does Buddhist introspection entail?

M. – One might reflect on such questions as, 'What is consciousness? What triggers a perception? Can the mind know itself?' The answer to this last question, for instance, is that from a relative point of view we're quite clearly aware of our minds and can observe the movements and nature of our thoughts. Indeed, we'd be unable to function without being aware of our thoughts. But, in the final analysis, no thought could both think and know itself at the same time, just as a sword can't cut itself and an eye can't see itself. So here, and in most examples of this kind, two kinds of reasoning or logic are distinguished. One is based on relative truth, or in other words on common sense, and the other on absolute truth. In the latter case, a final analysis shows that if consciousness existed as an independent entity, it could never both be and know itself at the same time. There are different philosophical schools in Buddhism, of different levels. Some say, in this case, that consciousness has an ultimate and independent reality and that it's self-aware by a process that doesn't imply a subject-object relationship, like a lamp flame that illuminates itself without needing any external source of light. Others would reply that a flame has no need to 'illuminate' itself as it doesn't contain any darkness, and that if light could illuminate itself, darkness would also have to be able to darken itself.

J.F. – I don't want to deny the originality of Buddhist thinking in this field, but in what you've just said I recognize a whole classic problem in Western philosophy. Can the mind know itself, for example? This is what we call the problem of the possibility of introspective thought. In perception, or in knowledge, can we be simultaneously aware of the object perceived or known, and of our own thought as a conscious agent? Some psychologists think that introspection is possible, while others think that we're not good enough judges to examine ourselves and that observing our inner life by itself is unreliable; only by observing behavior can we ever hope to find out where it comes from.

M. – That last point of view, of course, would exclude any contemplative knowledge, which is Buddhism's very essence. If you think about it, one of the main things that distinguishes what's conscious from what's inanimate is exactly that faculty of self-examination. It's the unique characteristic of the mind. So that reluctance to explore the nature of the mind through introspection, rather than limiting oneself to what's measurable or detectable by physical means, is self-defeating.

Buddhist and other contemplators have been applying themselves to the introspective approach for more than two thousand years. Using mechanical instruments is hardly likely to teach one anything about the nature of the mind, because what one will be studying and measuring will only be the nervous system's input and output. Consciousness itself will be left out of the investigation. Only the mind can know and analyze the mind.

J.F. – How would you analyze perception?

M. – In terms of relative truth, each instant of consciousness is born from contact with an object triggering a perception. You could say that there's a subject for each object, at each moment of perception. Despite an apparent continuity, perception and discursive thought arise and cease in each instant. But in the final analysis, even in the present moment, consciousness doesn't exist as an independent and distinct entity. It's just a flow, a continuity made up of ephemeral instants that have no individual existence. Only nondual 'awareness', which transcends discursive thoughts, never changes, because it's beyond time.

J.F. – The study of perceptions and sensations, beginning first of all with ideas, is an old problem that goes back to Greek philosophy and continued up to Kant's time and beyond. It's traditionally called the problem of the theory of consciousness, and includes the formation of images, concepts, sensations, the building up of thought and reasoning. On a more normative level, it's also logic, one of the most important branches of Western philosophy.

M. – Of Eastern philosophy, too. There are whole treatises on logic, some of them extremely complex.

J.F. – Logic as a process is not only how our thoughts unfold but also how we build up representations, how we organize them, how they hold together and lead to judgments, reasoning, and so on. But it's also the discipline required to avoid errors of reasoning and judgment, the whole science of linking concepts together. From Plato's *Theaetetus* until Kant's *Critique of Pure Reason*, via Descartes' *Discourse on the Method*, it's been a central theme. So, again, for me the most interesting thing so far is to see that the problems Buddhism has found itself dealing with, in the absence of practically any contact with the West until very recently, are much the same as those that Western philosophy has tried to confront.

M. – Buddhism doesn't claim to have discovered any new truths.

The very notion of 'newness' is, of course, foreign to any spiritual knowledge, which aims at recognizing the very nature of things – and that has no reason to differ from West to East, or from ancient times to the present day. But what distinguishes it from a purely intellectual analysis is that it's derived from direct contemplation of the nature of mind. It's acquired by experience, not just conceptual reasoning. Nor is it knowledge that's just left as theory, like a doctor's prescription left on your bedside table without the medicine ever being taken. It's actually put to work to eliminate from the stream of the mind everything that veils its underlying nature.

J.F. – The same distinction between discursive and contemplative knowledge is also central in Plato. Direct vision, or *theoria*, is for him the final stage in philosophical initiation.

M. – Let's come back to perception for a moment. Our perception of an object as desirable or undesirable doesn't reside in the object itself, but in the way we perceive it. There's no inherent quality in a beautiful object that does the mind any good, nor anything in an ugly object that might harm it. If human beings were to disappear, the phenomenal world wouldn't necessarily disappear along with them – but the world as it's perceived by humans would no longer have any basis for its existence. 'Worlds' as they're perceived by other sorts of beings would continue to exist, for them. The classic example is that of a glass of water, which is perceived as a habitat by a fish, as a drink by a human, as nectar of immortality by a god, as blood and pus by a being from the world of spirits tortured by want and as molten bronze by those who see the world as a hell. There's a Zen poem, too, which says, 'To her lover, a beautiful woman is a delight; to an ascetic, a distraction; to a wolf, a good meal.' Although they're triggered by objects, our perceptions are, in the end, built up by the mind. When we see a mountain, the first image that comes to us is a pure, unfabricated perception. But from the second instant onward, some people will think, 'Oh, that mountain looks dangerous and inhospitable,' while others might think, 'That would be a good place to do a retreat.' Numerous different thoughts will then follow. If objects were defined by themselves and possessed intrinsic qualities, independent of the subject observing them, everyone ought to perceive them in the same way.

J.F. – Those observations are all quite correct, although as I've already said they're classic fare for a philosopher. But how are they related to the sort of wisdom that can be applied in everyday life?

M. – If we investigate our perceptions through contemplation and analysis, we'll eventually stop believing in and being so attached to their substantiality. We'll understand, for example, the ephemeral relativity of notions such as 'friend' and 'enemy'. Someone we see as an enemy today might be greatly liked by other people, and in several months' time may become the best of friends for us, too. Somehow, we have to train our minds in such a way that the solidity of our judgments, of our perception of both other people and inanimate objects, melts away like a block of ice melting into water. Ice and water are the same element, but whereas one is hard and brittle and you can break your bones on it, the other is soft and fluid. We can perceive the whole world as potentially hostile and divide it into what's desirable and what's undesirable, or else we can see it as a continuous process of transformation, ceaselessly changing and devoid of any true existence. We could even recognize in phenomena an infinite purity, synonymous with emptiness. These different ways of perceiving things make an enormous difference.

J.F. – There are two attitudes toward reality, toward humankind as a whole. The first is common to the Epicureans, Buddhists, and Stoics. It consists of saying that the whole reality of the world and humankind can't be improved as such. The only thing that can be improved is the human psyche. The solution, broadly speaking, is to attain spiritual qualities, personal wisdom. To concentrate on the versions I know least badly, the Epicurean or Stoic sage is someone who basically says to himself, 'The less I get involved in all the complications of the world and leave the folly of men to unfold independently of myself, the more I'll succeed in keeping out of harm's way and won't find myself mixed up in potentially disturbing trouble. At all costs, I must avoid convincing myself that I can change anything. The only thing I can change is the way I behave and think in the face of those circumstances. And the worst thing I could do is take up causes or take sides in anything.' The opposite of such an attitude is one that consists of saying, 'Of course we can change reality, it can be improved, we can act upon it. The goal of philosophy isn't to master my thoughts to the point of no longer taking part in any objective situation, it's to transform that situation through technical and political means.' Plato tried to combine these two positions.

M. – I think that Buddhism recommends a marriage of those two attitudes, too, but a marriage based on principles that to my mind are more basic than nonintervention on the one hand and technology and politics on the other. First of all, there's no need to transform reality itself, or, let's say, the ultimate nature of things. According to Buddhism, perfection, the primordial purity of everything, is neither 'degraded' when we fail to recognize it nor 'improved' when we do recognize it. What we can and must change is our mistaken perception of the nature of things. It's within the framework of that transformation that we apply mastery of thoughts and the altruistic approach that consists of offering others the means of bringing about such a transformation. In the end, the Buddhist path consists of a new way of perceiving the world, a rediscovery of the true nature of the individual and of phenomena. It allows us to be much less vulnerable to the ups and downs of life, because we know how to take them not only 'philosophically' but also joyfully, using difficulty and success as catalysts to make rapid progress in our spiritual practice. It's not a matter of withdrawing from the world, but of understanding its nature. You don't look away from suffering, you look for a cure for it and go beyond it.

J.F. – What sort of a cure?

M. – All living beings possess within themselves the potential to become Buddha, or in other words to attain perfect liberation and wisdom. Everything that veils that potential and prevents it expressing itself is only adventitious and ephemeral. The veils are called 'ignorance' or 'mental obscurations'. So the spiritual path consists of freeing oneself from negative emotions and ignorance and, in so doing, *actualizing* the perfection that's already present within us. It's a goal that has nothing selfish about it. The motivation that makes us progress on the spiritual path is the idea of transforming ourselves to be able to help others be free of suffering. Through this altruistic point of view, we first acknowledge our impotence in the face of others' suffering, and then give rise to the wish to perfect ourselves in order to be able to do something about it. It's far from an indifference to the world. Invulnerability to the ravages of outer circumstances becomes the armor in which we clad ourselves for the battle to deliver others from suffering.

J.F. – In the book of the Harvard symposium, Daniel Goleman, who holds a doctorate in psychology, states at the beginning of his account: 'As a student of psychology at Harvard, I had come to assume, as is the tacit assumption in the West, that psychology is a scientific topic that originated in America and Europe within the last century.'

(I'd add here, by the way, that there's psychology in Greek philosophy.) He goes on to speak of scientific psychology in the sense in which it was understood in the nineteenth and twentieth centuries. But when he began traveling in Asia, he says, he discovered psychological systems there, particularly in Buddhism, that were very rich, diversified, and developed – and that looking back he was shocked to see how his professors in the West had never felt the need to teach about those systems of psychology in the same way as they taught about all the schools of Western psychology. So in the East there must have been a psychology defined according to the same criteria as what we call scientific psychology in the West – which by the way, to me has never quite seemed to deserve being described as a science, except for its neurophysiological side. So here's a professional psychologist telling us that this attitude of detached, scientific observation of the phenomena of mental processes isn't strictly Western at all. Such investigation had been going on for a very long time, particularly in Buddhism.

M. – I'd add, in passing, that Goleman isn't the only person to have been surprised by such a lack of interest in Eastern disciplines. The neurobiologist Francisco Varela, who's director of research at the National Centre for Scientific Research in France and a member of the Research Centre for Applied Epistemology at the Ecole Polytechnique in Paris, has also written: 'It is our contention that the rediscovery of Asian philosophy, particularly of the Buddhist tradition, is a second renaissance in the cultural history of the West, with the potential to be as equally important as the rediscovery of Greek thought in the European renaissance. Our Western histories of philosophy, which ignore Indian thought, are artificial, since India and Greece share with us an Indo-European linguistic heritage as well as many cultural and philosophical preoccupations.'[3]

J.F. – So what do they consist of, these Buddhist psychological investigations that aren't so much related to the idea of personal improvement or the attainment of serenity, but more to the pure study of mental and psychological phenomena?

M. – I'll take a simple example involving the study of perception, since that's one of the main topics in the study of how the mind works. When you perceive an object, even the simplest one, a blue square for example, you can distinguish the area of the square, its corners, its sides, and so on. These several elements are all perceived integrally as a square. Now, is there an instantaneous overall perception of the object with all its components, or does it happen rather through a rapid succession of brief instants of awareness of each detail of the object, assembled into an integrated image – like when you swing a torch rapidly around in a circle at arm's length and see a circle of light, even though it's actually composed of multiple perceptions of a point of light in continuous movement? There's a whole series of analyses of this kind in the Buddhist literature, and treatises several hundred pages long that deal with such phenomena.

J.F. – When do they date from?

M. – From the Buddha's sermons, in the sixth century B.C., right through to several great Tibetan commentators of these texts on perception in the nineteenth century. These problems continue to be discussed and investigated in a very lively way during the metaphysical sparring that goes on every day in our monasteries.

J.F. – I find that very interesting indeed, because these questions match the ones put by one of the most important twentieth-century schools of psychology. It's what's called Gestalt psychology, the psychology of form, founded in the first part of the twentieth century in Germany and America. Gestalt psychology arose from the following observation: psychology has been, until now, essentially analytic. That's to say, it believed that our perception of objects was built up from each of the elements of which the object consisted. We're supposed to arrive at the final, complete object step by step. But in fact, what happens in actual practice – Gestalt psychology was developed using laboratory experiments – is that we perceive integral objects from the start. Recent theories in cognitive science dealing with notions of 'complexity' and 'self-organization' also pose the problem of overall perception in terms that could be seen as comparable with the Buddhist analysis. So here's a problem that's already been asked in almost identical terms, six hundred years before Christ, in Buddhist studies of perception.

M. – No object is permanent, and the subtle impermanence of things is such that an object must be changing every instant. As consciousness is triggered by the object, there are as many instants of consciousness as of states of the impermanent object. This idea of the instant-by-instant impermanence of phenomena and the mind goes a long way, because it shows that if there were even one single, fixed, permanent, intrinsically existing entity in the phenomenal world, consciousness would remain as if stuck to that object, and would be prolonged indefinitely. In the end, all the consciousnesses in the world would find themselves trapped by that object, and wouldn't be able to detach themselves from it. It's the presence of this subtle impermanence that leads Buddhism to compare the phenomenal world to a dream or an illusion, to an ever-changing and ungraspable flux. Even things that seem solid to us, like a table, are changing every instant. The stream of our thoughts is also made up of infinitesimally short instants triggered by each of the infinitesimally tiny changes in the world outside. It's only the putting together of these instants that gives the impression of a gross reality.

J.F. – That's a view that takes the opposite stance to a very important Platonic idea. All the Greek philosophers, but especially Plato, took the view – almost obsessively, I'd say – that we can't know anything that moves or undergoes change. For them, a phenomenon – the Greek word, as you know, means 'that which appears', the world of appearances – being in a state of permanent motion, it can't be the object of any stable, certain, definite knowledge. Hence the efforts of the whole of Western philosophy, not only the Greeks but right through to Kant, to find *behind* the phenomenon some permanent and stable element that could be the object of definite knowledge. The model for such stability was supplied by mathematics, which at the starting point of Western thought was the first model that completely satisfied conceptual thought. So the permanent principles behind phenomena and governing them were sought. These permanent principles are laws. To escape from the chaotic motion of the phenomenal world, the structures behind it need to be found, and these are the relationships of cause and effect, the permanent laws. Epicurus, or to be more exact his disciple the Latin poet Lucretius, called these laws 'pacts' (*foedera*) by which the Gods guaranteed the matching of the human mind to reality. These pacts are the stable element behind the moving reality of phenomena.

M. – But be careful. The existence of laws doesn't mean that there actually are permanent entities that exist behind phenomena. Buddhism accepts perfectly that the phenomenal world is governed inescapably by the laws of cause and effect. But neither these laws nor the phenomena they govern are permanent, autonomous entities that exist in themselves. Nothing at all exists by itself and in itself; everything appears through the play of the interdependence of causes and conditions. The law of gravity doesn't exist in itself, in the absence of objects. A rock is composed of atoms, which are themselves equivalent to energy. A rainbow is formed by the play of a shaft of sunlight falling on a cloud of raindrops. It appears, but it's intangible. As soon as one of the factors contributing to it is missing, the phenomenon disappears. So the 'rainbow' has no inherent nature of its own, and you can't speak of the dissolution or annihilation of something that didn't exist in the first place. That 'something' only owed its illusory appearance to a transitory coming together of elements which aren't intrinsically existing entities themselves, either.

J.F. – But you can't reduce all natural phenomena to just rainbows.

M. – Well, all phenomena are certainly the result of a combination of transitory factors. Nowhere are there any phenomena that are permanent and exist independently. As the saying goes, 'Nothing independent could appear, just as a flower could never appear suspended in space.' To come back to laws, there's nothing that proves they exist as *permanent principles* underlying phenomena. Knowledge of them can only come through the mind, and it's a metaphysical choice that science makes when it states that with the help of our concepts we can discover the ultimate nature of a phenomenal world that exists independently of our concepts. Here Buddhism agrees with Henri Poincaré, who said in essence that whatever the nature of a reality independent of the mind conceiving it might be, that reality will forever be inaccessible to us. You could also say that in the absence of human beings, reality as human beings perceive it would cease to be.

J.F. – But mathematical laws do exist, all the same!

M. – That's not as obvious as it might seem. We might well suppose that the reality underlying the phenomenal world could be expressed in mathematical terms that exist outside a purely subjective domain. But, as Alan Wallace sums up, 'Plato and Aristotle agreed, though for different reasons, that mathematical axioms need not be proved, for their truth is unquestionably self-evident ... In the nineteenth century, several mathematicians suggested that none of Euclid's postulates are either true or false, they are simply the rules of the game ... During this century it began to appear that mathematical axioms are derived, directly or indirectly, from experience ... There is little justification for believing that mathematics contains truth in the sense of laws of physical reality as it exists independent of experience.'[4] To deny that there can be any detectable stable entities behind phenomena is also a refutation of the idea found in certain Hindu philosophies of 'general archetypes', like an archetype 'tree', that exists in every tree, or even the archetype 'exist' that would be the essence of everything that exists.

J.F. – That's the same as the *idea* in Plato.

M. – It's quite similar. Buddhism refutes such notions by saying that if such an archetype as 'tree' actually existed, it would have to be the same in each tree, and therefore all trees would have to grow at the same time and in the same way, because a permanent entity can't be the cause of something changing and multiple. In fact, the simple fact of producing or growing destroys the permanence of any entity, because afterward it's no longer the same as before.

J.F. – It's important not to confuse axiom and postulate, and not to assimilate knowledge in physics and biology, an ongoing to-and-fro process between observation, theory, and experiment, with the postulates of mathematics, an *a priori* science by its very essence. But our brief isn't to plunge into a seminar on the philosophy of science. To pursue the East-West parallel, Hindu philosophy seems to be closer to Plato's philosophy than Buddhism, because for Plato the 'tree in itself' exists in a suprasensory world, and all the trees that exist in the world of the senses, the phenomenal world, are, so to speak, copies of that tree-in-itself, 'perceptible' copies of that 'intelligible' tree. None of the copies, therefore, can fully reflect the perfection of the tree-in-itself. Hence the obsessive fear, the opposition between the perceptible world, unknowable because of its movement, and the suprasensory world of intelligible entities. Can Hindu philosophy be seen in such terms? How did Buddhism react to it?

M. – Let's say that Plato's *idea* and Hinduism's 'general entities' do have points in common, in the sense that both envisage fixed entities behind phenomena. As for Buddhism, it gets down to a complex discussion that refutes the existence of any permanent entity whatsoever. The Hindu theory that Buddhism contests most strongly is that of an all-powerful Creator, like the Hindu Ishvara. Debates on the subject took place with the holders of the main Hindu philosophies, of which there were many, several centuries both before and after Christ.

What we're talking about here is the idea of a permanent Creator entity, sufficient in itself, without any cause preceding it, creating things as a voluntary act. Point by point, Buddhist dialectics refute this idea. Let's take all-powerfulness, for instance. A Creator would have to be all-powerful. Either the Creator doesn't 'decide' to create, in which case all-powerfulness is lost, for creation happens outside his will; or he creates voluntarily, in which case he can't be all-powerful, either, as he's creating under the influence of his desire to create.

J.F. – That's as neat as the paradoxes of Zeno of Elea.

M. – Can a Creator be a permanent entity? No, because after creating he's different from how he was before he created. He's become 'he who created'. What's more, if he creates the whole universe, that necessarily implies that all the causes of the universe must be present within him. Now, one of the bases of the law of cause and effect, or *karma*, is that an event can't take place as long as all the causes and conditions for its arising are not assembled, and that it can't *not* take place once they are. That means that a Creator either could never create or would have to be constantly creating. This sort of reasoning, and many others like it, can be applied to all the traditions that envisage a Creator who's eternal, all-powerful, who exists intrinsically, and so on.

J.F. – I'm full of admiration. It's like listening to a Skeptic dialectician from classical times, or an Epicurean, or a Stoic, refuting the idea of a personal Creator God.

M. – In Asia, this form of dialectics continues even nowadays in philosophical debate and discussion. The relative aspect of phenomena, or in other words the world of appearances, is distinguished from the ultimate nature of everything. From an absolute point of view, Buddhism holds that an entity that truly existed could neither arise in the first place nor ever disappear. Being can't be born from nothingness, because even an infinitude of causes wouldn't be able to make something that didn't exist come into existence; nor can it be born from what already exists, as in that case there would be no need for it to be born.

J.F. – This is like listening to the replies in Plato's *Parmenides*.

M. – In any case, when you dissect the process of cause and effect from the point of view of absolute truth, you can only conclude that it's a process that can't link entities that have any sort of true, independent existence. Either the cause disappears before the effect appears, in which case the cause, as something which no longer exists, couldn't possibly have any relationship with the effect; or the cause is still present at the moment the effect appears, in which case it can't be the cause of the effect, because there can't be a cause and effect relationship between two things that exist simultaneously.

J.F. – Oh yes there can!

M. – No! If there were two things that really existed simultaneously, each as an independent entity, one couldn't be the cause of the other. If a seed and a plant were both entities with intrinsic existence, then the seed couldn't be the cause of the plant because the seed would have to be destroyed before the result, the plant, could appear. There could be no contiguity, and hence no causal relationship, between them. For the same reason, if a seed and a plant existed at the same time, that plant can't possibly have come from that seed.

J.F. – The relationship of seed to plant is the kind of causal relationship in which the cause precedes the effect, in temporal succession. But there are other types of causal relationships in which cause and effect coexist.

M. – For example?

J.F. – The fact that I'm breathing oxygen that keeps me alive. The cause, the oxygen in the air, and the effect, my body breathing it, coexist. Or the sunlight coexisting with a leaf absorbing its energy. Or a beam holding up a roof, the cause that prevents the roof collapsing – cause and effect are both present simultaneously. What I mean is that, classically, there are both concomitant and successive causal relationships. Not every succession is a causal relationship, and not every causal relationship is a succession. It's the old debate between Hume and Kant.

M. – The sunlight that caused the products of photosynthesis to appear in the leaf is no longer present once those products have appeared, even if more solar energy keeps coming and more products are synthesized. The same goes for the oxygen being loaded molecule by molecule into the red cells in your lungs. Of course, in a way, oxygen as a gross phenomenon remains present, but the same oxygen isn't present all the time. Oxygen isn't a permanent entity, it's constantly undergoing transformation. So is sunlight. Seeds and plants, beams and structurally intact roofs – none of them are entities with permanent, totally independent existence. The point I'm trying to make is that on a relative level, that of conventional truth as we all perceive it, the laws of cause and effect are inescapable. But if you look at things from the point of view of absolute logic, the laws of cause and effect couldn't operate with entities that had any permanent and solid existence. So nowhere in the whole phenomenal world is there a single fixed, independent, intrinsically existing entity.

J.F. – You're talking about cause and effect relationships between events, but there are also structural cause and effect relationships. For example, a system taken as a whole – a boat floating on water. The density of the water is the cause for the boat to float. Boat and water coexist.

M. – That's exactly what I mean. There are no cause and effect relationships between truly existing entities, but there are such relationships between transitory phenomena. You're calling them structural, and we'd call them relationships of interdependence: 'This exists because that is so, this is produced on the basis of that.' Nothing exists by itself, independently of other phenomena. Each of the elements of the chain of cause and effect is itself an aggregate of fleeting elements in perpetual flux. This is an argument that shows up the nonreality of independent, permanent phenomena, whether a divine Creator or an atom existing by itself, without causes or conditions, *independent* of other phenomena.

J.F. – There again, this is a problem that recurs throughout the history of Western philosophy. Sometimes phenomena are said to exist and are reality; that's the empiricist or realist view. Sometimes they're said to be a complete illusion; that's absolute idealism, like Berkeley's philosophy in the eighteenth century, for instance. Sometimes phenomena are seen as a chaos of things in succession, in which any relationship of cause and effect is utterly illusory; that's Hume's philosophy. Sometimes the phenomenon isn't reality in itself. It's a sort of synthesis, an encounter between reality in itself, which lies outside our knowledge, behind phenomena, and the building activity of the human mind, a sort of intermediate result between the primary matter supplied by reality in itself and the elaborative capacity of the human mind. In other words, it's at once real, partly supplied by the world outside, at the same time as being partly built up by the human mind. Such, in very broad outline, is Kant's theory in *The Critique of Pure Reason*. So just about all possibilities have been envisaged in

Western philosophy. My opinion is that this isn't a real problem. If phenomena don't exist in Buddhism, what does exist?

M. – Buddhism takes a middle path. It doesn't deny the reality of phenomena in the relative world of perception, but it does deny that there are any permanent, autonomous entities existing behind phenomena. That's why we speak of a 'middle path' that falls neither into nihilism, for which nothing exists outside our perceptions and everything is nothingness, nor into 'eternalism' – the realism you mentioned, no doubt – for which there's a unique reality that exists independently of any perception and is composed of entities that exist by themselves. The kind of solid entities that Buddhism refutes are, for example, indivisible particles of matter and indivisible instants of consciousness. It's close to the formulation of modern physicists, who have abandoned the idea of particles as being little cannonballs or infinitely small masses. What's called mass or matter is, rather, a sort of nonuniformity of the energy field. Buddhism leads us to the notion of the unreality of the solid world through an intellectual reasoning that doesn't claim to be a theory of physics but which examines intellectually the very possibility of the existence of atoms, of indivisible particles.

J.F. – Are there, according to Buddhism, two levels of reality, a level of phenomena, and behind that a real substrate of some kind, even if it's not made up of material atoms and can be reduced to energy?

M. – When Buddhism speaks of the 'emptiness' of phenomena, it says that phenomena 'appear' but don't reflect in any way the existence of fixed entities. Modern physics tells us that an electron, for example, can be seen either as a particle, or as a wave – two notions that common sense tells us are completely incompatible. Some interference phenomena caused by electrons can only be explained by supposing that an electron passes through two different holes at the same instant. According to Buddhism, atoms can't be considered fixed entities, existing according to one single, determined mode. So how could the macroscopic manifest world, which is supposed to be composed of such particles, have any fixed reality? All this helps to destroy our notion of the solidity of appearances. It's in that sense that Buddhism affirms that the ultimate nature of phenomena is emptiness and that emptiness carries within it an infinite potential of manifestation.

J.F. – Who formulated these premonitory hypotheses about the nature and insubstantiality of matter?

M. – The Buddha, and they were then compiled and commented in several treatises by two of the greatest Buddhist philosophers, Nagarjuna (around the second century A.D.) and Chandrakirti (in the eighth century). Here's how the atom is analyzed. Take an ordinary, gross phenomenon like a table. If you separate its constituent parts, it's already no longer a table. You'll have legs, the tabletop, and so on. If you then reduce them all to sawdust, these constituent parts in turn lose their identity. If you now examine one grain of the sawdust, you'll find molecules, and then atoms. The concept of atoms had already been formulated in the East by the time of Democritus.

J.F. – It's true that the notion of the atom makes its appearance in the philosophy of Democritus and that of Epicurus. But they never demonstrated it scientifically, any more than the other theories of ancient physics. These were purely theoretical views.

M. – And curiously the Greek word 'atom' means 'uncuttable'.

J.F. – Exactly. The ultimate nucleus that can no longer be cut into two.

M. – Buddhism uses the same word. It speaks of particles that 'have no parts', which can't be subdivided. These are therefore supposed to be the ultimate constituents of matter. Now, take one of these particles, considered as an autonomous entity. How could it combine with other particles to constitute matter? If these particles touch each other, the left-hand side of one particle, for example, would touch the right-hand side of another. But if they have left and right-hand sides, they can be divided, and thus lose their characteristic of being 'indivisible'. If they have neither sides nor directions, they must be like points in mathematics, without dimension, thickness, or substance. If you tried to put together two dimensionless particles, either they wouldn't touch and can't therefore be put together, or they do make contact with one another, in which case they merge with one another. A whole mountain of indivisible particles could then dissolve into a single one of them. The conclusion is, therefore, that indivisible, discontinuous particles with an intrinsic existence as the constituents of matter simply can't exist. What's more, if an atom had a mass, a dimension, and a charge, would it be identical to the whole set of its attributes? Would it exist outside its attributes? An atom isn't identical to its mass, nor to its size. But nor is it other than its mass and its size. So an atom *has* a set of characteristics, but *is* none of them. An atom is just a concept, a label that doesn't cover any entity that exists in an autonomous and absolute way. It exists only as a convention, in a relative way.

J.F. – In Democritus and Epicurus there's the idea that the ultimate constituents of matter, and indeed of living beings, too, are atoms organized into varying configurations to make up the different phenomena that appear to us in different forms. Those appearances are no more than illusions produced by the different ways in which atoms are organized. But to explain how atoms group themselves together, and why some atoms group together with specific other ones, the classical philosophers invented the theory – completely imaginary, of course – of 'hooked' atoms. Certain atoms have hooks which allow them to link up with other atoms, while others don't. They needed some way of explaining why atoms grouped themselves together in a particular way to produce particular phenomena.

M. – In a way, in terms of the selective interactions between what we now call atoms, they weren't so far off the mark. But in terms of trying to get down to the ultimate constituents of matter, Buddhism would object that if there are hooks, there must be parts – the tip of the hook, its base, and so on. So what they're calling an indivisible particle is divisible after all.

J.F. – There's truth in that, of course. But anyway, at that stage, in both the West and the East, all these brilliant theories belonged to the realm of metaphysics rather than physics.

M. – Yes, but the point is that in showing that indivisible particles can't exist, Buddhism doesn't claim to be trying to account for physical phenomena in the way modern science would. What it's trying to do is to break the concept we have of the solidity of the phenomenal world in our everyday experience. Because that concept is what underlies our attachment to a self and to phenomena, and is therefore the cause of the dualistic way we separate self and others, existence and nonexistence, attachment and repulsion, and so on, and therefore of all our torments. In any case, Buddhism is here quite close, intellectually, to certain viewpoints in contemporary physics, and its contribution ought to be included in the history of ideas. One of the great physicists of our time, Henri Margenau, wrote: 'Toward the end of the nineteenth century the view arose that all interactions involved material objects. This is no longer held to be true. We know that there are fields which are wholly non-material.' Heisenberg said, 'Atoms are not things,' and Bertrand Russell, 'The idea that there is a hard little lump there, which is the electron, is an illegitimate intrusion of common-sense notions derived from touch ... Matter is a convenient formula for describing what happens where it isn't.' Sir James Jeans, in his Rede Lectures, went as far as saying, 'The universe begins to look more like a great thought than like a great machine.'

J.F. – They're very striking, aren't they, those examples of intu-ition in classical philosophy, in Democritus, Epicurus, Lucretius in the West, and even earlier in Buddhism? They're very well thought out, and go very far. Some of them, even though they're derived from sheer reflection without any possibility of experimental verification, are quite astonishing premonitions of modern science. It would probably be possible to find some equally striking examples in Chinese philoso-phy. The thing is, though, that in the West it happened that such intu-itions led to the experimental revolution that gave birth to modern science. Why was there no evolution of the kind in Buddhism?

M. – Experimental verification does exist in Buddhism, of course. But it's important not to lose sight of the goal that Buddhism sets itself. That goal is inner science, a science that's been developed over more than two thousand years of contemplation and study of the mind. Especially in Tibet, since the eighth century, that science was the principal preoccupation of a large part of the population. The goal was never to transform the external world by acting physically upon that world, but to transform it in producing better human beings, in allow-ing human beings to develop an inward knowledge of themselves. That knowledge has several levels. Metaphysics deals with ultimate, tran-scendent truths, and the application of that knowledge in the relative world of phenomena is used to unravel the tangle of suffering. Suffer-ing, whether physical or mental, is the result of negative deeds, words and thoughts – taking life, stealing, deceit, calumny, and so on. Nega-tive thoughts arise from cherishing and wanting to protect oneself, attitudes that flow naturally from the notion of a lasting and unique 'I'. The belief in a self as an independent entity is just one particular aspect of the reification of phenomena. Recognizing that the self we're attached to isn't a truly existing entity, and dissolving our attachment to the substantiality of phenomena, it's possible to interrupt the vicious circle of suffering. So this theoretical refutation of the concept of independent particles certainly helps to lessen our attachment to the reality of phenomena and of our own individual selves, and thus to free ourselves from the negative emotions. Such analysis leads to a knowledge which, for all that it's inner knowledge, has no less immense repercussions on our relationship with the outer world and the influence we have on it.

J.F. – Yes, but then how was that possible, since the Buddhist theory is that of the unreality of the outer world, or at any rate of its characteristics…

M. – …appearing, yet empty.

J.F. – In other words, that theory of the atom having no ultimate reality as a building block of reality has never been subjected to any experimental verification. You can't be sure that it's correct. So you're building a science of the mind on a completely unproven theory of matter.

M. – The goal is simply to destroy our concepts of a solid, permanent reality by demonstrating that those concepts are illogical and unfounded. Here, the verification is in terms of the transformation of the individual. It's not an analysis that claims to summarize physics. Its goal isn't to shed light on molecular structure, explain the movements of the stars, or anything else of the sort, but to act in an extremely pragmatic way as an antidote to the suffering engendered by attachment to phenomena.

J.F. – Yes, but all the same the goal was attained not thanks to any scientific certainty about what the external world really is or isn't but thanks to a pure hypothesis, a convenient vision made of the external world without ever being experimentally verified by Buddhists.

M. – In fact this view of things has been verified experimentally – in the field it actually belongs to. Experimentally, aspirin gets rid of headaches, while working on oneself inwardly in this way gets rid of hatred, desire, jealousy, pride, and everything else that disturbs the mind. It's an experimental result that seems to me, to put it mildly, at least as useful as aspirin!

J.F. – But to me, it seems to be saying: let's take up a particular idea of reality because that idea's convenient to us, it helps us build ourselves a suitable moral philosophy.

M. – It's not just a convenient idea of reality. By negating the idea of an indivisible particle using an intellectual, logical analysis, we can destroy the mental image that we've hitherto had of the solidity of phenomena. What we're trying to do is to obtain an effective antidote to suffering. If that goal's attained, the goal of the spiritual path is attained too. When you shoot an arrow, you mustn't forget what your target is. Success could be defined as being able to land on the moon, or to have mastered matter to the extent of being able to blow up the whole planet – but such successes are certainly questionable. Science, at the cost of centuries of intellectual and material effort, at the cost of generations of human beings who've dedicated their lives to it, has attained some of the major goals it's set itself. Buddhism has other priorities, to which, over the generations, it's dedicated equally extensive efforts.

J.F. – Buddhism's approach is completely understandable. But that doesn't alter the fact that it's not an approach to spiritual salvation built on a foundation of objective knowledge, but on the basis of a helpful hypothesis.

M. – What do you mean by objective knowledge? The nature of elementary particles can't be known independently of the systems we use to measure them. In the same way, a universe independent of any human concept couldn't ever be known by the human mind. What is it that's attached to the reality of phenomena? It's the mind. And here, what are we working on? The mind! If we succeed in unblocking the solid way in which the mind perceives the world – a way of perceiving that leads to endless suffering – then that's undeniably objective knowledge, not of the physics of the natural world, but of the mechanisms of suffering, and it's undeniably an experimental verification of the results of that science of the mind.

J.F. – I'm not completely satisfied by that idea of what experimental verification is.

M. – Do you think experimental verification only applies to physical phenomena? From that point of view, only the quantitative and physical sciences would deserve to be called exact sciences. To be exact, any science must start from certain hypotheses, and then proceed with rigor in the field of experience in order to confirm or invalidate those hypotheses in the light of that experience. There's no reason why those criteria should be confined to the physical, so-called objective, domain. What's more, I don't see why it should be necessary, as you said before, to dissociate the sciences of the mind from the improvement of the individual. Surely the attainment of serenity is one of the experimental proofs of contemplative science, just as the falling of bodies is experimental proof of the law of gravity.

Nothing, other than the mind itself, can allow us to know the ultimate nature of the mind. If introspection has failed as a scientific method in the context of Western psychology and has been discarded, it's because those who used it didn't have suitable tools at their disposal with which to conduct their experiments. They had neither the slightest training in, nor the slightest knowledge of, the field of contemplation, and knew nothing of the techniques that allow the mind to be calmed so that its underlying nature can be observed. It's like someone using an unstable voltmeter and concluding that it's impossible to measure the tension of an electric current. Apprenticeship in contemplative techniques requires perseverance. You can't just dismiss them with a wave of the hand because they're far from the predominant preoccupations of the Western world – which are, let's admit, a great deal more material than spiritual – and because you don't feel inclined to have the experience yourself. It's easy to understand the skepticism, but not the lack of interest or wish to verify the validity of a different approach. In fact, the same problem also exists in the other direction. I know Tibetans who refuse to believe that men have been on the moon!

1. *Mind Science: An East-West Dialogue*, op. cit. See also *Gentle Bridges, Dialogues between the Cognitive Sciences and the Buddhist Tradition*, J. Hayward and F. Varela, Shambhala, Boston, 1992, and especially *Sleeping, Dreaming, and Dying, a Colloquium with the XIVth Dalai Lama*, coordinated and narrated by F. Varela, Wisdom, 1997.

2. Shantideva, *The Way of the Bodhisattva* (*Bodhicaryavatara*), trans. Padmakara Translation Group, Shambhala, Boston and London, 1997.

3. Varela, F., E. Thompson and E. Rosch, *The Embodied Mind: Cognitive Science and Human Experience*, MIT Press, Cambridge, 1991.

4. J.F. Allan Wallace, *Choosing Reality*, Snow Lion, Ithaca, 1996. A remarkable work bridging Buddhist concepts and modern physics.

~

FIVE

LOOKING FOR REALITY:

BUDDHIST METAPHYSICS

JEAN-FRANÇOIS – I think we should stop skirting round the subject and come to Buddhism's central theme. In particular, we need an answer to the famous question – is Buddhism a philosophy? A religion? A system of metaphysics? What's the very core of Buddhism, the way it sees the world and the human condition, that explains the way Buddhists live and what they do, and all the psychological techniques that we've covered in our preceding discussions?

MATTHIEU – Here, I can't help quoting André Migot, who gives the perfect answer to that question in his book *Le Bouddha (The Buddha)*:[1]

'There has been a lot of discussion about whether Buddhism is a religion or a philosophy, and the question has never been decided one way or the other. In these terms, it is a question that only makes sense to a Westerner. Only in the West is philosophy just a branch of knowledge like mathematics or botany, and only in the West is the philosopher a person, usually a professor, who goes through particular doctrines during his courses but, once he goes home, lives exactly like his lawyer or his dentist without what he teaches having the slightest influence on the way he lives his life. Only in the West is religion, for a large majority of believers, a small compartment that only gets opened on particular days, at particular times or in certain predetermined circumstances, and is firmly closed again before actually doing anything. Although there are professors of philosophy in the East, too, a philosopher there is a spiritual master who lives what he teaches, surrounded by disciples who want to follow his example. His teaching is never based on sheer intellectual curiosity, for its value lies only in its realization. In this light, there seems little point in wondering whether Buddhism is a philosophy or a religion. It is a path, a way of salvation, that which led the Buddha to enlightenment; it is a method, a means of attaining liberation by working intensely on the mind and spirit.'

So I think that the simplest possible way to define Buddhism is, first and foremost, to see it as a path. The goal of that path is to attain what can be called 'perfection', ultimate knowledge, enlightenment, merging with the absolute, or, technically speaking, the state of Buddhahood.

J.F. – Do you attain that state over several successive lives?

M. – Yes, but of course it's actually reached during one particular life, like that of the Buddha Shakyamuni (the historical Buddha), whose enlightenment, sometimes also called 'awakening', was the final result of numerous lives spent developing wisdom, love, and compassion.

J.F. – But at the moment you attain that discovery of perfect knowledge, do you disappear?

M. – Why? Who would disappear? It's quite the opposite. After having achieved his own welfare by attaining enlightenment, the Buddha begins to deploy his vast activity to help others, to teach and show them the path. His teachings are the direct expression of his spiritual realization. They're like travel guides that lead others along the same path he took himself.

J.F. – So his own self doesn't disappear?

M. – The only thing that disappears, and it disappears totally, is ignorance. Belief in the existence of a self is one of the main forms that ignorance takes. So that mistaken idea of a self disappears with it. Buddhahood is an awakening to the ultimate nature of things. It's not something that's built up anew, it's something that's discovered. The fundamental idea, in fact, is that all beings have within them the nature of Buddha. That capacity to attain ultimate knowledge, that potential for inner transformation, is present in each being like a nugget of gold whose purity is unchangeable, even when it's buried under the earth. In ordinary beings the potential perfection of the Buddha nature is buried under numerous obscuring layers formed by the negative mental factors we've already mentioned, which arise from attachment to the intrinsic existence of a self and phenomena. The path, therefore, consists of dissolving everything that hides this true nature from us so that we can actually see it as it is. As the scriptures say, if we didn't have that potential, wanting to attain Buddhahood would be as futile as trying to whiten a piece of coal. That's why the Buddhist way is a discovery rather than anything else.

J.F. – It reminds me a lot of Plato's theory of recollection. Learning, for Socrates, is a process of recollecting what one has forgotten.

M. – From another angle, it's also a process of purification, not of original sin or some inherent impurity, but of adventitious layers that conceal our deep nature from us. It's like when an aircraft goes up through the cloud layer. From the ground, the sky might look gray and misty, as if the sun didn't exist. But it's enough to be in the aircraft that emerges from the clouds – it's always a magnificent sight – to rediscover the sun shining brilliantly in an unchanging sky. The Buddhist path is just like that.

J.F. – Socrates' teaching on this point is set out in several of the dialogues, but especially in the *Meno*. His idea was that, strictly speaking, we never learn anything at all. When we study, we're in fact recollecting. We all possess knowledge within us present in our being before our birth, an innate form of knowledge. What's happened during life is that false knowledge, opinions, and artificial psychological states have covered over what you just called that central nugget of gold. To demonstrate that learning is fundamentally a process of recall, Socrates brings along a young slave belonging to Meno and asks his master, 'Are you quite sure that this slave was born in your home, and that he's never had any education?' Drawing diagrams in the sand with a stick, he makes the slave rediscover the proof of a geometrical theorem simply by asking him questions, making sure never to give him any hints. Hence the Socratic method of proceeding by asking questions – you don't teach, you make the pupil rediscover what he or she knew already without being conscious of it. So that's the idea that we all already possess knowledge, and we just need to put ourselves into the conditions that make that treasure emerge. But in Buddhism, there seems to be an additional postulate. I'm curious about Buddhism. There are things about it I don't understand and I'd like to know. Does Buddhism teach, or doesn't it, that beings go from one incarnation to another, and that the goal of ultimate happiness is to no longer be reincarnated, to be finally released from the succession of reincarnations and dissolve into the impersonal cosmos?

M. – It's not a matter of dissolving into some state of extinction, but of discovering ultimate wisdom within oneself. The goal isn't to get out of the world, it's to no longer be enslaved to it. The world in itself isn't what's bad, it's the way we perceive it that's mistaken. As a great Buddhist teacher said, 'It's not appearances that will bind you, it's your attachment to appearances.' What's called *samsara*, the 'vicious circle of the world of existences', which is maintained by ignorance, is a world of suffering, distraction, and confusion. We wander endlessly in it, impelled by the force of our actions, called *karma*. The notion of *karma* is rather different from what's usually understood as 'destiny'. It doesn't arise from divine will, as in Hinduism, nor does it arise by chance. It's the result of our actions. We harvest what we sow. Nothing forces beings to reincarnate in a particular way except the accumulated pattern of their actions, 'actions' here covering all our thoughts, words, and deeds, positive or negative. It's the equivalent of good and evil, but it's important to remember that good and evil aren't absolute notions. Our thoughts and actions are considered good and evil according to whether their motivation is to help or to harm, and according to their result, our own and others' happiness and suffering.

J.F. – We've come back to morals, in fact.

M. – You can call it morals or ethics, but it's actually a matter of the very mechanisms of happiness and suffering. In every instant, we're experiencing the result of our past actions, while our present thoughts, words, and deeds are shaping our future. At the moment of death, the pattern of all our actions hitherto is what determines the kind of existence we'll find ourselves in next. The seeds we've planted germinate, into flowers or hemlock. Another metaphor sometimes used is that of a bird landing on the ground. The bird's shadow – our *karma* – which was hitherto invisible, suddenly appears. A more modern metaphor might be that at the moment of death we develop the film we've been shooting all our life, a film that also incorporates everything filmed during all our previous lives.

J.F. – All our previous lives?

M. – During this present life which is coming to an end, we've been able to add or remove positive or negative actions to that accumulated *karma* and modify it, either purifying it or making it worse. After death comes a transitory state that we call *bardo*, during which the following life takes form and becomes clearer. In the *bardo*, the consciousness is swept along like a feather in the wind, as a function of the results of our positive and negative actions, and the outcome will be an existence that's happy, unhappy, or a mixture of the two. In fact, this gives us a very sane attitude toward whatever happens to us – we alone are to blame for what we are, we're the result of our past, and the future is in our own hands.

J.F. – So there actually is the idea of multiple lives and therefore of reincarnation?

M. – Actions, once they've been carried out, will eventually bring their results and propel us into other states of existence. So unless we apply the means to free ourselves from it, the cycle of rebirths is practically endless. As we never stop carrying out a mixture of negative and positive actions, we oscillate up and down from one life to the next, sometimes happy and sometimes wretched, like the buckets of a waterwheel rising and falling interminably. We'd say that as a whole the conditioned world has no beginning or end, but that each individual being can potentially break this vicious circle by purifying the stream of his or her consciousness, attaining enlightenment, and thus being released from the cycle of rebirths. In other words, we can put an end to the causes of suffering. To reach such a result, we have to cut through the root of the problem, the ignorance – the belief in a self – that causes it.

J.F. – So do you agree with this quotation from Alfred Foucher, who says, comparing ideas about the immortality of the soul and life after death in Christians and Buddhists, 'For Christians, the hope of salvation and immortality is the hope to survive. In Buddhists, it's the hope to disappear.'

M. – To no longer be born.

J.F. – He says 'to disappear'.

M. – It's the wrong word – that's the old idea about Buddhism as nihilistic still being handed down! The 'Middle Way' is so called because it avoids the two extremes of nihilism and eternalism. What does 'disappear' is ignorance, the belief in a self, but as it does so the infinite qualities of enlightenment appear in all their fullness. It's true that one's no longer reborn under the influence of negative *karma*. But one continues to appear in the conditioned world, through the force of compassion and wisdom, for the benefit of others, without being trapped there. *Nirvana* is translated by a Tibetan term meaning 'beyond suffering'. If anything is extinguished, it's certainly suffering and the confusion that it engenders.

J.F. – So *karma, samsara*, and *nirvana* aren't Tibetan words?

M. – No, they're Sanskrit words that are used more often in the West than the corresponding Tibetan because Sanskrit sounds rather more familiar to our ears than Tibetan does.

J.F. – I suppose that's because it's one of the Indo-European group of languages.

M. – Yes, whereas Tibetan belongs to the Tibeto-Burmese family. In most of the translations made up to the mid-twentieth century, Western interpretations often spoke of *nirvana* as a sort of final extinction. Dahlmann spoke of an 'abyss of atheism and nihilism', Burnouf of 'annihilation', and Hegel and Schopenhauer of 'nothingness'. Recently, Roger-Pol Droit in his book *Le Culte du néant* (*The Cult of Nothingness*)[2] has charted the historical circumstances of that misunderstanding. According to the Mahayana, or Great Vehicle, to which Tibetan Buddhism belongs, someone who attains the state of Buddhahood resides neither in *samsara* nor *nirvana*, both of which are designated as 'extremes'. He doesn't stay in *samsara*, because he's free of ignorance and is no longer the plaything of a *karma* leading him to reincarnate endlessly. Nor does he stay suspended in the peace of *nirvana*, because of the infinite compassion he conceives for all the beings still suffering.

J.F. – So what does he do, then?

M. – He puts into action the vow he took at the dawn of his enlightenment to continue to manifest deliberately – not under the constraint of *karma* but by the force of his compassion – until the conditioned world is emptied of all sufferings, or in other words for as long as there are still beings imprisoned in ignorance. So he's free of *samsara* but doesn't remain in *nirvana*. That's why we talk about Buddhas and Bodhisattvas manifesting numerous forms to accomplish the good of beings and guide them on the path to enlightenment. Among them are counted the great teachers who are perfectly realized.

J.F. – Is there any notion of transcendence in Buddhism?

M. – Yes, there is. One speaks, for instance, of the 'three bodies' of a Buddha. The 'absolute body' transcends all limitations and concepts, the 'subtle body' is pure love and wisdom, and the 'manifest body' is the person of a Buddha, like the Buddha Shakyamuni, whom we can meet in the flesh. But we shouldn't think that transcendence here refers to some kind of Almighty abiding on its own outside ourselves. The 'three bodies' are aspects of the Buddha nature present in every sentient being. This is the view held by the Mahayana.

J.F. – Historically speaking, when, how, and why did the Theravada separate from the Mahayana?

M. – Well, that's something, as you might have guessed, that followers of the Mahayana and the Theravada don't have quite the same views about. The teachings of the Theravada are all included in the Mahayana, which then adds a new dimension to them. This last point has generated numerous discussions within Buddhism itself. According to followers of the Mahayana, the Buddha taught both the Theravada and the Mahayana during his life. But, as he taught individuals according to their particular capacities, he only taught the Mahayana to those who had the openness of mind necessary to understand it. We're not talking here about esoteric teachings, which do also exist in Buddhism, but of different levels of teaching that weren't nominally distinct in the Buddha's lifetime.

The Mahayana emphasizes that to free oneself alone from suffering is a severely limited goal. At the same moment as committing yourself to the path, you should have the intention to attain Buddhahood for the sake of all beings. You transform yourself in order to acquire the capacity to help others free themselves from suffering. Since I'm only one person, while others are infinitely numerous, whatever happens to me, whether good or bad, is insignificant compared to the suffering and happiness of others. The depth of the Mahayana resides in its views on emptiness, on absolute truth. Emptiness has nothing to do with nothingness, but consists of understanding that phenomena have no intrinsic existence. Followers of the Theravada contest that view of things, as well as the authenticity of the Mahayana's teachings. I should mention here that there's also a third vehicle, which arose in India like the two others, but which was particularly widespread in Tibet. It's called the Vajrayana, or Adamantine Vehicle, and adds to the Mahayana a large number of esoteric techniques for the path of contemplation.

J.F. – When Buddhists talk about suffering, it seems to me that they're only referring to the suffering caused by negative emotions – jealousy, hatred, envy; disappointment caused by a hunger for power; rage and all the disappointments, failures, rancor, and subservience to negative states of mind that inevitably result. In short, that it's only a question of suffering caused by our own failings, the wrongs we do, our weaknesses, our excessive pride. Surely suffering has plenty of other causes? What about malnutrition, famine, extermination, or torture by tyrants, being put to the sword by a hostile population? In the case of sufferings like these, we're their victims, not their agents. Take just one example: what the Tibetans still living in Tibet are now subjected to – and what numerous peoples have undergone throughout history – is not their fault. The Chinese are inflicting it on them. Such things are conditions of life. To cure and eliminate evils like these is surely much more a matter of practical, material remedies than of the enlightenment of Buddhahood!

M. – Once the situation gets out of control, the emphasis has to be on practical remedies, although finally – even here – any lasting peace can only come from a change of attitude. But, first and foremost, let's not forget that the primary cause of torture and war is still hatred, the primary cause of conquest is greed, and that both hatred and greed are born from an exacerbation of selfishness, attachment to the idea of a 'me'. Up until now, we've been emphasizing those primary causes – ill-will, desire, pride, and so on. But most of the other evils that afflict us originate in these negative states of mind and are extensions of them.

J.F. – But, in this example, the hatred comes from the Chinese; the Tibetans didn't have it.

M. – In terms of the kinds of suffering for which we're apparently not responsible ourselves, those that are imposed on us by others and natural disasters or diseases, we've already talked about how they can be understood. Such wrongs are due neither to divine will, nor to fixed destiny, nor to chance, but to the long-term consequences of our own actions. They're arrows we've shot ourselves, coming back to us. I understand that the whole notion of *karma* can be quite disconcerting. Whatever happens to us, it teaches, is never just by chance. We've created the causes of our present sufferings ourselves. It's particularly disconcerting in the case of someone who seems completely innocent, like a severely ill child, or someone with many admirable qualities who's nevertheless going through some terrible tragedies. We're the result of a complex set of causes and conditions, a mixture of actions that are sometimes excellent, positive and altruistic, and sometimes unwholesome or destructive. Little by little, these causes ripen into results and are expressed as our successive lives unfold. From within a different metaphysical framework, of course, it would be difficult to see how our present happiness and suffering could be the result of our distant past. But in the context of a religion like Buddhism that accepts the idea of numerous rebirths, it all makes sense. So we've no reason to rebel against what happens to us. But nor should our attitude be one of resignation, because we now have the chance to redress this situation. The idea is, therefore, to recognize what we need to do, or to avoid, in order to construct our happiness and escape from suffering. If we understand that negative actions lead to suffering both for ourselves and others, and that positive actions lead to happiness, it's up to us to act now in such a way as to build our own future by sowing 'good seeds'. There's a saying that goes, 'As long as you keep your hand in the fire, it's no good hoping not to be burnt.' It's not that we'll be 'rewarded' or 'punished' – we're simply subject to the law of cause and effect. The Buddha gave numerous examples of karmic effects. For instance, those who've shortened the lives of numerous living beings, whether humans or animals, will have in some future existence a short life themselves, or might die an accidental death. But if at some other time they've also done something positive, that particular life, short though it may be, will be a happy and prosperous one. There are an infinite number of such combinations. It's said that only the omniscience of a Buddha can perceive the complexity of any individual's *karma*.

J.F. – Yes, but there are also natural kinds of suffering. Growing old, or death, for example.

M. – In his first teaching, the Buddha set out what are known as the 'Four Noble Truths' – the truth of the suffering of the conditioned world, the truth of the source of suffering (ignorance and the negative emotions that build up *karma*), the truth of the possibility of putting an end to suffering, and the truth of the path that leads to that cessation of suffering. Suffering here includes, of course, the suffering of birth, aging, illness, and death; of encountering adversaries, losing those dear to us, and so on. This isn't to be pessimistic about life. It simply stresses the need to become aware of suffering so that we can apply the proper remedy to it. Indeed, if there was no such remedy, there'd be no point in worrying about suffering.

J.F. – Suffering in terms of human destiny, therefore, or animal, or of any kind?

M. – The idea of suffering here covers the whole of the past, suffering in previous existences, and the whole future, suffering in future existences, for all the different kinds of beings.

J.F. – But the most fundamental kinds of suffering – birth, a life full of whatever negative actions and useless passions one can imagine, sickness, death – can all be experienced in conditions that are tragic to a greater or to a lesser extent. The scientific, technological, materialist West may be accused of having lost sight of certain values. But look at the spectacle of daily life in the streets of Kathmandu! It's all very well talking about some of the failings of Western economies, the extent of unemployment, and so on; but even so, compared to a Nepalese worker an unemployed Frenchman is a millionaire. In Nepal, a hundred dollars a month is considered a good salary, forty an average one. The conditions in which human life is lived in Western societies, despite all their inadequacies, have nevertheless eliminated, even for those we call the underclass, certain kinds of suffering, degradation, extreme and cruel physical miseries, that in the East continue to exist and are widespread. The idea of *practical* solutions seems to me all the same to have been a little lost from sight in Buddhism. In the philosophical sense, human destiny is human destiny. We know very well that an American millionaire can be psychologically less well off than a Nepalese porter. You can be a Rothschild and commit suicide out of despair, as we saw in 1996. Nevertheless, daily happiness and suffering, for most people, depend on a whole crowd of factors other than metaphysical.

M. – I think we should be careful about making hasty judgments about the filthy state of the streets of Kathmandu. Everyone can see how bad things are, and of course it's regrettable. Kathmandu, like many cities in the East, is suffering from chaotic expansion. This is due, on the one hand, to a population explosion and precipitous industrialization that have brought increasing poverty in rural areas, and on the other, to people's often unfulfilled hopes of a better life in the city. We're shocked by the poverty we see in India or Nepal, and quite rightly so, but as we make such observations we very often tend to ignore the progress that's been made over the last fifty years. In particular, India has managed to maintain a democratically elected government, and a large number of low-caste Indians have been given access not only to education but to jobs hitherto reserved for higher castes. There are still plenty of people below the poverty line in India, but a quarter of the population now has an acceptable standard of living. You're thinking of the social welfare entitlements our fellow citizens in the West now enjoy, but don't forget that they're a recent phenomenon that only goes back to the period between the wars. For countries as poor as Nepal and India, it's inconceivable that such social benefits – which are very expensive – could be extended in the near future to the whole population as it grows at such a giddy rate. They simply don't have the resources. Paris and London were veritable cesspools in the seventeenth century, but spiritual beliefs weren't to blame then, either. I don't think Buddhism loses sight of practical remedies, but the poverty to be tackled in the East is much greater for all sorts of reasons, whether geographical, climatic, or demographic. The greatest cause of misery in India is certainly not the importance accorded to spiritual values. If poverty's so widespread there, it's because there are nine hundred and fifty million inhabitants, and to overpopulation are added the rigors of an extreme climate. In Europe we don't suffer from drought every year, immediately followed by disastrous floods.

As for the suffering of war, the suffering of the tortured and of the oppressed, these are sufferings that can be observed, unfortunately, almost all the time. They're the result of ignorance, its unfortunate fruits. Faced with such suffering, any Buddhist, any Christian, any self-respecting human being, whether a believer in a religion or not, owes it to himself or herself to do everything possible to help others. For believers, that's part of the application of religion to everyday life, and for nonbelievers it's a natural, heartfelt expression of generosity. A good person will do whatever's possible to feed anyone who's hungry, shelter anyone who's cold, find medicines for anyone afflicted by illness, and so on. Not to do so is to lack any sense of human responsibility.

J.F. – But then we come back to the problem of moral philosophy. What you've just described is a highly commendable way of behaving that I'd say was a bit like that of saints and benefactors in the Middle

Ages in the West. Surrounded by a sea of poverty and suffering, a very low standard of living, you'd do whatever you could, out of Christian charity, to comfort and relieve the misfortunes of the poor, beggars, the sick, lepers. The other approach, which is the Western idea of things, is that the system itself has to be reformed, a kind of society has to be created where this type of poverty disappears and no longer simply depends on one individual's actions with respect to another. It would seem that, in Buddhism, the principal cause of suffering for a human is a lack of control over one's thoughts. But there are objective sufferings that are nothing to do with that.

M. – Of course, and we've just been talking about other kinds of suffering. But how does a war begin if not from thoughts of enmity and hatred?

J.F. – Well, yes, that's true.

M. – And why do people say that the Tibetans, on the whole, are a peaceful people?

J.F. – That's true, too.

M. – Surely it's because fundamentally there are other ways of resolving conflicts than war, and these other ways have visible reper-cussions, even seen on the scale of a society or a country.

J.F. – On that level, you're right.

M. – It's the practical consequence of a certain outlook, a certain idea of what life is about.

J.F. – Yes, but the poverty that reigns in southern Asia isn't only due to the wars that have taken place there. It's due to a lack of devel-opment, to the fact that economic structures haven't been mastered, and also perhaps that science's technical applications have been viewed with suspicion. The science of the material world has been neglected in favor of the science of the mind. Some kinds of suffering have disap-peared from Western societies because objective science has been applied to objective reality. Take disease, for example. You can't deny that the constant increase in life expectancy in the West is the result of better and better health care. Sick people, however poor they might be, are protected by a number of social welfare arrangements – extremely expensive, it's true – which shows that solidarity and humanity are Western virtues, too. They don't depend on a decision or a good act on the part of any particular individual, but form a system that's automat-ically triggered as soon as someone falls ill. Techniques that are the result of scientific knowledge also help to assuage physical and mental suffering. The misery of sickness entails intense mental suffering, too. So here evil is being tackled from its tangible, external side.

M. – I don't think any Buddhist would deny the good that's come from progress in medicine, in the organization of humanitarian aid, in social welfare, or from material and scientific development, when these things contribute to the relief of suffering. Let me mention some examples of attitudes in Buddhist communities. Sri Lanka, a country that has a Buddhist majority, has the highest level of literacy in southern Asia, as well as a remarkable healthcare infrastructure. Sri Lanka's also the only country in southern Asia to have succeeded in halting its population growth, thanks to birth control. This progress has been achieved by a lay government, the majority of whose members are nevertheless Buddhist. A few Buddhist monks in Thailand have taken a very active role in the fight against drugs and AIDS, some of them caring in their monasteries for drug addicts and HIV-positive people rejected by their families. Bhutan, a completely Buddhist country, spends thirty percent of its budget on education, which must be the highest percentage of any country in the world. It's also one of the only countries to have set in motion a very strict program of environmental protection before the environment was spoilt. Hunting and fishing are completely forbidden, as too is deforestation.

It's no good falling into any extreme. To reject or mistrust material progress when it's capable of reducing suffering would be ridiculous. But the opposite extreme's also unhealthy. To neglect internal development in favor of purely external progress might well, in the long term, have even more harmful consequences, because that's where intolerance and aggression come from, and therefore war, the insatiable thirst to possess, and hence dissatisfaction, the pursuit of power, and selfishness. Ideally, material progress would be used judiciously, without invading our minds and our activities, while we accorded priority to the inner development that could make us better human beings.

In Tibet, the tragedy of events notwithstanding, there are some areas, especially Kham, where you can see societies with a traditional way of life, living very simply, inspired by Buddhist values and to all appearances astonishingly happy, in spite of the sufferings inflicted upon them. Unfortunately, no doubt, they're deprived of access to modern hospitals – the Chinese communist system seems wary of bringing such improvements to Tibetans – but the feeling you get there is a very long way from the oppressive atmosphere in the streets of New York, or the sort of physical poverty seen in the slums around the great cities born of the industrial revolution.

J.F. – You're absolutely right. But let's go back to Buddhism's doctrinal and metaphysical ideas. I've been told that although Pope John Paul II has a good relationship with the Dalai Lama and has received him several times, he's thinking of taking part in a new ecumenical meeting, similar to the one at Assisi at which the Dalai Lama was present, but this time exclusively with representatives of the monotheistic religions, Christianity, Islam, Judaism. Buddhism won't be represented. Is that because there's no Buddhist God?

M. – The Dalai Lama has often expressed a wish that a second conference like the one at Assisi be held, and as a venue he's even suggested Jerusalem, the focus of several religions, with the idea that it's unacceptable that conflicts like those in Bosnia and the Middle East continue to arise at least partly through differences of religion. He's always emphasizing that any religion practiced in its true spirit has the well-being of all as its goal, and so surely ought to be a factor for peace. The message of Jesus Christ is one of love, and one of the meanings of the word 'Islam' is peace. Violence and coercion perpetrated in religion's name, and the use of religion to accentuate the divisions between peoples, can therefore only be abuses. Truth is strong enough by itself to convince, and should never be imposed by force. In other words, it should never be necessary for an authentic truth to need violence to be asserted.

J.F. – Such abuses are frequent, to say the least.

M. – That's why, in this deplorable state of affairs, one of the Dalai Lama's principal concerns as he travels the world is to encourage representatives of different religions to meet each other, to foster better knowledge and mutual respect. He emphasizes the points common to all spiritual traditions, principally love of one's neighbor and compassion for those who are suffering.

J.F. – The trouble is that religious leaders may respect each other without that necessarily filtering down to the mass of believers. It doesn't prevent Christians and Muslims exterminating each other in Bosnia, or Muslims and Jews exterminating each other in Palestine. But to come back to questions of doctrine, I suppose that Buddhism can't be considered as a monotheistic religion.

M. – No, because it doesn't have the idea of a demiurge who created the world and beings, as I've already said. But if by God you mean absolute truth, the ultimate nature of being, or infinite love, the difference is only a matter of words.

J.F. – In the history of religions, there's a very marked difference between polytheism and monotheism.

M. – Buddhism isn't a polytheism, either. In the Tibetan tradition you find a whole set of representations of divinities, but these are nothing to do with 'gods' in the sense of entities endowed with any independent, true existence. They're manifestations of wisdom, of compassion, altruism, and so on, and as objects of meditation allow those qualities to be actualized within us, using techniques of visualization that I'll come back to later.

J.F. – In the history of religions as we know them, it's often thought that monotheism is immensely more advanced than polytheism, because polytheism is held to represent various forms of superstition. But it seems to me that the major monotheistic religions, whether in the past or nowadays, involve lots of taboos, rituals, and prohibitions that I consider absurd and practices that I consider completely superstitious. So I can't really see how monotheism is better than polytheism. Quite the contrary, in fact – I'd say polytheism was more tolerant than monotheism.

M. – It still is. Polytheism still exists in India and here in Nepal.

J.F. – Intolerance is something that arose with monotheism. As soon as human beings allowed themselves to say, 'There's only one true God, and that's mine, so I have the right to annihilate anyone who doesn't believe in him,' the cycle of intolerance and religious wars began.

M. – Sad to say, yes.

J.F. – But it's a historical fact, and an evil that still plagues us, even nowadays when everyone talks only of tolerance and pluralism.

M. – Genocide continues to be perpetrated in the name of religion. There are two main forms that intolerance takes. The first is when people who haven't gone deeply into the real meaning of their religion, and don't practice it in an authentic way, use it as a rallying flag to arouse sectarian, ethnic, or nationalist passions. The second is when people who practice their religion sincerely are so deeply convinced of the truth of their beliefs that they think any means are justified to impose them on others, since by so doing they're helping them. The first part, their conviction in their faith, is admirable, but it's what follows that's so wrong. They don't know how to respect other people's religious traditions and the diversity of human beings. The Dalai Lama often says, 'We should have total conviction in our own spiritual path along with perfect respect toward other truths.'

J.F. – In terms of theology and cosmology, one element that all monotheist religions have in common is a creation myth. The one we know best, of course, is the one set out in the Bible, in Genesis, but there's also, for example, Plato's demiurge in the *Timaeus*. He's the Creator of the world. That idea of the creation of the world comes up in innumerable religions, including polytheistic ones. Monotheism goes further with the idea of a personal God who sees everything and surveys everything, an idea shared by Jews, Christians, and Muslims and taken up by the great philosophers. An omniscient and omnipotent God who created the world and who, according to Descartes, created the eternal truths, and accounts for the whole of reality, is found in the famous Book XII of Aristotle's *Metaphysics* as well as in later great philosophers, Descartes and Leibniz in particular. So doesn't Buddhism have that same idea? Wasn't there a creation? Is there no personal God whose eyes and ears watch over the whole of humankind?

M. – No, not at all. I've already mentioned the arguments Buddhism advances to show that no eternal, all-powerful, and autonomous entity could create anything without losing his qualities of being eternal and all-powerful. The world is governed entirely by the laws of cause and effect and interdependence. But if what's understood as God is 'infinite love and wisdom', as Christians sometimes say, then Buddhism would have no trouble accepting that understanding of divinity. It's just a question of words.

As for ultimate reality according to Buddhism, I'd like to say a few words about it. In fact, we'd distinguish two different aspects. The phenomenal world, as we perceive it, belongs to relative truth. The ultimate nature of things, transcending any concept of being or nonbeing, appearance or cessation, movement or nonmovement, one or many, belongs to absolute truth. Absolute truth is therefore the realization of emptiness, of enlightenment, of nonduality, which can only be understood by contemplative experience and not by analytical thought.

J.F. – What do you mean by emptiness? Is it nothingness?

M. – Some people find the notion of emptiness disorienting and even frightening. They think nothing can arise from emptiness, nothing could function properly, and no law – that of cause and effect, for instance – could operate in such a 'void'. Emptiness, they think, couldn't carry within it the slightest potential to manifest anything, and it makes them feel very uneasy. But that's confusing emptiness in the Buddhist sense with nothingness. In nothingness there's nothing at all, while 'emptiness' is in fact the opposite of nothingness – it's a universal potential, the universe, beings, movement, consciousness. No phenomena at all could ever be manifested if their ultimate nature wasn't emptiness. In rather the same way, though this is only an image, the visible world would not be able to unfold without space to unfold in. If space was intrinsically substantial and permanent, no manifestation, no transformation, would be possible. That's why the texts say, 'Since there is emptiness, everything can exist.' Emptiness thus contains all possibilities, and those possibilities are interdependent.

J.F. – You're rather playing with words. You use emptiness here not in the sense of the abolition of consciousness of a self, but in the sense of empty space, ready to be filled by realities.

M. – No, it's not really that. The analogy of space allowing worlds to be formed is only an image, to show that nothing in the phenomenal world is substantial, permanent, or intrinsically existing, neither the self nor the world outside. It's that absence of any true existence that allows phenomena to be manifested *ad infinitum*. So emptiness isn't like the empty space within a container, but the very nature of the container and whatever it contains.

Why is it so important to distinguish relative truth from absolute truth? As long as the ultimate nature of phenomena is confused with the way they appear, as long as we believe that phenomena have some intrinsic existence, our minds will be invaded by an incalculable number of thoughts and positive or negative emotions. Of course, we could try to apply a particular antidote to each of those emotions, sympathy to counteract jealousy, for example. But no such antidote by itself is capable of eradicating ignorance, our attachment to the reality of phenomena. To cut through that attachment, we need to recognize the ultimate nature of phenomena, what we've called emptiness. For anyone who's attained the omniscience of Buddhahood, there's no longer any discrepancy between the ultimate nature of things and the way they appear. The perception of apparent phenomena continues, but that perception's no longer distorted by the ignorance of taking such phenomena as entities that have some intrinsic existence. Their ultimate nature, emptiness, is also perceived at the same time.

J.F. – How does that happen?

M. – Emptiness isn't something distinct from phenomena, it's the very nature of those phenomena. In the domain of relative truth, the Buddhist idea of the world is close to that of the natural sciences, given the scientific knowledge of the age in which Buddhism arose. According to Buddhist cosmology, the world was first formed from a continuum of 'particles of space' that were condensed and modified to make the constituent particles of the four other elements, or principles, water, earth, fire, and air, of which the universe is composed. There's then mention of a vast primordial ocean churned up by the winds to create a sort of cream which, as it solidified, formed the continents, mountains, and so on. This whole process obeyed the laws of cause and effect. Buddhism says that the world has no 'beginning'. In fact you can't speak of time having a beginning, because any manifestation must have a cause that precedes it, and before anything manifests the notion of time is meaningless. Time is only a concept attached by an observer to a succession of instants. Time has no intrinsic existence, because you can't apprehend any time distinct from its moments. Time and space only exist relative to particular systems of reference and to our experience.

J.F. – That's rather like Kant's doctrine. Time has no existence in itself, but is a human mode of apprehending phenomena.

M. – Time doesn't exist outside phenomena. In the absence of phenomena, how could it exist? Time's related to change. The past instant is dead and gone, the future instant isn't yet born, and the course of time is imperceptible in the present instant. Buddhist metaphysics also speaks of a 'fourth time' that goes beyond the other three – past, present, and future – and represents the unchanging absolute.

J.F. – An unchanging time? That's a bit of a contradiction in terms.

M. – Not really. The 'fourth time' isn't a real time, it's just a symbolic expression to signify that the absolute is beyond time, which belongs to the relative truth of the phenomenal world. Buddhist cosmology also speaks in terms of cycles. The cycle of a universe is made up of four phases, a period in which it's formed, a period in which it remains present, a period in which it's destroyed, and a period in which nothing is manifested. Then a new cycle begins.

J.F. – The Stoics held the theory that the history of the cosmos perpetually starts again from a 'year zero' that returns periodically and is marked by a gigantic conflagration.

M. – Here, it's not a question of the eternal repetition of the same thing, which wouldn't make any sense, but of an infinite unfolding of phenomena following the law of cause and effect, *karma*.

J.F. – So apart from its archaic aspects, Buddhist cosmology isn't a dogma that would be fundamentally opposed to the discoveries of science?

M. – Certainly not, because it's a cosmology of relative truth, conventional truth, which changes according to the generally shared perception of people at different points in history. Nevertheless, it differs significantly from scientific theories in its view of the origin of consciousness. As I mentioned in one of our previous discussions, Buddhism would hold that nothing conscious could arise from something that was inanimate. A present instant of consciousness, which was itself set off by a preceding instant of consciousness, sets off the next instant of consciousness. We've said that the world has no real beginning in time, and the same goes for consciousness. This is also one of the reasons why we consider that at the moment of conception, the spark of consciousness that animates a newly formed being can only be caused by an event of the same nature, a conscious one, even in the case of a spark as primitive as the one we could imagine in an amoeba.

J.F. – According to traditional metaphysical ideas, whatever belongs to consciousness can only be born from what's conscious, and matter can only be born from matter. That's also something you'd find in Plato, in seventeenth-century philosophy and in Descartes' statement that there can't be more in the effect than in the cause. But then, on that very point, the whole of modern science shows the contrary, on the basis of experiment and observation that can't just be discounted or scorned. It's the thesis that your former boss, Jacques Monod, in particular, set out in *Chance and Necessity*: that the biological world arises from the material world, and consciousness arises from the biological world. There's an evolution, therefore, along those lines – the birth of life from matter, then the evolution of species leading little by little to consciousness and language. This, we could say, is the scheme of things now generally accepted by contemporary science.

M. – According to Buddhism, the conscious isn't just a more and more complex and perfect development of the inanimate. There has to be a qualitative change there, not just a quantitative one. There's nothing wrong with the observation that the gradually increasing complexity of the organization of the nervous system, as forms of life get higher, goes hand in hand with gradually increasing intelligence. But Buddhism holds that even very elementary forms of life are endowed with some form of consciousness – extremely primitive perhaps, but different from matter alone. As you progress up the evolutionary ladder, the faculty of consciousness becomes more and more effective, deep and developed, culminating in human intelligence. So consciousness is manifested to a varying extent in different supporting mechanisms and in different conditions.

J.F. – The fact that there is a psyche in animals is accepted. Only Descartes denied that. Nowadays there are numerous books on animal psychology. It's obvious that there is consciousness in animals. But in more elementary forms of life there can't be any self-consciousness, it's not reflective consciousness.

M. – I agree, but even so they're animate beings. For the higher animals, I wonder if those who still think that there's no animal 'intelligence' aren't still being subconsciously influenced by Judaeo-Christian culture, which refuses to accept that animals could have a 'soul'. Don't forget that only a few centuries ago there was a debate among Spanish Catholics as to whether South American Indians had a soul!

J.F. – So where would that consciousness come from, even the very primitive one in some microscopic creature?

M. – Buddhism answers that by saying that it can only come from a previous life, according to the law of 'conservation of consciousness' analogous to the conservation of energy in the world of matter.

J.F. – That's not, of course, what science would think at all. Science sees man as an animal among the other animals, an animal in whom one dimension of perceptual consciousness has been particularly developed because of the development of the brain. But it's true that the great mystery, or rather the great leap in the vision of modern science, is the passage from matter to life. When we ask ourselves whether there could be life in other solar systems, in other galaxies, or even on Mars, we're always trying to find out, basically, if the set of factors that have led to the chemical reactions that produced life within matter might have been able to happen on other planets or in other solar systems. But the shift from animal or vegetable life to consciousness over the evolution of living species is perhaps rather less mysterious than the shift from matter to life.

M. – I don't think we can go much further in reconciling these different points of view. While Buddhism doesn't contest the process of evolution toward more and more complex forms of life and more and more refined forms of intelligence, it doesn't think, as I've already said, that consciousness could arise in inanimate matter. Science says that as cells acquire a more and more complex structure, they react in more and more effective ways to external stimuli, and that this growing complexity might culminate in a nervous system whose consciousness is not something different from itself. For Buddhism, consciousness can't arise from any chemical reaction, whether complex or not.

J.F. – Well, that's quite clear. But let's go back to what you call absolute truth, the idea of emptiness.

M. – Emptiness is neither nothingness nor an empty space distinct from phenomena or external to them. It's the very nature of phenomena. That's why one of the most basic Buddhist *sutras* says, 'Emptiness is form and form is emptiness.' From an absolute point of view, the world doesn't have any real or concrete existence. So the relative aspect is the phenomenal world and the absolute aspect is emptiness.

J.F. – But the phenomenal aspect is perfectly concrete and tangible.

M. – The idea of emptiness is to combat the innate tendency we have to reify the self, consciousness, and phenomena. When Buddhism says, 'Emptiness is form and form is emptiness,' it's not that different an idea from the statement that 'Matter is energy and energy is matter.' We're not denying the ordinary perception we have of the world. What we are denying is that, in the final analysis, the world has any intrinsic reality. If atoms aren't things, to go back to Heisenberg's statement, how would a large number of them taken together – visible phenomena – suddenly become things?

J.F. – But doesn't Buddhism teach, for instance, that the world has no existence of its own because it's only produced by our perception? Isn't that what's called absolute idealism in Western theories of consciousness?

M. – There is a school of Buddhism called the 'Mind Only' school which says that, in the final analysis, only consciousness exists, and everything else is a projection of consciousness. But it's a monism that's been refuted within Buddhism itself.

J.F. – That's exactly what would be called absolute idealism. It's just like what Berkeley or Hamelin said.

M. – What the other schools of Buddhism reply to such a point of view is that, of course, the phenomenal world is perceived via the sense organs and is interpreted by the instants of consciousness that apprehend the information coming from those organs. So we don't perceive the world as it really is, we perceive only the images that are reflected in our consciousness.

J.F. – That's Emmanuel Kant's form of idealism, called 'transcendental'.

M. – An object is seen by a hundred different people like a hundred reflections in a hundred mirrors.

J.F. – But is it the same object?

M. – As a first approximation, it's the same object, but one that can be perceived in completely different ways by different beings, as we saw with the example of the glass of water. Only someone who's attained enlightenment recognizes the object's ultimate nature – that it appears, but is devoid of any intrinsic existence. Buddhism's final position is that of the 'Middle Way': the world isn't a projection of our minds, but it isn't totally independent of our minds, either – because it makes no sense to speak of a particular, fixed reality independent of any concept, mental process, or observer. There's an interdependence. In that way, Buddhism avoids falling into either nihilism or eternalism. Phenomena arise through a process of interdependent causes and conditions, but nothing exists in itself or by itself. Finally, the direct contemplation of absolute truth transcends any intellectual concept, any duality between subject and object.

J.F. – Does the world, then, not exist independently of ourselves?

M. – Colors, sounds, smells, flavors, and textures aren't attributes that are inherent to the objective world, existing independently of our senses. The objects we perceive seem completely 'external' to us, but do they have intrinsic characteristics that define their true nature? What is the true nature of the world as it exists independently of ourselves? We have no way of knowing, because our only way of apprehending it is via our own mental processes. So, according to Buddhism, a 'world' independent of any conceptual designation would make no sense to anyone. To take an example, what is a white object? A wavelength, a 'color temperature', moving particles? Are those particles energy, mass, or what? None of those attributes are intrinsic to the object, they're only the result of our particular ways of investigating it. Buddhist scriptures tell the story of two blind men who wanted to have explained to them what colors were. One of them was told that white was the color of snow. He took a handful of snow and concluded that white was 'cold'. The other blind man was told that white was the color of swans. He heard a swan flying overhead, and concluded that white went 'swish swish'. The world can't be determined by itself. If it was, we'd all perceive it in the same way. That's not to deny reality as we observe it, nor to say that there's no reality outside the mind, but simply that no 'reality in itself' exists. Phenomena only exist in dependence on other phenomena.

J.F. – So it's what we could call Buddhist cosmology, physics, and theory of consciousness, all at once. Without wishing to contest the originality of these reasonings and doctrines, because anyway they predate Western philosophies, I'm struck nevertheless by the number of common points there are, not with this or that Western school of thought as a whole, but with sometimes one phase, sometimes another, of the evolution of Western philosophy from Thales to Kant.

M. – I'd add that Buddhism doesn't claim any monopoly of the truth, nor to have discovered something new. It's not a matter of constructing dogma, but of using a science of the mind to bring about both a transformation of the individual and a realization of the ultimate nature of things through contemplation.

J.F. – But in any case, Buddhism evolved before the doctrines I mentioned, before the very beginnings of Greek philosophy, so there's no question of any borrowing having occurred. What's interesting is to see that when people reflect about what reality, consciousness, and truth might be, and about how to interpret the world, they all review a certain number of possible hypotheses. Before experimental science as such came in, as long as people were content to reflect and devise possible and plausible interpretations of reality, of consciousness's relationship to it, and how best to manage human destiny, the number of solutions that could be envisaged wasn't unlimited. Widely separated cultures, which could hardly have been able to influence each other, thought up and evaluated the same hypotheses. Buddhism had some influence on the West, but classical Greek philosophy can't have had any influence on the origins of Buddhism. Different minds were nevertheless led to envisage a series of hypotheses whose number was quite restricted.

M. – In one way, it's only to be expected that authentic contemplative traditions would yield similar results. But I'm not sure that the different cultures of the ancient world were as isolated one from another as we sometimes think. Travel took longer, of course, but merchants, envoys, and adventurers traveled extraordinary distances. At any rate, the gradual exchange of ideas, as well as of goods, from the Far East right through to Western Europe, is now known to have taken place in ancient times.

J.F. – We started out with the question whether Buddhism was a religion or a philosophy. I'd say that, for me, the answer's now quite clear. Buddhism's more a philosophy than a dogmatic religion. It's a philosophy with a particularly developed metaphysical dimension, but a metaphysics derived nevertheless from philosophy and not from revelation, even if it includes ritualistic aspects that resemble religious practice. Indeed, such aspects are also found in some of the ancient philosophies, in Neo-Platonism for instance.

M. – Well, in a way there is revelation in Buddhism, too. It's the revelation of the 'truth' the Buddha found upon his enlightenment. That awakening to the true nature of mind and phenomena is the result of an increasingly deep inner experience that would be difficult to attain using philosophy and intellectual concepts alone. But although it's a revealed truth, it's one that dedicated seekers can find for themselves by following the Buddha's example and teachings. There are also Buddhist scriptures derived from visionary experience, but these are not seen as revelations bestowed by external entities, rather as natural manifestations of innate wisdom.

Since we're talking about parallels, here's a quote that you include in your *History of Philosophy*, a summary by Aristotle of the philosophy of the Eleatic school, which was contemporary with the Buddha's life in the sixth century B.C.: 'No existing thing either comes into being nor yet perishes, because that which comes from being must have its origin either starting from what exists, or else starting from what does not exist. And both processes are impossible. That which is does not become, because it is already; and nothing can come from that which is not.' Next, here's a Buddhist text dealing with being and nonbeing: 'Something that exists with true existence, what need is there for it to have a cause? Something that is wholly inexistent, again what need has it to have a cause? Even a hundred million causes will never transform nonentity. For if nonentity keeps its status, how could entity occur? And likewise, what is there that could so change? When real and nonreal are both absent from before the mind, nothing else remains for mind to do but rest in perfect peace, free from concepts.'[3]

J.F. – Those two quotes are very striking, but the philosophy of Parmenides actually takes a position diametrically opposed to that of Buddhism. What Parmenides is trying to show is that change is impossible, evolution's impossible, motion's impossible. For Parmenides, being is totally given and immobile, once and for all. Now, in Buddhism, being is in permanent flux. The famous 'paradoxes' of Zeno of Elea are designed to refute the existence of motion. The arrow never moves, because if you take it in each instant of its flight, it's motionless in that instant. In the same way, the hare can never catch up with the tortoise, because each time it halves the distance separating them, the other half is still left, even if that half becomes smaller and smaller. So all these 'paradoxes' are designed to break motion down, to show that there is no motion.

M. – In his *Metaphysical Principles of Infinitesimal Calculus*, René Guénon says that Zeno's paradoxes simply try to show that without envisaging the notion of continuity no motion would be possible, and that the limit doesn't belong to the series of successive values of the variable; it's outside that series, and going to the limit involves a discontinuity. Buddhism uses reasoning similar to Zeno's to show that, from the point of view of relative truth, what seems to be a play of causes and effects has no real existence. Such that, from an absolute point of view, things can undergo neither birth, real existence, nor cessation. The goal isn't to deny that there's any such thing as the phenomenal world as we perceive it – what Buddhism calls conventional truth – but to show that the world isn't as real as we think. In fact, coming into existence seems impossible, because, once again, being can't arise from nothingness, and if it already exists it doesn't need to arise. At the same time, it doesn't 'cease', because it's never come into existence. This is what leads Buddhism to say that the world is *like* a dream or an illusion. It doesn't say the world *is* a dream or an illusion, because that would be falling into nihilism. According to this 'Middle Way', appearances are emptiness, and from emptiness arise appearances.

J.F. – But then, according to that way of seeing things, even if one accepts the relative reality of the phenomenal world, the world is like an illusion, meaning that deep down it has no existence?

M. – It has no existence in itself – no true, independent existence.

J.F. – Doesn't that lead to a philosophy of nonaction? What would be the point of acting on something that didn't exist?

M. – Absolutely not! On the contrary, it leads to a considerably greater freedom to act and to be open to others, as we're no longer held fast by our attachment to the self and to the solidity of phenomena. Certain Hindu philosophies did, in fact, oppose Buddhism with the argument you've just brought up. If everything's like a dream, if your suffering is like a dream, what's the use of being free from suffering? What's the use of trying to attain enlightenment? And the reply is this. Since beings do undergo the experience of suffering, it's right to dissipate it, even if it's illusory. If your argument, which is quite like that Hindu one, was valid, it could also be applied to science. What's the use of taking any action, as we're just a bunch of cells directed by a bunch of neurons? What's the use of taking any action, as we're made up of atoms and particles that 'are not things' and which, in any case, are not 'us'?

1. Op. cit.
2. *Le Culte du néant: les philosophes et le Bouddha,* Editions du Seuil, Paris, 1997.
3. *The Way of the Bodhisattva (Bodhicaryavatara),* op. cit.

∾

SIX

ACTING ON THE WORLD

AND ACTING ON ONESELF

JEAN-FRANÇOIS — If, as a layman, I've properly understood it, Buddhism says that the whole fabric of our ordinary life is pain, to release ourselves from which we have to free ourselves from the mistaken feeling that we are a substantial and lasting entity, a self distinct from the world and continuous in time. That illusory self is the source of the desires, appetites, ambitions, and jealousies that make us suffer. Release, therefore, consists of becoming aware of the illusory nature of the self. What even such a brief outline reveals straight away is the extent to which Buddhism is the antithesis of a dominant tendency in the West. While many philosophers, moralists, and religious guides, even in the West, have often denounced the illusory nature of the thirst for power and preached the salutary virtue of detachment and abstention, that doesn't change the fact that the central current of Western thought is built around two essential and complementary poles. The first is the achievement of personal autonomy and the strengthening of individuality, of personal judgment, and of will as a conscious agent and center of decision making. The second is action on the world. The West is a civilization of action – action on human history through politics, and action on the world through knowledge of the laws of nature, with all the assurance of being able to transform it and bend it to man's needs. Now, it seems to me that all of this jars with the Buddhist ideal of nonattachment. Isn't there a basic and irreducible opposition between these two attitudes?

MATTHIEU – First of all, when you say in your summary that the fabric of ordinary life is pain, it's important to specify that the truth of suffering taught by the Buddha in his first sermon belongs to relative truth, and doesn't describe the ultimate nature of things. Someone who attains spiritual realization experiences an unchangeable state of bliss and perceives the infinite purity of all phenomena; all the causes of suffering, for such a person, have disappeared. Why, then, do we put so much emphasis on suffering? It's in order to become aware of the conditioned world's defects, as a starting point. In this world of ignorance, sufferings pile up, one on top of another. One of your parents dies, and several weeks later the other dies too. Passing joys turn into torments; you go for a cheerful family picnic and your child gets bitten by a snake. Reflecting on pain should therefore incite us to take to the path of wisdom. It's often said that Buddhism is a philosophy of suffering, but in fact the more you progress on the path the more that perception of suffering gives way to a happiness that impregnates your whole being. To begin with an acknowledgment of the unsatisfactoriness of the ordinary world is, in practice, to take the opposite direction from pessimism and apathy. Once suffering has been acknowledged, Buddhism lucidly identifies its causes and energetically applies remedies to them. A Buddhist thinks of himself as ill, the Buddha as the doctor, his teachings as the treatment, and spiritual practice as the process of getting cured.

J.F. – Buddhism may be one way of escaping from suffering, but hasn't the West found another way of doing the same, by transforming the outer world and human societies?

M. – Transforming the outer world has its limits, and the effect that such outer transformations have on our inner happiness also has its limits. It's true that improvement or deterioration of outer, material conditions has a major effect on our well-being, but in the final analysis we're not machines, and it's the mind that feels happy or miserable.

J.F. – Does Buddhism preach that we shouldn't try to act on the world?

M. – Not at all, but it thinks that wanting to act on the world without having transformed oneself can't lead to either lasting or profound happiness. You could say that action on the world is desirable, while inner transformation is indispensable.

As for the strengthening of the personality as it's encouraged in the West, you're right in pointing out how that goes against Buddhism's goal of uncovering the 'imposture of the ego', this ego that seems so powerful and causes us so much trouble while having no existence in itself. Nevertheless, as a first step it's important to stabilize this feeling of a self in order to distinguish all its characteristics. You could say, paradoxically, that you first need to have an ego in order to be aware that it doesn't exist. Someone with an unstable, fragmented, amorphous personality has little chance of being able to identify that powerful feeling of 'me', as a prior step to recognizing that it doesn't correspond to any real entity. So you need to start with a healthy and coherent self to be able to investigate it. You can shoot at a target, but not in fog.

J.F. – But that's a simple step. Surely, in the end, the real goal is to recognize that the ego is an imposture, as you said.

M. – Yes, that is the goal, but it's important not to think that once the imposture of the ego is unmasked you find yourself in a state of inner nothingness, to the point that the destruction of the personality renders you incapable of acting or communicating. You don't become an empty container. It's quite the opposite. When you're no longer the plaything of an illusory despot, like the shadows in Plato's cave, your wisdom, love for others and compassion can be freely expressed. It's a freedom from the limitations imposed by attachment to a self, not at all an anaesthesia of the will. This 'opening of the eyes of wisdom' increases your strength of mind, your diligence, and your capacity to take appropriate and altruistic action.

J.F. – The 'cult of the self', as Maurice Barrès has called it, the cult of the ego, has objectives quite opposite to those of Buddhism. Western civilization, on the other hand, places a premium on the strong personality. It's superior individuals, in all fields, that have left their imprint on its exceptional periods. Thus, in *The Civilization of the Renaissance in Italy*, a classic book that appeared in 1860, the Swiss-German historian Jacob Burckhardt attributes the Renaissance in Italy, which can justifiably be taken as a very important moment in Western civilization, to a series of strong personalities, whether cultivated princes like Frederico d'Urbino or artist-scientists like Leonardo da Vinci. It's not just by chance that Burckhardt influenced Nietzsche. In the same way, for better or for worse, we find among the idols of the West such action heroes as Alexander the Great, Julius Caesar, Christopher Columbus, and Napoleon, rather more than St. Francis of Assisi. Of course, we also admire great philosophers, artists, and writers, but not nearly as much as men of action, men who transformed the world, organizers who reformed societies. It seems to me that in that basic tone there's something that contrasts with the spirit of Buddhism. Today, as these two different outlooks meet once again, what can we expect from that contact, given the fundamentally different orientations of those two mentalities?

M. – If by personality you mean exacerbation of the ego, simply to have a strong personality seems to me, unfortunately, a highly dubious criterion of success. Hitler and Mao Tse Tung had very strong personalities.

J.F. – Alas, they did indeed!

M. – So irreversible determination, impossible to stop, isn't in itself a positive quality. It all depends on the motivation behind it.

J.F. – That's a very valid objection.

M. – It's important not to confuse strong individuality and strength of mind. The great teachers I've been able to meet had indomitable strength of mind. You could say they had very impressive personalities, and that they radiated a sort of natural strength that everyone who met them could perceive. But the big difference was that you couldn't find the slightest trace of ego in them. I mean the kind of ego that inspires selfishness and self-centeredness. Their strength of mind came from knowledge, serenity, and inner freedom that were outwardly manifested as an unshakable certainty. They were worlds apart from Hitler, Mao Tse Tung and the like, whose powerful personalities arose from an unbridled desire to dominate, and from pride, greed, or hatred. In both cases, we're faced with immense power, but in the first that power is a flow of constructive altruism, while in the second it's negative and destructive.

J.F. – That's true, but the desire for action inherent in Western thought has two sides to it. A death-oriented side, which gave rise to Hitler and Stalin, and a life-oriented side, which gave rise to Einstein,

Mozart, Palladio, Tolstoy, or Matisse – people who brought truth and beauty to the world. Nevertheless, there is a shared trait, which is that the majority of great Western thinkers have always had at least some desire to put their thoughts into action. Plato draws up a constitution in the *Republic,* because he wants to transform society. Descartes says that man must make himself 'master and possessor of nature'. Rousseau developed the notion of the social contract. Karl Marx instituted *praxis,* meaning the translation of thought into action, this being the supreme criterion of the truth of a doctrine. So, to come back to my question. Buddhism conceives of life in the world as a captivity from which one must escape by extracting oneself from the cycle of rebirths. But for the Westerner, on the contrary, human suffering is to be attenuated by transforming the world and reforming society. Isn't that an antithesis difficult to overcome?

M. – If a prisoner wants to free his companions in misfortune, he must first break out of his own chains. It's the only way to do it. You have to gain in strength to act appropriately. An artist has to begin by discovering the roots of his art, acquiring a technical skill, developing his inspiration and being capable of projecting it on to the world. The sage's approach is similar, even if it doesn't have the same goals. The spiritual path begins with a period of retreat from the world, like a wounded deer looking for a solitary, peaceful spot to heal her wounds. Here, the wounds are those inflicted by ignorance. To try to help prematurely is like harvesting wheat when it's still grass, or like a deaf musician playing beautiful tunes that he can't hear. To be able to help beings, there should no longer be any difference between what you teach and what you are. A beginner might feel an immense desire to help others, but generally doesn't have sufficient spiritual maturity to be able to do so. Where there's a will, however, there's a way, and the strength of that altruistic aspiration will one day bear fruit. One of Tibet's greatest hermits, Milarepa, said that during the twelve years he'd spent in solitary retreat in caves, there wasn't a single instant of meditation or a single prayer that he hadn't dedicated to the good of all beings.

J.F. – No doubt, but altruism like that is much more in the realm of understanding than of action.

M. – Tibet's great lamas have had a considerable influence, not only on their disciples but on the whole of society. Their powerful personality was seen in a completely positive way by those who lived around them. In the case of the lama I spent most time with, Khyentse Rinpoche, he spent some seventeen years in solitary retreat in his youth, interrupted only by visits to his teachers from time to time. Then, when he was thirty-five, his teacher told him, 'Now the time has come for you to transmit your knowledge and experience to others.' From that moment onward, he never stopped teaching, indefatigably, for the rest of his life. Rising well before dawn, he'd spend several hours praying and meditating. Toward eight in the morning, he'd break his silence and begin to receive a constant flow of visitors, who'd already have been gathering at his door. According to their needs, he'd give them spiritual instructions, practical advice about their lives, teachings, or simply a blessing. He'd often teach all day for months on end, whether to a dozen people or a crowd of several thousand. Even at the end of such full days, he'd still try to fulfil individual requests and, late into the night, would teach one person or a small group. He was completely accessible to everyone and never refused a request for teaching. Such people certainly have a very strong influence on the society around them, of which they may well even be the focal point.

J.F. – All the same, such an attitude is hardly comparable to that of Western scientists, or even artists, whose activity isn't limited to just teaching others what they've understood themselves. What distinguishes the Western artist isn't thinking that the self is just a fantasy or an imposture, but quite the opposite – that an artist's creative originality comes from the fact that his or her individual self is unique, incomparable to all other selves, and is therefore capable of inventing something in literature, art, or music that no one else would have been able to think of. So everything in the West, if you like, converges on two specific goals. The first is the enhancement of the value of the self as such, which is the opposite of the Buddhist teaching, since that Western emphasis on the self isn't just a step taken with the idea of being able to pass knowledge on to others. The second is the use of discoveries made with this inventive originality in terms of political, economic, artistic, or cognitive action, the application of such discoveries to the real world. Here, it seems to me, there's a fundamental divergence of orientation.

M. – In Buddhism, the equivalent of that enhancement of the value of the self is the most perfect possible use of the extraordinary potential that human life offers. And its creativity is to put into action all the means necessary to attain wisdom. On the other hand, the enhancement of a self infatuated with itself, which pushes the individual to want to invent something original at any price, to do something different, is seen as a puerile exercise. That's particularly true in the realm of ideas. As for the overenhancement of the self as such, it's simply keeping a hand in the fire in the hope of cooling it down. Dissolving the mind's attachment to the reality of a self does go hand in hand with annihilation, but what's annihilated is pride, vanity, obsession, touchiness, and acrimony. As that attachment dissolves, the field is left clear for goodness, humility, and altruism. By no longer cherishing and protecting the self, you acquire a much wider and deeper view of the world. The sage is said to be like a fish swimming with wide-open eyes, moving through the phenomenal world with the eyes of wisdom wide open. Attachment to the self makes you completely self-centered, according more importance to yourself than others, reacting only in terms of what's pleasing or displeasing to that self, and always wanting to make a 'name' for yourself. Such an attitude places severe limits on your field of action. Someone free of egocentric perceptions can have a much vaster effect on the world. You said that the only thing sages did was to teach, but their teaching remedies the very causes of suffering. That's more fundamental than material remedies which only relieve the temporary manifestations of suffering. Nor, in fact, does it exclude other forms of action. In Tibetan civilization, the flourishing of architecture, painting, and literature was extraordinary. Khyentse Rinpoche, for example, wrote twenty-five volumes of poetry, essays on the contemplative life, and biographies of past masters. While he was building our monastery in Nepal, he had as many as fifty artists and craftsmen around him – painters, sculptors, goldsmiths, costume-makers...

J.F. – Wait a minute. I think there's a misunderstanding between us about what 'acting on the world' means. You're describing the influence a lama can have on those like him. But let's be more concrete. When I say that the West's been a civilization of action, I'm thinking of the transformation of the world by knowledge of its laws. I'm thinking of technological invention, I'm thinking of the invention of the steam engine, the use of electricity, the invention of the telescope and the microscope, the use of nuclear energy – for better or for worse, there's the atom bomb but also nuclear power stations. All that comes from the West. So acting on the world isn't just a matter of having some spiritual influence on people like oneself, but of a real change in the very substance of the world we live in, and the creation of instruments that were totally unimaginable five centuries ago. These are tools that have radically changed human life. If I've understood it properly, Buddhism says that action of that sort on the world, in the end, is superfluous, doesn't it? At any rate, it was never something Buddhist societies developed.

M. – As I've already put it, Western efficiency is a major contribution to minor needs.

J.F. – Minor needs! How can you possibly say that?

M. – From one point of view, it's true. The well-being that the improved living conditions resulting from technological progress bring are certainly not to be despised. Far from it. But experience shows that such progress only solves the secondary problems. You can travel faster, see further, go up higher, go down lower, and so on.

J.F. – Live longer, cure more diseases … Again, let's take a concrete example. In India, next door to here, man's life expectancy has risen from twenty-nine in 1900 to fifty-three today. Of course, one could say that if a man is too miserable there's no point in his living long. In that case he'd do better to die at twenty-nine than at fifty-three! But for someone profiting from all these discoveries, his life is both longer and more tolerable. That introduces a dimension that didn't exist in ancient philosophies. Not to be sick and not to die at twenty-nine is also a way of escaping from suffering. The Western conception of happiness includes, among other things, the prolonging of human life, being able to treat disease more effectively, being able to travel fifty kilometers without having to walk in the mud for two days, and other 'minor' aspects of the kind, like not dying of appendicitis at the age of ten, which is probably what would have happened to me had it not been for the invention of modern surgery and antisepsis. If Western-style happiness was of so little interest, why so much frenzy in the East to copy and adopt it?

M. – The right way is often the middle one. By all means, let's live a longer life thanks to medical progress, and use it wisely thanks to spiritual values. I'm not trying to minimize the importance of any material progress that allows suffering to be assuaged. The East is grateful to the West for progress in medicine and increased life expectancy. These are things everyone appreciates. But on the other side, a civilization oriented almost exclusively toward that form of action on the world clearly lacks something essential that material progress can never bring – indeed, it's not what it's designed to do. The proof is that Western society is now feeling just that, and, with a frenzy that's sometimes clumsy, is seeking all sorts of recipes for wisdom borrowed from the East or from the past. That lack appears clearly in the confusion so many minds are plunged into, in the violence that reigns in the inner cities, in the selfishness that governs so many human relationships, in the sad resignation of all those spending their last years in old people's homes, and in the despair of suicide. If spiritual values stop being an inspiration for a society, material progress becomes a sort of facade that masks the pointlessness of life. Of course, to live longer is to profit from an increased opportunity of giving meaning to life, but if you neglect that opportunity and just aspire to a long and comfortable existence the value of human life becomes altogether artificial. Study of the aging process, at a cellular level, has made considerable progress. In the laboratory the lifespan of nematodes and flies can now be doubled. It's not inconceivable that, one day, it might be possible to double or triple the length of human life. But such a perspective underlines even more the need to give some meaning to it. Otherwise, we'll just run the risk of having to live out two hundred years of depression, or three hundred years of bad moods. What's more, the destructive sides of technological progress have developed no less than its beneficial sides, and in some cases, pollution for example, have overtaken them.

J.F. – It's clear that industrial civilization, the creation of technological society, has been very polluting. But, at the same time, we're also now creating the antidote to that pollution, which was inconceivable in the past. Now it's the industrialized countries that are fighting pollution the hardest. It's even become one of their major growth industries.

M. – What a consolation!

J.F. – On the other hand, it's the less-developed countries that protest, and don't want to apply measures to protect the environment, claiming that such protection prevents their development.

M. – Unfortunately, they don't have the means. They're caught between uncontrolled industrial development and an incapacity to palliate its side effects. In India and Nepal, people keep repairing a car or a lorry for twenty years, by which time it's emitting terrible clouds of black smoke, before they can afford to buy a new one.

J.F. – I want to come to a more fundamental question. I completely accept all the criticisms that can be made of the negative aspects of technological civilization. Such criticisms have been made in the West by a large number of writers, from Jean-Jacques Rousseau to Aldous Huxley, as well as what we call the spirit of May '68 in Europe and the counterculture of the sixties in the United States. I could also quote Jacques Ellul, a French thinker who is unjustifiably little known in Europe but whose book *The Technological System*[1] was widely read in America in the sixties. He expressed the same criticisms as you've just made. But the question I wanted to ask you, as someone who's taking part in both cultures, is whether it might be possible, now that Buddhism's spreading in the West, to pencil-in the main features of some sort of compromise by which the East would absorb some Western values, and vice versa?

M. – I don't see why there'd need to be a 'compromise', which would imply that both parties would have to renounce some of their values. Instead, why not use whatever's beneficial in material progress, while keeping everything in a truer perspective? Is there anyone who wouldn't want progress in medicine and hygiene? That mutual benefit would be typical of the 'Middle Way' that I've spoken about, to which Buddhism keeps referring. A doctor, for instance, could only deepen his or her sense of vocation by being more and more impregnated with Buddhism's altruistic principles. But it would be wrong to fall into the extreme of steaming ahead in only one direction, that of material progress. The West has got rather carried away by that tendency. Its quest for material comfort and possessions is excessive. There's a Tibetan proverb that says, 'Wanting two of something when you've already got one is to open the door to the demon.' You're right that traditional cultures, like Buddhism, have given priority to action on oneself, and not to action on the external world.

There's an interesting example of this choice. In the nineteenth century there lived a sort of Tibetan Leonardo da Vinci, a lama called Mipham Rinpoche. Plans for flying machines and all sorts of other extraordinary inventions were found in his notebooks. However, he burned most of his sketches, explaining that it was better to dedicate oneself to inner transformation than to spend one's life inventing machines and getting lost in the multitude of everyday occupations. It's true that for the last two centuries the West has put huge effort into inventing technologies for using and mastering natural forces. We've been able to reach the moon, and to bring a considerable increase in life expectancy. Over the same period, and for many of the preceding centuries, Tibetan civilization dedicated itself to the contemplative life, to developing a very pragmatic knowledge of how the mind works, in such a way as to enable people to free themselves from suffering.

The West has produced antibiotics that save human lives, and Tibet has spent its time giving meaning to existence. The ideal of medicine is to allow everyone to live to a hundred or more without losing any teeth. The goal of the spiritual path is to eliminate any trace of pride, jealousy, hatred, cupidity, and so on from the current of consciousness, and become incapable of doing anything harmful to others. Our Western society, by and large, is no longer oriented toward quests of that kind; to us they seem out of reach. Why not combine both approaches? There's nothing to stop a sage using the benefits of medicine, or air travel, but he'd never give such conveniences the same importance as the spiritual quest. Spiritual and temporal can be combined in an intelligent and constructive way, as long as one remains aware of their respective importance.

J.F. – So does it seem possible to you that a real synthesis can be achieved, something more than just mutual tolerance? Does it seem possible to you that Western Buddhists – or Tibetans, Japanese, Vietnamese, and so on, transplanted into the West – instead of being a group treated with respect but set a bit apart from the rest, might contribute to transforming the concepts and behavior of Western society from the inside, however slowly and imperceptibly, without the latter renouncing what's been its main trajectory for the last two thousand five hundred years?

M. – Why not? Of course, everything depends on the interest the West has in the principles of Buddhism. It's Buddhism's ideas that could help fill in what's missing, not Buddhist culture as such. The Western world doesn't need fifteen-foot long Tibetan trumpets, however original they might be. But the quest to explore and master consciousness concerns everyone, as it can eradicate suffering.

J.F. – What you mean is that to become a Buddhist you're not obliged to adopt the cultural context in which Buddhism was born and in which it was able to develop in the East.

M. – I mean that the essence of Buddhism isn't 'Buddhist', it's universal, because it touches the basic mechanisms of the human mind. Buddhism considers that each person has to start where they are and use the methods that match their nature and their personal capacities. That flexibility and richness of possibilities could be useful in the West, without Buddhism renouncing its basic values. It's not a matter of adapting the teachings of Buddhism, but of being sure to understand its very essence – which doesn't need any adaptation, for it corresponds to the deepest preoccupations of anyone, wherever they might be.

J.F. – So it seems to you that the interest aroused by Buddhism in the West could be more than just a passing fashion that'll quite quickly come up against some sort of limit. You think that it's compatible with the overall Western attitude to life.

M. – What makes it different from just a vogue, to my mind, is that people are seeing it as a particularly lucid explanation of life's problems. Buddhism is compatible with everyone's deepest aspirations. What Buddhism could help to change is the overall attitude that consists of giving priority to 'having' over 'being', something it identifies as not very healthy. It's a matter of establishing a new order of values, giving priority to the quest for inner well-being.

I'm convinced that Buddhist ideas could make a tremendous impact on Western culture and give new life to the way we see religion. As a tradition that so closely combines study with inner experience, Buddhism could help people see how basic qualities like love, compassion, tolerance, and patience can actually be cultivated, and that it's possible to master one's own mind and tame the wild thoughts and emotions that destroy our own and others' peace. But I don't subscribe to the idea of a Western Buddhism that tries to make the rules of the game easier, so that it can join in. Whether we like it or not, the goal is to dissolve attachment to the ego, and it would be a great loss if people tamper with the tried and trusted methods that allow that goal to be attained. The danger is to imagine that there are certain essential points of Buddhism that can be adapted. It would be fruitless to put particular aspects of the teachings gradually to one side because they don't happen to correspond to our present ways of seeing things.

J.F. – There could be another problem, on a more mundane scale: Buddhism confronted by the Western religions on their own territory. First of all, Christianity in its various forms – including Orthodox, if one day the orthodox countries come into contact with Buddhism.

M. – That's already happened, a long time ago in the ex-Soviet Union, where Buddhist Buryats and Mongols lived alongside Russian Orthodox Christians.

J.F. – Then there's Judaism, and Islam, too, because that's now to some extent become one of the Western religions. In France, for instance, Islam is the country's second religion in terms of numbers of adherents. There are more Muslims than Protestants or Jews. Although I was born a Catholic, I'm not at all a believer, so for me personally it's a question I can ask with total detachment, and first and foremost out of cultural curiosity. Since Buddhism, unlike Western religions, recognizes neither a substantial soul that could hope for immortality in another world, nor a God to whom we can address our prayers to intervene during this life and welcome us in the hereafter, isn't there some risk of conflict, or at least competition between newly arrived Buddhism and the already-established religions?

M. – There's no real basis for any such competition. To make a noise, you have to clap two hands together. If from one side there's no intention to enter into competition, any competition from the other will come to an end by itself.

J.F. – I'm not so sure. Some people from those other religions could react competitively and take umbrage at your influence, even if you're not trying to extend it.

M. – It all depends on their openness of mind. Buddhism doesn't try to convert anyone. The fact that a growing number of Westerners feel drawn toward Buddhism might be irritating to a few people, but the risks of conflict are minimal. Buddhists are quite careful to avoid dissension and friction, and to promote mutual respect.

For instance, I was lucky enough to be able to visit the inside of the Grande Chartreuse with His Holiness the Dalai Lama in 1993. We were told that not more than twenty people, apart from the monks, had been allowed inside since the monastery's foundation, which goes back to the eleventh century. In the high-speed train approaching Grenoble, where the Dalai Lama was to meet the scientific community and take part in a conference at the university, I'd told him that there were monks living in silent retreat behind the mountain we were traveling past. He was immediately very interested. By a curious coincidence, the mayor of Grenoble asked the Dalai Lama whether he'd like to meet those monks and offered to try to arrange a visit. So a messenger was sent up to the Grande Chartreuse and the Father Superior replied that he'd be delighted to meet the Dalai Lama as long as there wasn't too much publicity involved. To escape the journalists, the mayor pretended to be organizing a lunch at his residence for the Dalai Lama, and then, instead of going there, we took a helicopter into the mountains and were landed – the Dalai Lama, one of his monks, and myself as interpreter – a few hundred meters from the Chartreuse.

The Father Superior and a monk were waiting for us at the door. For one hour, which passed very quickly, we talked in a small room. The conversation was entirely taken up by the contemplative life; what the monks, both in the Chartreuse and in Tibet, do in retreat; the timetable of prayers; what was done when a monk died; how prayer was transformed into pure meditation; and so on. It transpired that the hermit's way of life in both traditions was very similar. The Father Superior even said, jokingly, 'Either Christian and Tibetan Buddhist contemplatives must have had contact more than a thousand years ago, or they received the same blessing from heaven!' It was an inspiring and joyful encounter. They spoke the same language, that of the contemplative life. Afterward, the Dalai Lama asked if we could meditate in the chapel, and we did so for a quarter of an hour. He then looked at the Book of Hours, decorated with beautiful musical notation, before we left.

Later on, he told me that his visit there had been the most interesting moment of his stay in France. Between spiritual practitioners, there was no barrier. They'd understood each other perfectly. That's why I think that it's only between those who neglect the contemplative life and take up intellectual and sectarian points of view that clashes can occur.

J.F. – I find your account of that visit to Grande Chartreuse fascinating, and very reassuring. However, eliminating sectarian points of view from human behavior in general, outside monastic circles, will be a tough job. Let's hope you succeed.

M. – Wherever the Dalai Lama goes, he asks the organizers of his visits to invite all the local representatives of the different religions found there. In France, when we went to Grenoble, Marseilles, Toulouse, and everywhere else, the first people we met, along with the mayor and the préfet, were always the bishop, a rabbi, an imam, or an Orthodox priest. The Dalai Lama would immediately take them by the hand and the ice was broken. He thinks that the gulfs that seem to separate the different religions are only due to lack of communication.

J.F. – That's rather optimistic of him, but an admirable attitude all the same. Unfortunately, religions – and philosophies, too – have more often left their mark on world history by their sectarian side than by their sense of exchange and tolerance.

M. – It's an ever-poorer understanding of religions that, over the centuries, has led certain peoples to use religion for the purposes of oppression and conquest. Christ himself professed nothing other than love of one's neighbor. Personally, I don't think he would have approved of the Crusades and wars of religion. As for the Inquisition, how could those who took part in it dare to call themselves Christians?

J.F. – There's one question you haven't answered. That visit to the Grande Chartreuse, to my mind, underlines the fact that in the end the ideal of Buddhism is monastic life. Perhaps not the life of the hermit, because that's a wanderer's life, isn't it?

M. – A monk or nun, in the Buddhist world, is someone who's renounced the world and family life. Literally, 'one who's gone from home to homelessness'. But the monasteries are open communities. Laymen come there in large numbers to meet the teachers and listen to their teachings. A hermit, however, dedicates himself entirely to the contemplative life and lives alone, or in the company of a small group of retreatants, in the remotest places in the mountains or forest. Whether or not they're monks or nuns, hermits generally take a vow to stay in retreat for three years, five years, or more, without meeting anyone other than those taking part in their retreat. There are also hermits who go from one hermitage to another without settling anywhere permanently.

J.F. – So, whether it's monastic life or the life of a hermit, it seems to me – from the few Buddhist texts that I've read and from what I've seen while traveling, thanks to you, in Darjeeling, Bhutan, or here in Nepal, and on my own journeys to Japan – that monastic life or the life of a hermit are, in the final analysis, the ideal of Buddhist wisdom. Doesn't that limit its capacity to merge into all the aspects of a civilization which, like ours, is essentially secular? Doesn't that make Buddhism here a phenomenon that's bound to be marginal, just by vocation?

M. – Choosing to live as a monk or nun, or in retreat, is a sign that the mind is directed completely toward spiritual practice. When I took my monastic vows, I had a feeling of immense freedom. At last I could dedicate every moment of my life to do what I really wanted. That day, my teacher told me, 'You've been very fortunate to have taken vows.' But there are all sorts of other possible situations between a life of renunciation and the ordinary life of a Westerner. Buddhist ideas can perfectly well impregnate someone's mind and bring them many benefits without their necessarily renouncing what they do. Monastic life was highly developed in Tibet, since before the Chinese invasion up to twenty percent of the population lived in monastic orders. I agree that we can hardly expect anything of the sort in the West. But at the same time I don't think that needs to be a barrier to the understanding of Buddhism in our countries. Someone can have a very rich spiritual life while only spending several minutes or an hour a day actually in contemplative practice.

J.F. – How can that be reconciled with everyday activities?

M. – We make a distinction between 'meditation' and 'post-meditation'. Meditation isn't just to sit down for a few moments to acquire a beatific calm. It's an analytical and contemplative approach that allows the functioning and nature of the mind to be understood, to perceive how things really are. What we call 'post-meditation' consists of avoiding slipping back into our habits exactly as before. It consists of knowing how to use the understanding acquired during meditation in everyday life, to gain a greater openness of mind, goodness and patience – in short, to become a better human being. It's also very much what happens in the Tibetan lay community, which lives in symbiosis with the monastic community and the spiritual teachers. It's nourished by that inspiration, so that everyday life is better lived.

J.F. – But Western philosophies and religions, in theory, also offer the possibility of living according to one's chosen philosophy or religion while still taking part in the action, in our own times. Priests and monks have often been statesmen, writers, artists, philosophers, or scientists, as well as being committed to their religion. Plato's dream was of the philosopher-king, who'd be, he thought, a guarantee of good government for the city-state. If, as Buddhism affirms, the world is just an illusion, a sequence of images that have no reality, and the self too, what would be the point of managing a business, getting involved in politics, or doing scientific research? It would be useless, you'd just be an accomplice in a misleading illusion.

M. – For a hermit, that's true, ordinary activities have little meaning. They seem like children's games. But, in any case, I'd like here to go a little more into the meaning of the term 'illusion' in Buddhism, which seems quite difficult to understand in the West. For those of us living in that illusion, the world seems as real as it possibly could be. But just as ice is only solidified water, the solidity we ascribe to the world isn't its ultimate reality. This illusory nature of the world doesn't stop the laws of cause and effect being inescapable. Physicists would say that electrons aren't tiny cannonballs but concentrations of energy. Such a statement doesn't even slightly lessen the need to develop medicine, to allay suffering and to solve all the problems of everyday life. Even if the self is only an imposture, and even if the external world isn't made up of entities endowed with true existence, it's perfectly legitimate to remedy suffering by all available means and to do whatever can be done to increase the well-being of all. In the same way, a scientist who understands that we're only made of particles that can be reduced to just energy won't thereby be rendered indifferent to happiness and suffering.

J.F. – Once again, I'm struck by the similarity of that theory to Kant's view – the phenomenon isn't the thing in itself, and yet it's reality for us. You've answered my question. I'm going to ask you another, final one which is a bit specious, I admit, but one that is a classic question asked by commentators and historians of Buddhism. If the active self, and the influence that the self can have on the real world, are just illusions, what about moral responsibility? I'm nothing, so I'm not responsible. To my mind, there's a contradiction here, and I hope it's only an apparent one, between Buddhism as a system of ethics and morals, and Buddhism as metaphysics.

M. – Buddhist practice involves three complementary aspects – view, meditation, and action. The 'view' is what corresponds to the metaphysical perspective, investigation of the ultimate nature of things, of the phenomenal world and of the mind. Once this view has been established, 'meditation' consists of familiarizing oneself with that view and integrating it through spiritual practice into the stream of consciousness, in such a way that the view becomes second nature. 'Action' is the expression in the outer world of the inner knowledge acquired through view and meditation. It's a matter of applying and maintaining that knowledge in all circumstances. This is the phase in which ethics, or morals, enters into things. Ethics doesn't become invalid when you realize the illusory nature of the world. Someone whose eyes of wisdom are open sees even more clearly and finely the mechanisms of cause and effect, and knows what should be undertaken and what should be avoided in order to continue making progress on the path and bringing happiness to others.

J.F. – I'm sorry, but surely if I'm nothing in terms of a self, I'm not a moral agent. And if I'm not a moral agent, how can I be responsible for the harm that I cause others?

M. – To transpose the view of Kant that you quoted, we could say, 'The self has no existence in itself, and yet it's our reality.' Before, we likened the flow of consciousness devoid of a self to a river without a boat. So there's no solid and permanent self that's traveling like a boat on the river. That doesn't prevent the water of the river from being either poisoned with cyanide or remaining pure, crystalline, and thirst-quenching like that of a mountain stream. So the fact that there's no personal identity doesn't in any way stop every action having a result.

J.F. – Yes, but let's be careful. Moral responsibility doesn't follow from an inescapable law of cause and effect. On the contrary, the notion of moral responsibility arises the moment there's some relationship between an agent and the consequences of his act, which isn't something inescapable. It's the moment when the agent has the choice between several possible actions.

M. – The continuity of consciousness ensures that there's a link between the moment of an action and the moment of its consequences, whether happy or unhappy. Hindu philosophy used an argument similar to yours against Buddhism. If there's no self, it said, the person who lives out the result of the act is no longer the same person. So what's the point of avoiding evil and doing good? To that challenge, Buddhism replies with a parable. A man drops a flaming torch from a high terrace where he'd been eating his supper. The fire catches the thatch of his own roof and soon sets the whole village ablaze, house by house. When accused of causing the fire, he replies to his judges, 'It wasn't my fault. The fire of the torch I was eating by wasn't the same as the fire that burned the village.' But, of course, he's found to be responsible for the fire. So even in the absence of an individual self seen as an independently existing entity, what we are at present is the result of our past. Acts certainly bear their results. The most important point is therefore the continuity, not the identity. A negative act isn't translated into happiness, just as a hemlock seed doesn't grow into a lime tree. Consequently, the fact that a positive or negative action has a corresponding result, in terms of happiness or suffering, justifies our undertaking or avoiding it, even if the person who experiences the result doesn't have an eternal self.

1. Continuum, New York, 1980.

∾

SEVEN

BUDDHISM AND

THE WEST

JEAN-FRANÇOIS – All the problems we've discussed, everything you've explained about Buddhism's metaphysics, its theory of consciousness, its cosmology, and the repercussions of these great philosophical and metaphysical edifices on the conduct of human life, are still the subjects of living and animated debate among today's Buddhists. For them, it's not a matter of the history of philosophy or of ideas, it's philosophy and metaphysics lived in the present, just as disciples of Socrates and Plato lived them in the fifth and fourth centuries B.C. Public debate of such subjects on any such scale disappeared in the West a long time ago. The philosophies are still there, but that's no longer how they find expression. It's true that 'café philosophers' have appeared in Paris recently, holding sessions in public, open to all free of charge; but the debate they occasion isn't often on a much higher level than the talk at the bar. In spite of the West's undeniable success in other fields and other sectors, could it not be that big missing element – the absence of any discussion worthy of interest – that's behind the astonishing curiosity Buddhism arouses in the West these days? It makes me think of what the English historian Arnold Toynbee once said, that for historians of the future one of the most significant events of the twentieth century might turn out to be the encounter of Buddhism with the Christian West.

MATTHIEU – I think that all the interest in Buddhism nowadays is due to several factors. First of all, to people who want to commit themselves to the spiritual life and make it a major element in their lives, Buddhism offers not only a living system of metaphysics and wisdom, but also the means by which to integrate that wisdom into their innermost being. Then – and it's perhaps here that Buddhism has most to offer the West – it provides everyone, believers or not, with a vision of tolerance, open-mindedness, altruism, quiet confidence, a science of the mind through which to find their own inner peace and allow others' inner peace to blossom. Finally, Buddhism makes its ideas available but doesn't try to impose them, and even less to convert anyone. It simply offers to share an experience with anyone who wishes.

J.F. – There's no forced conversion in Buddhism, not even a missionary spirit?

M. – The Dalai Lama often says, 'I haven't come to the West to make one or two more Buddhists, but simply to share my experience of the wisdom that Buddhism has developed over the centuries.' And at the end of his lectures he always adds, 'If you find anything I've said useful, make use of it. Otherwise, just forget it!' He goes as far as advising Tibetan lamas who travel to different countries not to emphasize the teaching of Buddhism too much, but to offer their experience, as one human being to another. Trying to convert people may not only fail but could also inadvertently weaken their faith in their own religion. That approach is best avoided, he says. It's better to encourage those who believe in something to deepen their own faith. The point isn't to convert people but to contribute to their well-being.

That doesn't stop anyone who feels a particular affinity for Buddhism as a spiritual path from committing themselves freely to it if that's what they want. They should then study and practice seriously, and follow up their efforts to the end, like someone digging a well who perseveres until he actually finds water. While keeping a tolerant and open mind toward other religions, it's important that people dedicate themselves to the one they've chosen. It would be pointless for someone to half-finish a dozen wells without ever reaching the water he's looking for.

Several hundred Westerners have completed the three-year, three-month, three-day retreat, one of the traditional ways of Tibetan Buddhist contemplative practice. Three years of retreat, in small groups, during which the participants live in isolation from the world and get down to intense practice. During those three years, they spend an hour or two a day studying philosophy and the texts that deal with the contemplative life, and sometimes learning Tibetan. The rest of the time, from the early hours of the morning until after dark, they try to integrate what they've studied into their innermost being.

J.F. – Being? What being?

M. – Into the flow of their minds, you could say. The point is to make sure that philosophy doesn't become a dead letter, pure theory. For example, we've already mentioned the techniques that aim to 'liberate' thoughts the moment they arise, to stop them linking one to another in chains and proliferating to the point of invading the mind completely.

J.F. – Liberate? It's more like learning to discipline one's thoughts, isn't it?

M. – We've already seen how thoughts can be disciplined by applying antidotes specific to the different negative emotions, but also – and it's a more fundamental method – you can liberate a thought by watching it at the moment it arises, tracing it to its source, and observing its complete lack of substantiality. The moment you begin to watch it like that, it dissolves like a rainbow fading into space. That's what's called 'liberating' or 'untying' a thought, in the sense that it'll no longer trigger a chain reaction of further thoughts. Thoughts vanish without leaving a trace, and are no longer translated into the words and actions that are the usual expression of an emotion – anger, desire, and so on. Whatever the circumstances, you no longer fall under the sway of your thoughts. You become like an expert horseman, who might at first have found it hard to stay in the saddle, but later on, like a Tibetan rider, can even pick up an object from the ground at full gallop without falling off.

J.F. – Let me slip in a small comment here. I accept that Buddhism presents this self-discipline in a new way, in a language that's new for the West. Nonetheless, it's an exercise that's far from unknown to us. In all Western philosophical systems a very clear distinction is made between disorganized and organized thought. We know very well that there is, on one side, a disorganized way of thinking that lets associations of ideas flow in a purely fortuitous manner; and on the other, an organized form of thought which is directed and disciplined – mathematical analysis, for instance, or any reasoning conducted with properly constructed logic. Westerners are great logicians. From Aristotle through Leibniz to Bertrand Russell, the art of directing the mind and not leaving it at the mercy of mere associations of ideas has been an important discipline throughout the ages. It was even one of the principal goals of philosophical training.

M. – But do you really think mathematicians and logicians are less susceptible to negative emotions? I hope so, for their sake. In any case, Buddhism, as I've emphasized, doesn't claim to lead to any new discoveries. But unlike some of the other philosophical and religious traditions of our time, it does put theoretical, intellectual understanding into practice in an extremely vital and energetic way. It could well be that pragmatic approach that attracts people who are interested in metaphysical points of view but haven't hitherto been able to apply them, in everyday life, to find inner peace.

J.F. – Is Buddhism relevant to all sorts of people, even those who can't or don't want to opt for a life of retreat or some kind of monastic situation?

M. – That's another interesting side. For reasons of family and job, there aren't many people who could – or would even want to – live in isolation in a three-year retreat, or join a monastery. But the same techniques for transforming the mind can be applied at any moment in life, allowing people living a completely ordinary life to profit greatly from them. Buddhism is first and foremost a science of the mind, but that also gives it the capacity to respond to many of society's problems, thanks to its tolerance and its notions of nonviolence toward living creatures and the environment. There's a path for everyone, laypeople as well as monks and nuns. In Asia, Buddhism continues to show signs of great vitality. The Tibetan refugees in India and Nepal, for example, started rebuilding monasteries as soon as they could, despite their initial destitution thirty years ago. Those monasteries are now packed with aspiring students, and of the hundred and thirty thousand Tibetan refugees in India ten percent are again in the monasteries.

J.F. – And in the West?

M. – Buddhism's arousing a growing interest, based on a wish for exchange and openness. People don't necessarily study it with the idea of becoming Buddhists. Sometimes it's in order to understand the practice of their own religion better, or rediscover its truth and inner strength, with the help of some of the techniques that Buddhism offers.

J.F. – Isn't that syncretism – mixing up bits borrowed here and there from different doctrines? Syncretism is hardly the most elevated form of thought.

M. – No, it's not syncretism at all. The Dalai Lama has emphasized that it's quite useless trying to 'stick a yak's head on to a sheep's body'. Syncretism can only make the traditions it tries to mix insipid, or distort them. I was referring to certain techniques used to train the mind, contemplative techniques whose value is universal. In 1994, the Dalai Lama was invited to spend a week commenting on the Gospels in England. At the beginning, he wondered, 'How am I going to do this? I've never studied the Gospels. How am I going to start from the principle of a Divine Creator, something Buddhism doesn't believe in? It seems quite a difficult thing to do. Anyway, let's try. Why not?' So he commented on selected passages from the Gospels to an audience of priests and laypeople. The extraordinary thing was that while he was reading those passages aloud and making his comments, some Christian priests, monks, and nuns, moved to tears, had the impression that they were hearing certain passages for the very first time, even though they'd been reading them all their lives. Why? Because when the Dalai Lama spoke of love or compassion, everyone felt that his words were a direct expression of his experience. He was really living what he said.[1] Westerners are sensitive to that living aspect of the tradition. Sogyal Rinpoche's *The Tibetan Book of Living and Dying*[2] has run to almost a million copies and has been translated into twenty-six languages.

J.F. – Is it an old text, a classic?

M. – No, it's not a translation of the classic *Tibetan Book of the Dead*, the *Bardo Thödröl*, which explains the intermediate state after death. *The Tibetan Book of Living and Dying* is a simple and direct explanation of Tibetan wisdom, interspersed with autobiographical anecdotes about Sogyal Rinpoche's encounters with his teachers. But first and foremost it's a manual for living. How can we really live properly, how should we approach death, how can we help the dying, how can we give meaning to life and make a good death the culmination of a good life? These are some of the main questions it tackles.

J.F. – It seems significant to me that the younger generation of philosophers in France refer more and more often to Buddhism. I've been reading a book by Luc Ferry, *L'Homme Dieu ou le sens de la vie* (*Man as God or the Meaning of Life*),[3] which is a remarkable essay that appeared in early 1996 and has been very widely read. It opens with a reference to the very book you just mentioned, *The Tibetan Book of Living and Dying,* and develops a number of Buddhist-derived ideas in which the author makes clear his sincere interest in them. After several pages of discussion, however, he raises a basic objection which consists of saying, 'Well, that's great. There's a lot to be said for retreating into oneself like that, escaping from the world, isn't there? But, even with a great deal of compassion for the whole of humankind, that's not what's going to solve the problem of Auschwitz or of Bosnia!' What would you reply to that objection?

M. – First of all, there's a major misunderstanding there which needs to be cleared up. The same misunderstanding forms the basis of Pope John Paul II's criticism of Buddhism. In his book *Crossing the Threshold of Hope,*[4] the Pope states that, according to Buddhism, 'To liberate oneself from evil, one must free oneself from this world, necessitating a break with the ties that join us to external reality,' and that 'the more we are liberated from these ties, the more we become indifferent to what is in the world'. He also describes *nirvana* as 'a state of perfect indifference with regard to the world'. These are unequivocally misinterpretations – due to lack of information, no doubt – that many Christians and Buddhists have found regrettable. For in fact, the goal of Buddhism is a complete and ultimate understanding of the phenomenal world, both inner and outer. Subtracting oneself from reality solves nothing at all. *Nirvana* is the very opposite of indifference toward the world. It's infinite compassion and love toward all beings in their totality. It's a compassion that's all the more powerful in that it's born from wisdom – from the understanding that each individual living creature intrinsically possesses the nature of Buddhahood – and in that such compassion isn't just confined to a few beings, like ordinary love. The only thing we need to 'break with' is our childish and egocentric attachment to the endless fascinations of the race for pleasures, belongings, fame, and so on.

J.F. – John Paul II also thinks that for Buddhism 'detachment from the world of the senses' is an end in itself.

M. – In fact, the goal is to no longer be enslaved to the world of the senses, to no longer suffer from it like a moth attracted to a flame and then burned to death by it. Someone free of all attachment not only freely enjoys all the beauty of the world and beings but can also return within that very world to deploy unlimited compassion, without being the plaything of the negative emotions.

J.F. – The Pope states that for Buddhism 'To save oneself means, above all, to free oneself from evil by becoming indifferent to the world, which is the source of evil.'

M. – Well, it all depends on what you call 'the world'. If you mean the conditioned world of suffering, of those tortured by ignorance, who wouldn't want to be free from it? But the world in itself isn't evil; for an enlightened Buddha it's 'infinite purity' or 'unchangeable perfection'.

Finally, for the Pope to affirm as he does that 'Carmelite mysticism begins where Buddhism ends' seems rather incongruous. How can one judge from the outside how deep the Buddha's enlightenment was? Perhaps by what the Buddha himself said about it just afterward: 'The truth I have found is like nectar, deep, peaceful, simple, uncompounded, radiant, and free from all elaborations of the intellect.' The Buddha's enlightenment far transcends our ordinary, deluded mind. It's a merging with absolute truth, a final awakening in which there isn't a trace left of the darkness of ignorance, nor any possibility of a return to it. I don't want to be polemical, but to my mind this contrasts starkly with the poignant doubt that Carmelite mystics apparently experience in their 'dark night of the soul'. In any case, no one without firsthand experience of both mysticisms can so lightly assert the superiority of one over the other.[5]

All of these statements of the Pope's about Buddhism are based on an outdated understanding that goes back to the first translations of Buddhist texts, made in the nineteenth and early-twentieth centuries. On the basis of incomplete knowledge, the authors of those preliminary interpretations grasped the Buddha's insistence on suffering as the primary characteristic of the conditioned world and so understood the 'cessation of suffering' as referring to some process of extinction – whereas in fact it's simply what happens when one fully understands the nature of suffering, and is of enormous help and significance both for oneself and others. Fortunately, there are other eminent Christians who have formed a high opinion of Buddhism, like Thomas Merton, an

American Trappist monk whose writings have had considerable influence worldwide and who was sent to the East by Pope John XXIII. Merton took the trouble to seek out the real essence of Buddhism. Having spent some time with several Buddhist teachers, he wrote in his *Asian Journal*:[6] 'It does seem that Tibetan Buddhists are the only ones who, at present, have a really large number of people who have attained extraordinary heights in meditation and contemplation.'

During the remarkable seminar on the Gospels I spoke of just now, which, according to Father Laurence Freeman, the Benedictine who organized it, was a 'model of dialogue in mutual listening', the Dalai Lama, true to his customary openness of mind, declared, 'I feel that between the Buddhist and Christian traditions there is an exceptional closeness and a potential for mutual enrichment through dialogue, especially in the field of ethics and spiritual practice – as well as in the practices of compassion, love, meditation and progress in tolerance. I also feel that such dialogue can go very far and reach a very deep level.' But he also warned his audience of the temptations of syncretism, which is always pointless.

J.F. – Let's come back to that reproach that Buddhism is ineffective in the face of problems like those in Bosnia – although, if you ask me, Buddhism is hardly alone in that respect.

M. – Whenever people ask the Dalai Lama how he explains what happened in Bosnia, he replies that the problem was that people's negative emotions, particularly hatred, grew to the point of getting completely out of control.

J.F. – That's a somewhat rhetorical explanation! More of a description than an explanation, in fact.

M. – But surely it's much more rhetorical to reproach Buddhism for being impotent faced with the horrors of Bosnia, isn't it? It wasn't Buddhism's values that shaped the conditions for what happened there – it was Western ones. Suppose Bosnia had adopted values like Buddhism's several centuries ago, and those values had impregnated its culture. It would be most unlikely that a conflict of that sort could have broken out. In fact, the Bosnian flare-up was rooted in intolerance. It used religions, not to promote harmony between peoples but to set one against another by exacerbating hatred. Wars have certainly ravaged Buddhist countries, too, like Vietnam, Cambodia, Laos, and Sri Lanka, but such wars have never been waged in Buddhism's name or with its blessing. I think it's fair to say that they can be blamed on those who distanced themselves from Buddhism, or even fought against it. The communists in Vietnam and Cambodia, or the Tamils in Sri Lanka, for example.

J.F. – You're not obliged to subscribe to what I'm going to say, but my personal judgment is that the three religions that coexist in Bosnia and throughout ex-Yugoslavia, that's to say Islam, Catholicism, and the Orthodox Church, are all three of them religions that have supplied innumerable proofs of their intolerance toward other religions and toward free thinkers. They're conquering religions. Indeed, many of the written statements by Bosnian representatives of those three religions display a quasi-official wish to destroy the other beliefs. So a Buddhist can justifiably reply that if Bosnians had all been Buddhists or the like, it's highly unlikely that the Bosnian conflict would ever have reached such a level of atrocity! What one can concede to Luc Ferry, though, is that Buddhism has no practical remedy to contribute to the Bosnian problem, or to other tragedies of the kind. But for that matter, I don't see what the West, either, for all its claims of rationality and effective action, has succeeded in doing during the whole long conflict.

M. – In all the interreligious meetings the Dalai Lama has taken part in, he's always emphasized the fact that those who use their religion to oppress others are almost certainly distorting its true spirit. Love of one's neighbor is a point shared by all religions. It ought to be enough to relegate their differences to second place.

J.F. – As regards love, the great religions that dominate the world, ever since they began, have had two objects of hatred: infidels and heretics. And they've unashamedly set about eliminating both – with all the love in the world.

M. – According to Buddhism, it's a serious fault to scorn other religions, even if you don't agree with some of their metaphysical ideas.

J.F. – But what about Buddhism's engagement in the world? You sometimes hear people wondering how Buddhism could help bring peace, as it's a philosophy of detachment that encourages withdrawal from society. Monks live alone in the mountains and pray for others, but in fact they do nothing for humanity. They dedicate themselves to their personal perfection, but to what end?

M. – A retreatant withdraws temporarily from the world to gain the spiritual strength required to help others effectively. The spiritual path begins with an inner transformation, and it's only when that's been achieved that an individual can usefully contribute to the transformation of society. How can Buddhism help to bring peace to the world? Take the example of Tibet. As a Buddhist country, Tibet has never had a war of religion. The Dalai Lama preaches unconditional nonviolence, and proposes very concretely to turn his country into a zone of peace – if only the Chinese communists would release it from their clutches. He wants to create a buffer state between the great powers of the East, for in fact Tibet is right in the middle between China, Burma, India, Pakistan, Afghanistan, Tajikistan, Kirgiztan, Kazakhstan, Russia, and Mongolia. If Tibet recovered its independence and declared its neutrality, it would become an important factor for stability in the region. It would also be a zone of environmental protection, for the greatest rivers of Asia, the Yellow River, the Yangtse, the Mekong, the Brahmaputra, the Indus, and so on, all rise in Tibet. The Dalai Lama has suggested this idea several times.

J.F. – Forgive me for saying so, but that's the kind of idea everyone thinks is great, and no one ever actually applies.

M. – In this case, its application is only a matter of the release of Tibet from the yoke of Chinese occupation. If such ideas too often fail, it's simply because our leaders lack the deep and unbending determination to do something for peace. Why has it taken so much time to get round to nuclear disarmament? To demilitarizing countries? To a situation in which there'd only be a single multinational force, one that would be there not to make war but simply to prevent countries from rebuilding their war machines?

J.F. – That's the goal of the United Nations. Why do you think they're failing?

M. – The Dalai Lama says that outer disarmament can only take place through inner disarmament. If the individual doesn't become more peaceful, a society that's the sum total of such individuals will never become more peaceful either. Individuals who embraced and cultivated the Buddhist ideals simply couldn't conceive the idea of deliberately harming others.

J.F. – Do you mean that the only way to attain lasting peace in the world is the reform of individuals?

M. – To think otherwise is surely utopian. The reform of individuals would, of course, have to include our leaders as a first step! The Dalai Lama is always pointing out the completely unacceptable extent to which the Western nations indulge in the arms trade – even if it means the arms they've sold get fired back at them later. It's unacceptable that Western countries, calling themselves civilized and claiming to be establishing peace in the world, sell instruments of death for commercial gain. Remember that ninety percent of the arms exported to developing countries are sold by the five permanent members of the UN Security Council. This is a display of blatant hypocrisy by countries that keep on saying they want to promote peace – and, like France and the United States, make so much noise about being the very fountainhead of human rights and democracy. They're actually promoting war on a huge scale.

Last month I met someone who was doing de-landmining work in Laos, and who told me that the Fiat factories are one of the main world producers of antipersonnel landmines. Now they make them entirely out of plastic – what a miracle of progress! – without any metallic components at all, so that they can't be detected. I hope the board and shareholders of Fiat are proud of their product reliability, as witnessed by the number of women and children that get reliably blown up by their mines after the wars are over. Logically, the next business to get into to turn a bit more profit might be making artificial limbs for the survivors. Sixty-five out of the eighty-five Afghans mutilated every month by mines in the region of Kabul are children. There are ten million more mines waiting for them. Royal Ordinance in Britain and IBM in the United States also make parts for these same mines. And of course there are plenty of factories making arms in France, too. It's a pity such companies can't stick to selling cars, computers, and so on to make their money.

J.F. – I agree completely. It's monstrous!

M. – While we're speaking, eight million Chinese are working ten to fifteen hours a day in more than a thousand forced labor camps, the *laogai.*[7] One third of certain manufactured products exported by China comes from such camps. The Chinese dissident Harry Wu, who spent nineteen years in the *laogai,* has provided ample evidence for these figures. What sort of leaders authorize imports of such merchandise? Are toys made in prison at the cost of so much suffering the sort of thing you'd want to give your children for Christmas? True ethics can only come about through inner transformation. Anything else is just a facade. The Dalai Lama often says to journalists, 'It's really good that you poke your noses into things and uncover the state's scandals. An authentic politician should have nothing to hide.' Do we have to wait for the final collapse of Asian communism for anyone to speak openly about the Chinese gulags? Before the Second World War, world leaders courted, accommodated, or tolerated Hitler, just as today's leaders do to Li Peng and his comrades.

All of this applies to the environment, too. The Dalai Lama speaks of nonviolence not only toward humans but also in relation to nature. In Bhutan, fishing and hunting are forbidden on a national scale, a good example of the way in which Buddhist ideals can be achieved on the level of a society. A Buddhist state wouldn't hesitate for an instant to prohibit the use of dragnets forty kilometers long that catch not only fish but also turtles and dolphins, and lay waste to the marine ecosphere. All such violations of the environment are based on people wanting to make a profit, and feeling they have the right to kill an incalculable number of animals simply because they have the power to do so.

J.F. – The European Union has, in principle, banned dragnets.

M. – But Japan and Taiwan, notably, are still ravaging the seas with them.

J.F. – In all that you've just mentioned, a certain number of ideas are specifically Buddhist ones, and others have already been expressed by everyone who's thought about such things. The idea of creating a multinational force that keeps national forces in check was the idea of the League of Nations between the two world wars, it's what the United Nations wants to do today, and it's the idea behind the European Union's plan to create a sort of European army into which national armies are integrated. It's an ideal that returns periodically, just as there are periodic conferences on disarmament. But you're taking it a step further when you say that it's never going to be possible for groups of humans to stop killing each other, like in Bosnia, until we get a change to take place in the individuals themselves, until the individuals themselves have all been made nonviolent, one by one. Now there's a task! Lots of philosophies base their hopes of universal peace on a transformation of human nature. I'd even say that all the systems

of wisdom, the great utopias, and all the main religions, too, have reck-
oned on that hypothesis. But it's never worked hitherto. The idea of
making men peaceful one by one, in such a way that adding them all
together ends up making a human race opposed to violence, seems
impossible to realize in practice. Our century, at least, has hardly made
any progress at all in that direction.

M. – That's true, but the alternative, change imposed from the
outside, which consists of forcing more and more restrictive laws on
recalcitrant individuals – a totalitarian system, in the end – is not only
impossible to realize in the long term but is also fundamentally flawed.
You can tighten the screws for a certain amount of time, but the
oppressed always end up expressing their malcontent and freeing
themselves from the oppressor's yoke, whether by peaceful or violent
means. They'll find ways of getting hold of arms and of using them.

J.F. – Not only the oppressed, alas!

M. – True. Humans aren't perfect, and even in a Buddhist country
they don't always apply Buddhist principles. Tibetan civilization, nevertheless, was essentially peaceful. Many travelers there stressed the
'Buddhist gentleness' that, as André Migot says, 'is not just an empty
phrase; it's a gentleness that you can breathe around you, and which
has struck all who've lived in Buddhist countries. It's an attitude of
goodwill toward all living creatures.'[8]

J.F. – Is there any hope that we might see the rest of humanity
adopting such attitudes?

M. – Let me give you an example. On March 17, 1989, several
months after the Dalai Lama received the Nobel Peace Prize, the people
of Lhasa decided to stage a demonstration for Tibetan independence –
knowing full well what to expect, as Lhasa is surrounded by garrisons
of Chinese troops. It was just before Tiananmen. The police in Lhasa
fired on the crowd, and there were about two hundred deaths. Of
course, the Chinese said that provocateurs had attacked the police, that
the majority of the wounded were among the security forces, and that
there were only eleven deaths overall. Everyone believed them. I
arranged a meeting, here in Nepal, between eyewitnesses who'd just
escaped from Lhasa and some journalists from some major French
newspapers who were visiting Kathmandu at the time. But the journalists didn't dare say anything about it, fearing their information had
been too partisan. Two months later came the massacres of Tiananmen

Square – eight days after which the Chinese were claiming that nothing had happened, that the army hadn't fired, and so on. Even recently, the Chinese government were still maintaining that no one had been killed. So retrospectively, the blood of Tiananmen spoke for the blood of Lhasa. There were certainly two hundred deaths in Lhasa.

But the most extraordinary thing that happened at that time is that during the confrontation, whenever Tibetans managed to grab guns from the Chinese, instead of using them to return fire they broke them. So even in the heat of the action they remembered what the Dalai Lama had told them: 'Whatever happens, no acts of violence, which can only provoke an escalation of repression.' Nonviolence had been imprinted on their being. This example was a great encouragement to the Dalai Lama. His message had been heard. Another time, an old monk who'd spent twenty years in Chinese prisons in Tibet came to see the Dalai Lama in India. During the conversation, the Dalai Lama asked him if he'd been afraid during his long imprisonment, which had been interspersed with torture and brainwashing. The monk replied, 'My greatest fear was to lose my love and compassion toward those who were torturing me.'

J.F. – Such examples do indeed show how loath Buddhism is to resort to violence to impose its point of view, or even to defend itself effectively. The great religions we're familiar with have often turned their backs on their own ideals. Christianity, for example, is founded on nonviolence. Didn't Christ say, 'If someone slaps you on the right cheek, turn and offer him your left,' and 'Love one another'? Despite which, the Church has spent its time exterminating those who refused to convert to Christianity, or heretics who dared to profess theories different from the pope's. It has even interfered in scientific problems it knew nothing about, like the question in Galileo's time about whether or not the earth spins on its axis. Man's capacity to behave in flagrant contradiction to the ideals he pretends to profess has been constant throughout history. I wonder if that doesn't impose certain limits on the influence that Buddhism might be able to have in the West.

M. – Not necessarily. On the contrary, the fact that people who find their inspiration in Buddhism try to put those principles of tolerance into practice could be what makes them appreciated in the West. In any case, the first thing is to make peace within oneself – inner disarmament; then peace in the family; then in the village; and finally in the nation and beyond. In expressing such ideas, the Dalai Lama hopes to help people rediscover their own spiritual traditions. So we're quite a long way, here, from a missionary spirit. The resurgence of religious extremism and fundamentalism is no doubt born from the feeling that traditional values are sorely missing from our age. But that feeling shouldn't lead fundamentalists to brutally reject those who've gone astray for the very reason that they're deprived of spiritual reference points. Such a reaction is devoid of any wisdom, and even of good sense. People have to be taken as they are, wherever they might be, and helped with love to appreciate the essential values of life. It's certainly no good exterminating them.

1. Dalai Lama, *The Good Heart*, Rider, London, 1995.

2. Op. cit.

3. Grasset, Paris, 1996 (not available in English translation).

4. Knopf, New York, and Jonathan Cape, London, 1994.

5. Since publication of the original French edition of this book, a detailed analysis of the pope's criticisms and an outspoken reply to them from a Buddhist point of view has been published: Thinley Norbu, *Welcoming Flowers from across the Cleansed Threshold of Hope: An Answer to the Pope's Criticism of Buddhism*, Jewel Publishing House, New York, 1997.

6. Thomas Merton, *The Asian Journal*, New Direction, New York, 1973.

7. *Laogai* are forced labor camps or prisons to which the inmates have been sentenced after a trial, usually summary; *laojiao* are camps where prisoners are put to work without having stood trial at all, for an indefinite period.

8. Op. cit.

◊

EIGHT

RELIGIOUS AND SECULAR
SPIRITUALITY

JEAN-FRANÇOIS – Given the currently growing interest in Buddhism in
the West, one interesting side of what's happening at the moment sur-
faces in a particularly noticeable way: the relationship between Buddhism and some of what the new generation of philosophers are
writing. I've already quoted Luc Ferry. I'd also like to mention André
Comte-Sponville, who two years ago published a book called *Petit
traité des grandes vertus* (*A Small Treatise on the Great Virtues*).[1] It's
a series of pieces of well-thought-out practical advice, and belongs to
what we call in France the tradition of the moralists. The author
expresses his observations on human behavior and psychology, and –
not without getting close to platitudes in some places – gives practical
advice about how to conduct daily life. A book like that represents a
sort of revolution in the way people think in this last decade of the
twentieth century. Moralists always used to be held in profound contempt by professional philosophers, who saw what they had to say as
being no more than a string of anecdotal and purely psychological
points. The great builders of systems who dominated philosophy during my youth relegated even the greatest moralists to the realm of

worldly literature, belittling their works as unconnected, empirical and arbitrary observations that lent themselves to no systematization whatever. But now it looks as if the public, to the extent it's still interested in books on 'philosophy', has a taste for works that go back to those old moralists' recipes, which give advice, with much humility and practical good sense, on the daily functioning of the human animal.

The most original of the modern moralists, E.M. Cioran, who's a master of art and style, was for forty years a writer very much on the fringe, with a readership of only two or three thousand. But suddenly, around 1985, everyone started quoting him. It's symptomatic of the same change that Comte-Sponville's book has been such a huge success in France. It shows how much people want directing principles. They want someone to explain to them how to rediscover the art of living. These are needs that our philosophy hasn't been meeting for a long time. Now, Comte-Sponville, too, often refers to Buddhism. In particular, the following few sentences are interesting because they establish a parallel and a contrast between Buddhism and Christianity in terms of compassion and charity. He says, 'Compassion is the great virtue of the Buddhist East. As we know, charity – at least in theory – is the great virtue of the Christian West. Do we need to choose between the two? Why should we? One doesn't exclude the other. But if we do have to choose, it seems to me that there's this to be said about it. There's no doubt that charity would be worth more, if we were really capable of it. But compassion is more accessible, and in its gentleness it resembles charity and can lead us to it. In other words, Christ's message of love is more exalting, but the Buddha's message, which is of compassion, is more realistic.' Now, there are two things I'd like to say about that. Comte-Sponville is right to say that charity is the great virtue of the Christian West – 'in theory at least', for Christian charity has too often been rendered as the extermination of the American Indians, the burning of heretics at the stake under the Inquisition, or the persecution of Jews and Protestants. Secondly, although paying homage to the Buddhist idea of compassion, Comte-Sponville, at the end of his reflection, seems to be saying that after all it's a somewhat inferior version of Christian charity. What do you think, and what exactly is Buddhist compassion?

MATTHIEU – First of all, I'd like to say something about the first part of your question. Why is there such renewed interest in these collections of advice based on practical wisdom? Perhaps it's to compensate for the fact that our educational systems these days hardly deal at all with becoming a better human being. Modern education, more secular than ever, is primarily designed to develop the intellect and accumulate knowledge.

J.F. – Even in that field, its success is hardly unmitigated.

M. – Intelligence is a two-edged sword. It can do so much good or so much bad, and can be used to build as well as to destroy. In the past, religions – when they weren't betraying their own ideals – taught people to become better human beings, to love their neighbors, to be good, upright, generous, magnanimous. Nowadays, if you asked such virtues to be taught in schools, it would cause a general uproar. You'd be told that such matters were for personal development, that it was the role of parents to inculcate human values in their children. The current generation of parents have themselves been brought up in schools where nothing of the sort is inculcated, and few of them have had a religious education or known any sort of spiritual quest. People even go as far as saying that love and compassion are exclusively matters for religion to deal with. The Dalai Lama often says that we can do without religion, but no one can do without love, compassion, and tenderness. He readily distinguishes between religious and secular spirituality, the latter being aimed at simply making us better human beings, and developing the human qualities that we all have the capacity for, whether or not we're believers. In the absence of any spirituality, adolescents would have nothing and no one to show them what those human values are and how to develop them, unless they happen to read something about it by chance. So it's encouraging to see this resurgence of interest.

J.F. – I'm glad you mentioned what the Dalai Lama says about secular spirituality, because I was going to reply that in my opinion there's no reason why education in ethics shouldn't happen just because the context is secular. 'Secular' implies that what's taught is neutral and isn't dictated by any particular dogma, whether religious or political. That doesn't exclude a training in ethics, indeed it demands one, centered on respect for the law, for others, for the social contract and for the proper uses of freedom – in brief, everything that Montesquieu called republican virtue. Lately, the notion of secularity has gone wide off the mark.

M. – True secular education doesn't mean eliminating religious education classes altogether, as some countries have done. It means making sure that children in school get to know something about all the different religions and philosophical views – why not include agnostic materialism, too – and giving the pupils themselves the choice of attending the course or not, as they wish. That would at least give children and adolescents the chance to get an idea of what was on offer. Why should they wait until they're sixteen and start classes in philosophy before anyone opens their minds to the basics of human values?

J.F. – That's certainly something that would generate some animated discussions among the powers that be in national education! So then, what do you think about Buddhist compassion compared to Christian charity?

M. – The whole idea of compassion is a typical reflection of how difficult it is to translate Eastern ideas in Western terms. In the West, the word 'compassion' sometimes suggests condescending pity, a commiseration which presupposes a certain distance between oneself and the person who's suffering. But in Tibetan, *nyingjé*, which we translate as compassion, means literally 'lord of the heart', that's to say that which should reign over our thoughts. Compassion according to Buddhism is the wish to remedy all forms of suffering, and especially to tackle its causes – ignorance, hatred, desire, and so on. So it's a compassion that refers partly to the suffering being and partly to the mind in which it arises.

J.F. – Would you include compassion in charity?

M. – Charity is one way of expressing compassion. To practice giving is certainly one of the cardinal virtues in Buddhism. Several forms of gift are distinguished. There are material gifts of food, money, clothing, and so on; the gift of 'protection from fear', which consists of protecting those in danger and saving the lives of others; and lastly the gift of teaching, which gives beings a way to free themselves from the yoke of ignorance. These different forms of charity are practiced all the time in Buddhist communities. Sometimes benefactors give away everything they possess to those in need. In the history of Tibet, there are numerous cases of people who, inspired by the ideal of charity, have given their very lives to save those of others. This is what corresponds to Christian charity. Then, to eliminate long-term suffering, it's also important to reflect on the origin of suffering, and one then becomes aware that it's ignorance that nourishes war, the thirst for revenge, obsession, and everything else that makes beings suffer.

J.F. – What's the difference between compassion and love?

M. – Love is the necessary complement to compassion. Compassion can't live, or even less develop, without love, which is defined as the wish that all beings might find both happiness and the causes of happiness. Love, here, means total, unconditional love for all beings without any distinction or partiality. Love between men and women, and love for family and friends, is often possessive, exclusive, limited, and mixed with selfish feelings. There's an expectation of getting back at least as much as one gives. Such love might seem quite deep, but it easily vanishes if it doesn't live up to expectations. What's more, the sort of love we feel for those close to us is often accompanied by a feeling of distance, or even hostility, toward 'strangers', those who could pose a threat to ourselves and to those we love. True love and true compassion can be extended to our adversaries, while love and compassion mixed with attachment can't include anyone we see as an enemy.

J.F. – So in fact love is as important in Buddhism as it is in Christianity?

M. – It's the very basis of the path. But true love can't be polarized, restricted to one or two specific beings, or contaminated with partiality. What's more, it should be completely disinterested and not expect anything in return. One of the principal topics for meditation is to begin by thinking of someone you love deeply, and letting that feeling of love and generosity fill your heart and mind. Then you break out of the cage that restricts that love to a particular person and extend it to all those for whom your feelings are neutral or indifferent. Finally, you include in your love all those you consider as enemies. That's true love. To know that someone wants to harm you can't affect true compassion, because that compassion's based on the profound comprehension that this 'enemy', like all of us, wants only to be happy and not to suffer.

J.F. – So what's the difference between Buddhist compassion and Christian charity?

M. – Love of one's neighbor, as described in the Bible, corresponds completely to love and compassion in Buddhism. In fact, it's common to all the great religions, in theory at least. In Buddhism, love and compassion are combined with two other virtues. One consists of rejoicing in the good qualities and happiness of others and making the wish that their happiness might last as long as possible and only increase; to feel such joy about others' happiness is the antidote to jealousy. The other is impartiality, or equanimity, in the sense of feeling love, compassion, and sympathetic joy not only toward those who are dear to us but also to strangers and our enemies. If we weigh up our own well-being against that of the infinity of beings, it's clear that the importance of the former is negligible compared to the latter. It's also important to be aware that our joy and our suffering are intimately linked to those of others. We can see in everyday life what a difference there is between people who are completely preoccupied with themselves and those whose minds are constantly turned toward others. The former are always ill at ease and dissatisfied. Their narrowness of mind gets in the way of their relationships with others, from whom they have a hard time obtaining anything at all. They never stop knocking on closed doors. The latter, on the other hand, who have open minds and are very little concerned about themselves, are always focused on what might be best for others. They enjoy such strength of mind that their own problems hardly affect them, and others are always ready to listen to what they have to say.

Finally, as I've mentioned already, love and compassion in Buddhism are indissociable from wisdom, or in other words from knowledge of the true nature of things, and are aimed at freeing others from the ignorance that's the primary cause of their misfortune. It's that wisdom and intelligence that gives so much strength to compassion.

J.F. – Couldn't it be objected that it's all rather intangible and abstract? People these days are very preoccupied by what are called the problems of society. Inequalities of all kinds, delinquency, drugs, abortion, what we should do with criminals – from the question of the irreversible punishment of the death penalty, to whether it's better to send delinquents to prison or try to reeducate them. And the problems you brought up just now about education: should it be compulsory, or based only on the pupil's own aspirations?

M. – The problem of education is whether young people should be taught what they want to hear or what they really need to hear. The first is an easy way out. Only the second is a responsible attitude.

J.F. – And then all the problems of welfare and social protection, unemployment, violence, the integration of immigrants and interracial conflict in modern society. Has Buddhism thought about such problems, and does it have any solutions?

M. – Western society has more means than ever before for dealing with suffering due to outer conditions, but seriously lacks any means for developing inner happiness. For the real problems of life and society, there aren't any reference points; spiritual principles are less and less used to light the way. In 1993, when I accompanied the Dalai Lama as his interpreter on a three-week visit to France, I was very struck by the way students welcomed him everywhere. It was in the universities, in fact, that he received the most enthusiastic welcome. In Grenoble, the huge university amphitheater was packed out, and although it was December, eight in the evening, and very cold, three or four thousand people stood outside for hours to watch him on a giant screen and listen to what he had to say. In Bordeaux, it was much the same – a packed lecture hall and thousands of young people outside. And what was astonishing was the feeling of overflowing energy and enthusiasm that surrounded him in the question and answer sessions he took part in. The discussions covered all sorts of questions, the death penalty, abortion, birth control, violence, love – the impression I had was that at last the students had found someone to put these questions to.

J.F. – And what were his answers?

M. – Speaking of birth control, he said that life is the most precious thing we possess. Each human life is extraordinarily precious, as it's the boat that can carry us toward knowledge. But when all those precious lives become too numerous, they begin to be a problem for the human race in general, because the Earth's resources are insufficient to allow so many billions of humans to lead a decent life. The only solution is to curb population expansion using birth control. What the Dalai Lama advocates is 'nonviolent' birth control, meaning the use of all the available methods of contraception.

J.F. – Prevention of births?

M. – Doing everything possible to avoid an excessive birth rate using nonviolent means.

J.F. – So that would be much less in favor of abortion.

M. – Yes. Buddhism defines the act of killing as 'taking the life of a living being or a living being in the process of being formed'. It's a logical consequence of the idea of rebirth, since from conception onward the consciousness from a previous life is present, even if it's in a very primitive or almost undetectable form. In certain cases, when the mother's life is in danger, or when you know that the child's going to be born with terrible malformations, abortion can be justified, but it's not acceptable simply for reasons of personal convenience dictated by egotistical concerns – the parents took no precautions, it might be annoying for them to have a child, and so forth. It's important that effective methods of contraception continue to be developed so as to avoid as much as possible any recourse to abortion. The Dalai Lama's reply seems to have satisfied his audience. 'But the best way of all to stop the population explosion,' he then joked, 'would be to increase the number of monks and nuns.'

J.F. – I'd add that the overpopulation argument is no longer valid in the developed countries, where the birth rate has fallen below the level necessary to maintain a stable population. The only argument to be discussed is that of personal liberty, the freedom of choice. Another problem of society is the death penalty. In fact, in most modern Western societies, it's a problem that's been dealt with already. Hardly any of them have retained it. Even in the United States, there are only a few states that still have it, although several have recently reintroduced it. There remains, in general, the repression of delinquency and of organized crime. Nonviolence by itself could never be the answer to organized crime. How could we defend ourselves against the Mafia if we didn't use violence, if we didn't put criminals in prison, and make sure they weren't in a position to do any harm?

M. – Nonviolence has nothing to do with weakness. The goal is to reduce the suffering of others at any price. So neutralizing criminals by appropriate methods is necessary. But it doesn't justify either revenge or punishment inspired by hatred and cruelty. On the radio recently, I heard the moving statement of the parents of a child killed in a terrorist attack. The day before the terrorist was to be sentenced, they said, 'We don't need another death.' Compared to life imprisonment, which allows a criminal to be prevented from doing more harm, the death penalty looks like an act of revenge. This is what the Dalai Lama says about it in *Terre des dieux et malheur des hommes* (*Land of Gods and Sorrow of Men*):[2] 'To condemn someone to death is a serious act. A human being is going to be simply eliminated. Now, to have the possibility of changing, of modifying his or her behaviour, it's important that the individual concerned can continue to live. I am quite sure

that even in the most dangerous criminals some possibility of transformation and making amends still remains. If such people are allowed
to live, they still have that chance to accomplish the kind of change of
which we are all potentially capable.'

Recently, in 1996, in the state of Arkansas, a prisoner was executed
twelve years after being sentenced to death. In the meantime, he'd
realized how horrible his crime had been and wanted to devote the rest
of his life to others in order to make whatever amends he could for the
wrong he'd committed. He'd also taken monastic vows during his
imprisonment. He managed to make himself heard on local radio by
telephone and said, 'I've become another person. Accept my redemption. Don't kill me. We want to believe that we live in a humane society, but it's not true. It would be better if the government officially
considered the death penalty as revenge. It's clear that capital punishment doesn't fulfill the function of punishment by example, which is
what would effectively reduce crime levels.' And he asked, 'Why do
you always execute prisoners at a time unknown to anyone, in the
middle of the night? If the act you were committing wasn't inhumane,
if you didn't feel guilty, why not execute us in the daytime, in front of
the television cameras?' The governor of Arkansas, a former pastor,
refused to pardon him and brought the date of his execution forward
by a month to avoid him taking any further opportunities to make
himself heard.

J.F. – I think there's a fairly general agreement on that point. The
only large democratic country to have retained the death penalty is the
United States, and that's only in a minority of states. It's led to many
contested cases recently. In Europe, it's practically disappeared. Otherwise, capital punishment today only still exists in totalitarian states
like China, a certain number of African countries, Malaysia, Singapore,
Iraq of course, Iran...

M. – In China there are a hundred executions every day. What's
more, the prisons often sell the organs of executed prisoners on the
black market for transplants in the Hong Kong hospitals and make the
family pay for the bullets used in the execution.

J.F. – A hundred executions a day in China! But anyway, in almost
all states under the rule of law, capital punishment is a problem that's
been solved already. On the other hand, there's still a debate on the
prevention of crime, and its sanctions. You can't always take the point

of view of the offender. Sometimes you have to take the victim's side, meaning to protect people as much as possible from repeat offenders. That's particularly the case when defending society against terrorist groups and against organized crime. In that respect, it's quite difficult to see any strictly nonviolent solutions.

M. – It's certainly not a matter of feeling more sorry, in an unhealthy and unrealistic way, for the criminal than for the victim. The goal is very much to prevent a harmful person from continuing to do harm.

J.F. – And all the more so when it's a harmful organization.

M. – The goal of nonviolence is specifically to diminish violence. It's not a passive approach. So it's crucial to evaluate the suffering concerned. The best solution would consist of finding one way or another of neutralizing those who do major wrongs to others, without adding further forms of violence. During a meeting of winners of the Prix de la Mémoire at the Sorbonne, someone in the audience asked the Dalai Lama, 'Will we see a Nuremberg-type trial in Tibet one day, if the country regains its freedom?' The Dalai Lama replied that there would probably never be such a trial, and if there were its purpose would be to bring out into the open the horrors perpetrated in Tibet, where more than a million people died following the Chinese occupation. But there wouldn't be any acts of vengeance against those Tibetans who'd collaborated with the Chinese. It's like a dog that goes around attacking everyone, he said. Such a dog urgently needs to be put out of action. He'll be muzzled and kept in isolation – if necessary until his death, should he remain dangerous that long. But if not, and he grows old and toothless and spends his time dozing in a corner, nobody's going to shoot him just because he bit fifteen people ten years before.

J.F. – The problem isn't so much that people are put on trial like they were at Nuremberg; that certainly serves a valuable educational purpose. It's more about what you do with those found guilty. Do you execute them, as most of those found guilty at Nuremberg were? The trials going on at the moment in The Hague are to examine the cases against war criminals from the Bosnian conflict. I don't think any of them will be either sentenced to death or actually executed, and in fact the legislation of the countries concerned doesn't even allow that possibility. It's a position that the Dalai Lama would completely agree with.

M. – His actual words on the occasion I mentioned were, 'We must forgive, but not forget.'

J.F. – Yes, not to forget. That's absolutely right. But all that reasoning applies to individual criminals, whereas today's crime is essentially organized. There's political crime, like that of ETA or IRA terrorists, or the Sikh separatists a few years ago in India. Then there's the organized crime of the Mafia, whether Italian, Russian, Chinese, or Colombian. These are bands of people who feel they have the right to act criminally, whether out of self-interest or because of some fanatical ideology. It's not enough to do something just about this or that individual. When the head of the Sicilian Mafia, Toto Rina, was arrested in Palermo, it was a big success for the Italian police – but five minutes later Toto Rina must have been replaced by someone else as the boss of the Mafia. So the real adversary is the organization, not any one person. Now, it happens that society has a tendency to keep on giving rise to criminal gangs, lured by profit or political influence, or both. And society has hardly any means of defending itself against them other than the use of violence. It's counterviolence.

M. – Organized crime is, in the end, just criminals grouping together. Making sure that criminals are prevented from doing any harm is only to palliate the wrong and suppress the symptoms. But if you want to treat the causes, it's the individuals that need to be reformed. They need help in changing themselves.

---

1   PUF, Paris, 1998; to be published in English, as *A Small Treatise on the Great Virtues*, by Metropolitan Books, New York.

2. Gilles van Krasdorf, Editions J.-C. Lattès, 1995.

∾

NINE

TRACING VIOLENCE

TO ITS SOURCES

JEAN-FRANÇOIS – What we've just been talking about leads us to a metaphysical question – if indeed the Mafia could ever lead to metaphysics – which is the problem of evil. I'd like to know Buddhism's position on this particular subject. One of the things that characterizes the major Western religions and philosophies is that they accept the problem of evil as something to be considered. That's to say, they agree that evil exists in itself. It's one of the biggest problems in metaphysics and ethics, both in the main religions and in the major philosophies, particularly in Christianity where the notion of evil is related to the idea of original sin. In the major philosophies, classical philosophies like those of Descartes and Leibniz, the existence of evil is the source of a certain amount of anguish. These philosophers were Christian, and based their philosophies on the idea of divinity, an all-powerful God who was identified with supreme intelligence and at the same time with supreme good. How could he allow evil to exist? It's a problem that most philosophers came up against – and theologians even more so – as an insurmountable obstacle, and it's never really been solved within the terms and metaphysical context in which it was formulated. All the solutions that have been put forward to overcome that inherent contradiction are really quite specious. Does Buddhism accept the existence of evil in itself?

MATTHIEU – No. Fundamentally speaking, evil has no more existence than a mistake. The ultimate nature of all living beings is perfect. That perfection is always there, deep within us, even when it's hidden from sight by ignorance, desire and hatred. The problem of evil seems particularly hard to solve for those who consider everything to be the direct creation of God, and who are therefore obliged to see him as responsible for evil as well as for good. But according to Buddhism, the essential perfection of the Buddha nature is inherently present within each living being in the same way that there's oil inherently present within sesame seeds. In fact, it's the very nature of living beings. That perfection may be hidden from sight, but needs only to be revealed and expressed as we rid ourselves of what hides it, the obscuring layers of ignorance and of the negative emotions that form under ignorance's influence. Those obscuring layers don't belong to the Buddha nature. They hide it from sight but they don't change it in any way. Nonetheless, it's all too easy for us to lose track of that essential nature and get involved in dualistic, negative ways of thinking that are translated into negative words and deeds, and hence into suffering.

The apparent opposition between good and bad doesn't really exist. It's simply the result of our way of seeing things. It exists for us, but only for us. It's a sort of hallucination. The false doesn't have any real existence and isn't in any way a component of the truth. So evil is only an aberration, just as a mistake is only an incorrect perception of reality. The confusion of the relative truth in which we live is the result of truth being fragmented, by our failure to see the primordial purity of all beings and phenomena. Evil, therefore, only exists in an illusory way. That confusion is one possibility, but once you realize the Buddha nature, you can see how it's a mistake that never really existed.

J.F. – So Buddhism doesn't hold that there was an original fall into sin, like Christianity?

M. – No. There's been no fall, and there isn't any sin, there's only a forgetting of our original nature, a state of somnolence or amnesia. Once that nature's forgotten, a distinction between self and others appears, along with all the powerful ego-centered tendencies related to either attraction or repulsion that make negative emotions and intense suffering flare up.

J.F. – But where do they come from, those negative tendencies? If man is basically good, how do they ever form?

M. – In actual truth, the emotions and suffering never are really 'produced', for none of them have any solid reality; it's all, as it were, just a bad dream you wake up from when you attain enlightenment. Ignorance has never really existed. Someone who's enlightened, like the Buddha, sees beings' ignorance in much the same way as someone reading the thoughts of a sleeping person in the grip of a nightmare. He knows what the nightmare's like, but isn't taken in by it himself.

J.F. – As an image, that's all very well. But even if evil is only an appearance, we're still tortured by it. You're only moving the problem from one place to another. If everything's basically good in reality, how does evil appear?

M. – Well, it only does just that – it appears, but that doesn't mean it has any true existence. When you mistake a piece of rope for a snake, the snake has never actually existed, at any time or in any way, except as an illusion. The mistake only has a purely negative way of existing, it has no inherent existence in itself. It's because the ultimate nature of ignorance is wisdom that ignorance can be dispelled. A piece of gold can be cleaned, but there's no way to whiten a piece of coal.

J.F. – The way you formulate it is different from the way Christianity puts it, and also from the way seventeenth- and early eighteenth-century classical metaphysics put it. But the problem's quite similar. Our Western philosophies have quite a hard time explaining how a God who is goodness alone has been able to allow evil to exist. It's all very well to say that evil's only an illusion, that it's only relative to a particular situation, that it doesn't really exist in itself – but it's still not a satisfactory answer.

M. – When you're not aware of the true nature of things, you believe in their apparent mode of existence. The duality between self and other, beautiful and ugly, pleasant and unpleasant, and so on, develops and triggers a whole chain reaction of negative mental factors. This is ignorance, and appears as a covering layer that conceals our true nature from us and makes us act in a way that goes against our deep nature. It's a deviation, like a mirage that attracts the mind toward what's harmful to ourselves and to others.

J.F. – But why do they appear in the first place, those negative factors, those 'agents of evil'? If man is fundamentally good, there shouldn't be any way for them to come into being.

M. – The whole thing is a false problem. If you press on your eyes while you're looking at the moon, you see two moons. It would be quite useless to wonder who or what made the second moon. But imagine someone who never stops pressing on his eyes, and is therefore convinced that there are two moons. It's a truth for him, and he'll develop all sorts of theories about the origin and the nature of the second moon. Now, for someone else looking at the moon in the normal way, there's not even any question about whether or not the second moon exists. But that won't prevent the normal person having the greatest difficulty getting the one seeing double to understand the truth of there being only one moon. The only way he'll ever be really convinced is for him to stop pressing on his eyes. You could say that ignorance, the very source of evil and of suffering, is an accidental misunderstanding, a sudden forgetting that makes no difference to the ultimate nature of the mind but gives rise to a whole chain reaction of painful experiences – just as a nightmare doesn't make any difference to the fact that you're lying comfortably in bed, but can nevertheless cause a great deal of suffering in the mind. The fact that ignorance is a possibility is enough for it to make its appearance. Ignorance appears within wisdom, but doesn't belong to wisdom's ultimate nature. It's own nature is that it's an illusion. That means that when wisdom is realized, in reality nothing at all has happened. Now, that's an explanation that might seem a bit far-fetched, but it comes from the observations of contemplative experience. Someone who wakes up has absolutely no need of an explanation to be able to understand the illusory nature of the dream he's just been having.

J.F. – But those nonexistent events have nevertheless made him suffer, haven't they?

M. – They certainly have. Even in dreams, suffering is well and truly suffering for the person experiencing it, and the fact that the suffering is illusory in no way lessens the need to remedy it. That's what justifies altruistic action – intervening to dispel the sufferings that beings are experiencing – and the spiritual path, which aims at remedying hatred and the other causes of suffering. The way suffering appears is governed by the laws of cause and effect – the results of our actions, words, and thoughts. However tragic suffering might be, in the final analysis only one single thing is always present, and that's innate perfection. Gold never changes, even when it's coated in mud. The sun is always shining, even when it's hidden by the clouds.

J.F. – Well, OK … But I still don't find that a satisfactory answer. It's a bit like what Leibniz said to try to resolve the antinomy between a world in which evil exists and the creator of that world, a God who's goodness alone. Any number of contortions have been used to try to explain that the appearance of evil in the world isn't due to God himself but to all sorts of adventitious factors. But you can't have it both ways. Either he's all-powerful, in which case he must be responsible for evil, or else he's not all-powerful, in which case he's not God.

M. – That's one of the reasonings Buddhism uses to refute the idea of an all-powerful creator.

J.F. – Leibniz, with his absolutely inexhaustible metaphysical imagination, developed the famous theory of the best possible world, which Voltaire made fun of in Candide. Lisbon has just been destroyed in an earthquake, and amidst the ruins, while the victims groan under the smoking rubble of the city, the Leibnizian philosopher Pangloss explains to his disciple Candide how we live in the best possible world. It's a satirical but striking illustration of what is, in fact, an insoluble problem. Mani's famous theory said that there were two independent and distinct powers that existed, Good and Evil. That gave rise to the doctrine called Manichaeanism, which was refuted and condemned as a heresy by the Christian Church, and has generally been challenged by philosophers, in particular Immanuel Kant. So this is a metaphysical problem that even on the level of words is one of the most difficult to solve. In any case, what distinguishes Buddhism from Christianity is its rejection of the notion of sin, especially original sin.

M. – The great virtue of sin is precisely that it doesn't have any true existence. There's therefore no negative action or thought that can't be dissolved, purified, or repaired.

J.F. – And on the other side, there's no question in Buddhism of evil being the responsibility of God, because there isn't any God!

M. – There are no such things as 'good' and 'bad' as such, there are only actions and thoughts that lead to suffering, and others that lead to happiness. We ourselves are responsible for the evils that befall us. We inherit the past and create the future. But in any case, much more important than the metaphysical problems of suffering and evil are the means by which suffering and evil can be remedied. One day, the Buddha picked up a handful of leaves and asked his disciples, 'Are there more leaves here in my hand, or in the forest?' The disciples replied that there were, of course, more leaves in the forest. 'In just the same way,' the Buddha continued, 'I have realized more things than I have taught, for there are many things that, although they can be known, would nonetheless be of no help for putting an end to suffering and attaining enlightenment.'

J.F. – If man's essentially 'good', how can you explain that there's so much violence in the world?

M. – The idea of man's true nature can be understood as a state of balance, while violence is a state of imbalance. The proof that violence isn't part of man's deep-seated nature is that it causes suffering in both victim and perpetrator. Man's deepest wish is for happiness. Don't we say of people under the sway of hatred that they're 'beside themselves' with rage, or 'no longer themselves'? No murderer has ever felt even the slightest peace or feeling of fulfillment after indulging his hatred by killing – at most there's sometimes a rather short and unhealthy feeling of jubilation. In the longer term, it's quite the contrary – murderers often find themselves in a state of profound confusion and anguish that sometimes leads them to suicide.

It's also possible to become desensitized to crime, like those African children that mercenaries first force to execute a member of their own family in order to destroy all sensitivity in them and turn them into implacable killers. Some of the Serbian snipers in Sarajevo, too, said that killing had become so natural to them that they found it hard to imagine doing anything else. When asked whether they'd pull the trigger if one of their former Muslim friends appeared in their sights, they replied that they would. Those snipers had clearly lost touch with their own true nature. Isn't it said of inveterate killers that 'there's nothing human left in them'? On the other hand, when it happens that sworn enemies who've really hated each other for a long time are finally reconciled, they feel an enormous relief and great joy, which no doubt comes from their being reunited with their true nature.

J.F. – I'm personally a bit less optimistic than you are about the remorse of great criminals pushing them to the point of suicide. Remember that Stalin, Mao, and Franco all died in bed, and Hitler killed himself because he'd been beaten – not at all because he felt the slightest remorse for the crimes he'd committed. I regret to say that Saddam Hussein hasn't killed himself yet and is still having other people shot every day. His latest craze is to cut people's ears off, deserters for example, and if his doctors and surgeons refuse to perform the operation he has them hanged. Suicidal regret among criminals, I'm sorry to say, is statistically very marginal.

M. – It's not so much a question of remorse as of suffering, a total absence of inner peace. Mao died practically demented, his wife committed suicide, and Stalin on his deathbed asked that his mistress be assassinated as he couldn't bear the thought of her being with someone else.

J.F. – I'm very pessimistic about the eradication of evil. Unlike Rousseau, I believe that humans are bad and that it's society that makes them good, as long as society is constituted according to law. From time to time, some types of society can make man a little less bad. Why? Because evil's irrational.

M. – And against nature, too.

J.F. – If there were ways of using violence and practicing evil that could be defined as – what could we say? – realistic, perhaps, they would, of course, still be morally wrong, but at least there'd be something to discuss. When I say realistic, I mean that people would be using violence only in their own interest, in a way that was calculated to attain a specified goal. It would be a cynical and selfish use of violence, but it would be rational. That would already limit its use. Above all, it would be founded on some sort of reasoning, however amoral, against which some other reasoning, even more realistic, could be brought to bear. Unfortunately, experience shows that the use of violence is almost always completely mad, and goes well beyond the pursuit of realistic objectives. The most fearsome use of violence is psychopathic, recent examples being in Algeria, ex-Yugoslavia, and Rwanda. The true interest of the different peoples of Yugoslavia would have been to take part in realistic negotiations. If you look at most wars, the people responsible for them go far beyond any political or strategic goals that they may initially have set themselves. That Hitler wanted to take back the left bank of the Rhine, or recapture a few territories in Czechoslovakia that he considered German, could all pass as *realpolitik*. But to hurl himself into a war against the whole world, to exterminate almost all the Jews in Europe, to launch himself into a foolhardy campaign against his old ally Russia, can all only be explained as suicidal behavior – which was shared by the German people. It was obvious, in the light of any even remotely rational analysis, that such an operation could never succeed.

People who use violence often go much further than their concrete objectives. At the end of the eighteenth century in France, it was when the Convention had already crushed the revolt in the Vendée, and there was no longer any military danger from the borders, that the worst massacres of civilian populations took place. Chinese history contains numerous accounts of emperors or warlords who had ten, fifteen, or thirty thousand people beheaded, when in terms of realistic objectives it served not the slightest purpose. A purely sadistic desire to shed blood. And to come back to another example that Luc Ferry gives in his book, something on which he says Buddhism would have no hold – the genocide in Rwanda.

M. – Well, just as we've already said about Bosnia, obviously in the immediate situation Buddhism wasn't in a position to do much about the massacres in Rwanda! But you'll agree with me that no one else was able to do anything about it either, and that the grand so-called realistic policies, the New World Order of the Western powers, were all incapable of preventing it or of stopping it once it had started.

J.F. – But what's still more striking about the genocide in Rwanda is that it's so absolutely impossible to see any end point in it. When criminals commit a crime that brings them something in return, I condemn them but I can understand it. In any case, I can explain their actions as greed, the wish for power, a realistic calculation. But when it makes no sense, when that massive extermination of humans is in absolutely no one's interest and brings nothing to anyone whatsoever, one's forced to conclude that evil could exist in itself – or in man.

M. – It's more a question of losing all reference points, which is what happens when we get off the track of our own true nature. Anything becomes possible. It's a sort of deep misunderstanding or deviation. What you're saying ties up with the ideas of some anthropologists who've studied such events through history, and who conclude that when the individuals of a group are left completely to their own devices without anything to regulate them – whether religious principles or human conventions – they end up killing each other.

J.F. – But how could that ever be proved?

M. – By examples like Bosnia and Rwanda. Once you accept that you can kill a neighbor, you start killing all your neighbors, even if you were on good terms with them up until then. The survivors of the mutiny on the *Bounty*, despite being united in the same cause to begin with, ended up killing each other on the island they'd settled. Perhaps in the tribal context of prehistoric times there was some underlying evolutionary reason for the formation of groups that exterminate each other, but in the context of modern society it's a totally irrational form of behavior.

J.F. – To justify itself, each side claims to be acting in legitimate defence. One thing is certain, that no amount of reasoning has any effect in such situations.

M. – But even if this tendency to violence exists, it's up to intelligence to try to remedy it and not give in to its influence. Where does that hatred come from? If you trace it back to its source, everything begins with a single thought.

J.F. – Yes, in Rwanda it was just pure hatred. Going back to the Bosnian example again, each side there started out with territorial claims that they considered justified by history, geography, prior land occupation, and so on. At the outset, therefore, it was a matter of classical geopolitics which could have been dealt with by discussion. But no one wanted to negotiate, and so it turned into a war. At that point, it was a war that could be described as rational – war as Clausewitz described it, politics being pursued by other means. But then it turned into a bloodbath that was completely unjustified, because it not only went beyond any political objectives that had been determined but also put any such objectives completely out of reach. The butchery became so unacceptable that the international community intervened, tried to keep everyone under control and sent troops to make that possible. Nevertheless, a total and bloody anarchy supervened, with Croats killing Muslims, Muslims killing Croats, and Serbs killing everyone. For several years no one managed to get the different factions to stick to any peace agreement at all. What we were witnessing, in fact, was the self-destruction of all the communities involved.

M. – In place of an analysis of the political and geographical causes, I find it more useful to put it in terms of the mental processes that lead to such an eruption of hatred.

J.F. – Absolutely. What I'm also trying to say is that the political and geographical causes don't explain anything. If that's what it had all been about, a rational solution could have been found.

M. – All the causes of war in the world, whether territorial claims, the sharing of irrigation water, or whatever else it might be, come down to a feeling of oneself being wronged, which then gives rise to hostility. That's a negative thought, a divergence from the natural state, and is therefore a source of suffering. The obvious conclusion is that before such thoughts completely invade and take over the mind, we need to gain mastery over them. A fire is easiest to put out at the very moment the first flames appear, not once the whole forest is ablaze. It's all too easy to get a very long way from the basic goodness within us.

J.F. – But how do you explain the fact that we stray away from it so much more often than staying faithful to it?

M. – When you're following a mountain path, it doesn't take much to put a foot wrong and tumble down the slope. The fundamental goal of a spiritual discipline is to maintain perfect watchfulness all the time. Attention and awareness are basic qualities that the spiritual life helps to develop.

J.F. – Yes. But if to eradicate evil from the world we have to wait for six thousand million individuals to reach that spiritual path, it could be a long wait!

M. – As an oriental proverb says, 'With patience, the orchard becomes jam.' That it might take a long time doesn't alter the fact that there's no other solution. Even if violence doesn't stop arising overall, the only way to remedy it is the transformation of individuals. That transformation can then extend from an individual to his family, to the village, and to the whole of a society. There have been societies that have managed to establish a microclimate of peace at particular times in their history. It's a goal that can be attained, to the extent that each person contributes whatever he or she can. This is where people's sense of 'universal responsibility' toward one another takes on its full meaning.

~

TEN

WISDOM, SCIENCE,

AND POLITICS

MATTHIEU – What do you think of this quotation from Erwin Schrödinger, the great physicist who was awarded a Nobel Prize in 1933? 'The image of the world around us that science provides is highly deficient. It supplies a lot of factual information, and puts all our experience in magnificently coherent order, but keeps terribly silent about everything close to our hearts, everything that really counts for us.'

JEAN-FRANÇOIS – I'd say it was rather trite. The insight that science doesn't speak to the heart of each one of us in our individual quest for happiness is hardly very original. Science has never claimed to provide answers of that kind, anyway, with the possible exception of some of the human sciences. The West's failure doesn't have to do with science – quite the contrary, in fact. Science is the West's success. The problem is whether science by itself is enough, and there's a whole domain in which it quite obviously isn't. The West's failure is first of all a failure in nonscientific areas of Western culture, especially in its philosophy. In what sense has philosophy failed? We could say that overall, up until the seventeenth century, the twin dimensions of philosophy, as practiced ever since its very beginnings, both still survived. On the one side was the scientific dimension; and on the other was the attainment of wisdom, the discovery of meaning in human life, and perhaps beyond human life. That twofold reach of philosophy was still present in Descartes. Although he speaks of ethics as 'provisional', for him philosophy was nevertheless both science and wisdom. The last philosophy in which both aspects were present together and united, how-ever, was that of Spinoza. His is the final appearance of the idea that supreme knowledge can be identified with the joy of the sage who, having understood how reality works, thereby knows true happiness, the sovereign good.

M. – But why does philosophy no longer supply us with models by which we can live?

J.F. – Over the last three centuries, philosophy has abandoned its function as a source of wisdom, and has restricted itself to knowledge. But at the same time it's gradually been dispossessed of its scientific function by science itself. As astronomy, physics, chemistry, and biology appeared, developed, became independent and followed criteria which no longer had anything to do with philosophical methods of thinking, the goals of philosophy's scientific function were correspondingly emptied out, as it were. Kant points this out very clearly in his *Critique of Pure Reason*, even if subsequent philosophers have taken very little account of it. Basically, philosophy's been killed off by its own success, since its purpose was to give birth to these different sciences. As for its other branch, that of wisdom, including the search for justice and the search for happiness, the attainment of wisdom by the individual is something that's no longer maintained on a personal level, as was still the case in Montaigne's or Spinoza's time.

M. – Isn't that the West's main problem?

J.F. – Not necessarily, because during the eighteenth century this second branch moved over to the field of politics. The attainment of justice and happiness were to become the art of organizing a just society that delivers happiness to its members through collective justice. In other words, the attainment of good, justice, and happiness all together became the Revolution – social, cultural, and political. At that moment, the whole ethical branch of philosophy was reborn in the form of political systems. In the nineteenth century, we come to the age of the great utopias that wanted to rebuild society from top to bottom. The main utopia of this kind was socialism, especially Marxism, which was to dominate political thought almost up to the end of the twentieth century. The ethical function of philosophy, from this perspective, sets itself the goal of building up from scratch a society that's completely just. The first major attempt of this sort was the French Revolution, in which the modern concept of revolution emerged. Now, the moment the authors of a revolution have in mind a model of a society they consider perfect, they feel they have the right to impose it on others, and if necessary to eliminate anyone who resists their attempts. This became even clearer when Marxist-Leninist theory could be put into actual practice, with the Bolshevik revolution, and later in China under Mao. All of these systems share a central idea, which is that the search for goodness, the building of the 'new man', evolves from utopia to the exercise of power through the revolutionary transformation of society.

M. – What do ethics consist of, once the meaning of liberty and personal responsibility have been obliterated by the political system?

J.F. – They consist of serving that ideal, of making it possible to realize the absolute Revolution. So there are no more individual ethics and there's no longer any personal quest for wisdom. The individual's ethic is to participate in collective ethics. In fascism and nazism too, the idea of the regeneration of man is found. For both Mussolini and Hitler, bourgeois capitalist society, as they saw it, with a parliamentary system enslaved to money, to a plutocracy, to the Jews, was immoral. It became a matter of regenerating mankind by building a new society from top to bottom, from zero to infinity, by liquidating whatever might be suspected of opposing it. Revolutionary action replaced philosophy, and even religion.

M. – Yes, with the success we saw in Russia, and are still seeing today, unfortunately, in China. The problem with the kind of utopias that aren't based on the development of human qualities is that even when they preach egalitarianism – the sharing of property, for example – ways to get round such ideals are soon found, and those who hold the reins of power turn them into an instrument with which to oppress and exploit their 'comrades'.

J.F. – All those great systems failed. They crashed straight into absolute evil. Even in their final throes they uncovered the most outrageous characters, like Pol Pot in Cambodia, who pushed the logic of such systems to its ultimate extreme. To create a new kind of human, eradicate the past and erect a society which will at last be an absolutely just one, the first thing to do was to destroy all the humans currently alive, who had therefore been corrupted by the preceding societies to a greater or lesser extent. Without all having gone to such grotesque and deadly excesses, the majority of intellectuals over the last three hundred years have accepted that making man more moral and achieving justice can only be done by creating a new society that's more just, more balanced, and more egalitarian.

The failure of these utopian political systems in practice, and their moral discrediting – the major event of these final years of the twentieth century – is what I call the failure of Western civilization in its aspects other than scientific. Social reform was supposed to replace ethical reform, but it's led to a disaster, such that we now find ourselves completely distraught and faced with an utter vacuum. Hence the renewal of interest in more modern philosophies, which consist of providing some practical, empirical, ethical advice about how to lead one's daily life. Hence, too, the renewal of curiosity about wisdom doctrines like Buddhism, which talk about human life and compassion and don't claim to be remaking the world by destroying it, or to be regenerating the human race by murdering it. The renewal of interest in such ideas can be explained by the spectacular failure of the great political systems, the grand utopias I've just briefly described. Science isn't responsible for the catastrophe. It was caused by fanaticism quite outside its ranks.

M. – I don't think any Buddhist would disagree with your analysis. But let me just add one or two ideas, not to criticize science itself but to shed light on why science, if too hastily taken for a panacea, can also eclipse the search for wisdom. Science is essentially analytical and therefore tends to get lost in the inexhaustible complexity of phenomena. Science covers such a vast field of discovery that it's captivated the interest and energy of many of the brightest minds of our times. It's like a never-ending gold rush. The spiritual approach is a very different one, because it deals with the principles underlying knowledge and ignorance, happiness and suffering. Science only takes account of tangible or mathematical proofs, while the spiritual approach recognizes the validity of intimate conviction arising from contemplative experience.

J.F. – We should be careful here to distinguish science from scientism. The examples of science's successes have had the effect of making people believe that everything can be approached in a scientific way. Remember that the phenomenon of the restrictive utopia we've just been talking about was called 'scientific' socialism. There was, of course, nothing scientific about it. Quite the opposite. But it's very interesting that people claimed to be applying scientific criteria to the reform of human society. That's a perversion of the notion of science that's done a lot of damage.

M. – The risk of science, real science, is that it gets carried away by its analytical momentum and goes too far, so that knowledge gets too horizontally spread out. There's an Arab proverb that says once you begin counting you'll never be able to stop. When I studied geology at the science faculty, we did some practical studies on the morphology of grains of sand. There were 'polished round' grains, 'shiny round' ones, and so on. From them one could deduce how old rivers were, where the sand had come from, or whether it was river sand or sea sand. It could be fascinating, but is it really worth the trouble?

J.F. – The study of grains of sand happens to be highly informative in working out the history of the earth, its climate, the alternation of warm periods and ice ages, and so forth. Knowing about the laws of nature is incontestably one of mankind's legitimate aspirations, and all of philosophy began from that.

M. – Yes, but I don't think that the study of such things, however interesting, should take precedence over the search for wisdom.

J.F. – Science – good science – becomes a form of wisdom when it's totally disinterested. Great scientific discoveries have often been made by scientists who were being told that the field they were exploring was completely unfruitful. But research first of all follows the desire to know, and only then the demand that it be useful. The history of science shows that it's always been at the moment when people were only following their intellectual curiosity that they've made the most useful discoveries. But they weren't looking for anything useful when they started. There's a sort of detachment in scientific research that's a form of wisdom.

M. – But the desire to know still needs to be applied to something that deserves dedicating a lifetime to, and that 'wisdom' ought to lead scientists to make better human beings of themselves and others. Otherwise, what sort of wisdom is it? Is curiosity, however disinteres-ted, an end in itself?

J.F. – What you're saying is rather what Pascal thought. In my view, the limitation of scientific culture in our Western society lies more in the fact that though everyone can benefit from it, very few people actually take part in it. Only a tiny minority of people know how the universe, matter, and life really work. But millions of people every day – including myself – take aspirin without having much idea about how aspirin relieves their momentary aches and pains. When people say that the human race is now living in a scientific age, it's not true at all. The human race is living in parallel with a scientific age. A completely illiterate person enjoys all the benefits and spin-offs of science to the same degree as a top scientist. But, given that a majority of the population even in the West – where classical and modern science took birth – play no part whatsoever in science from the inside, they need to be provided with something else. Until quite recently that something else was religion, and the political utopias. Religion no longer fulfils such functions, with the possible exception of Islam, and the utopias have collapsed in bloodshed and ridicule. So there's a vacuum.

M. – It's interesting to reflect on how and why we choose to spend our lives doing whatever we do – to the extent that we choose at all. I'd like to mention the Buddhist definition of laziness, which seems quite relevant here. We speak of three kinds of laziness. The first is simply to spend all your time eating and sleeping. The second is to tell yourself, 'Someone like me will never manage to perfect themselves.' In the Buddhist context, such laziness makes you feel that it's pointless even trying, you'll never attain any spiritual realization. Discouragement makes you prefer not even to begin making any effort. And the third kind, the one most relevant here, is to waste your life on tasks of secondary importance, without ever getting down to what's most essential. You spend all your time trying to resolve minor problems, one after another in an endless sequence, like ripples on the surface of a lake. You tell yourself that once you've finished this or that project you'll start giving some meaning to your life. I think that the horizontal dispersion of knowledge has something to do with that third form of laziness, even when people work hard on something for a whole lifetime.

J.F. – You've been talking in terms of minor problems, but to my mind that's not the right distinction. It would be better to talk in terms of problems that have some relationship to spiritual realization and problems that don't. A problem can have nothing at all to do with spiritual realization, but still be a major problem.

M. – Well, that all depends on how you see it. Financial ruin is a major problem for an ambitious banker, but a minor one for someone who's weary of worldly ways. But let's come back to laziness. The antidote to the first kind of laziness – only wanting to eat and sleep – is to reflect on death and the impermanent nature of everything. We never know when we're going to die or what circumstances are going to lead to our death. So there isn't a moment to lose in getting down to what's really essential. The antidote to the second kind of laziness – feeling too discouraged to commit ourselves to spiritual practice – is to reflect on the benefits that such inner transformation will bring. The antidote to the third kind – attending to the details rather than to the essentials – is to realize that the only way to get to the end of our endless projects is to drop them, and then turn to what gives life its meaning without waiting any longer. Life is short, and if we want to develop our inner qualities it's never too soon to start getting down to it.

J.F. – What you're saying is just what Pascal said when he defined 'diversion' as what 'diverts' us from the essential. He, too, classified scientific research, *libido sciendi*, as a diversion, even though it was something he himself excelled in. But that's a mistake. Just as it's no good asking spiritual realization from science, it's also no good thinking that spiritual realization can replace science. Science and technology respond to a number of questions. First of all, they satisfy the appetite for knowledge, which is, after all, one of the most basic dimensions of human beings. And in their practical applications they solve a large number of human problems. In this respect, I'm a son of the eighteenth century. I believe in the betterment of the human condition through technological progress, when it's in the right direction. But it does leave a gap in what we'd call, roughly, the domain of ethics and wisdom, of the individual's search for harmony and salvation.

That gap, to my mind, can be filled by two different things. The first is the sort of system of which Buddhism is an example. This explains why we're seeing Buddhism spreading in the West at the moment, and that's all the more interesting in that it uses no militant propaganda, unlike fundamentalist Islam. It spreads somewhere only when it's invited – or else, alas, when it's been forced to move by being expelled from somewhere else. The second instrument that can fill that gap is still, I think, the political reorganization of society. To my mind, that basic intuition of the eighteenth century remains sound. It's just that the way we've been setting about doing it is wrong. I believe in the value of democratic society, and the Dalai Lama agrees with it, too. There's a profound morality in the fact of endowing each individual with the possibility of taking part in democratic responsibility, and of calling to account the representatives that he or she has elected to exercise power. The socialist deviation and the collapse of totalitarian systems shouldn't make us think that we ought to abandon the hypothesis of building a just world society. On the contrary, it should remind us that we've considerably delayed the building of such a system by letting totalitarianism usurp our democratic ambitions.

M. – What we're lacking in that domain is a wider vision – what the Dalai Lama calls a sense of 'universal responsibility'. It's unacceptable that certain parts of the world develop at the expense of others.

J.F. – Yes, but each part of the world is free to do what it wants, including making stupid mistakes.

M. – To go back to the failure of modern philosophy, what strikes me most about philosophy from the seventeenth century onwards is how little use it is to those looking for reference points or principles that could give meaning to their life. Those philosophies, cut off from the practical application that any spiritual path requires if its goal is to bring about a veritable inner transformation, were able to indulge themselves in an unimpeded proliferation of ideas, intellectual games of extreme complexity and minimum usefulness. The gap between the world of ideas and that of the individual's life has become such that those who promulgate these philosophical systems no longer themselves need to be the living illustration of them. It's completely accepted nowadays that you can be a great philosopher at the same time as living in a way that no one would even think of taking as an example. We've already emphasized that the principal quality of a true teacher is that he's a living illustration of the perfection he teaches. That perfection can't just be the coherence of a system of ideas; it should be transparently manifested in all the person's different sides. A philosopher can completely lose his way in his personal problems, or a scientist in his emotions, but a disciple committed to the spiritual path knows at once that he's on the wrong track if he notices that over the months and years his human qualities – goodness, tolerance, being at peace with himself and others – have been declining instead of growing. So I'd explain the failure of philosophy by the fact that its ideas can be run in neutral gear, and have no impact on the person at all.

J.F. – Yes, that's all absolutely true. There are instances to be found everywhere in Western societies. That's where there's been a big gap left behind by scientific achievement, extraordinarily precious though that achievement has been. I've only known one thinker whose way of life completely matched what he wrote, and that was Cioran, a French moral philosopher of Romanian origin. Cioran was a very pessimistic writer with an acute awareness of the limits of human life – of its finitude, as humanist philosophers say – and lived completely in accordance with his principles. To my knowledge, he never had a proper job, and always refused any honors offered him. Once, I telephoned him with the proposal that he accept a literary prize which also happened to involve the award of a substantial sum of money. I knew he was in considerable need and thought he'd be happy to have it. But he refused outright, saying that he'd absolutely no wish to receive any official reward, whatever it might be. Here was one case of an intellectual living by his principles, or at least by the analysis he'd made of the human condition.

The picture you've just sketched sums up what could be called the essential wound of Western civilization, which is basically the contrast and contradiction between the intellectual and artistic prowess that individuals can attain on the one hand, and the frequent poverty of their moral life, or of their ethics, on the other. And it's true that it's the result of the gap left when philosophy abandoned the individual quest for wisdom. Ever since the seventeenth century, that place has traditionally been filled by what we call the moralists. The contributions of La Rochefoucauld, La Bruyère, or Chamfort to our knowledge of human psychology are among the finest. But they don't indicate much of a path for us in terms of how we should behave. Their ethics are based on retreat from the world. They see how mad everyone is – there are only people blinded by ambition, politicians demented by their lust for power, senile courtesans following them to extract whatever advantages they can, vain hypocrites who think they're geniuses, or who to obtain some derisory honor or other would stop at nothing, even at having themselves cut into pieces. So the best one can do is to refuse to mix with any of them, and just sneer at the spectacle while taking care not to fall into such foibles oneself. Well, I suppose it's the beginning of some sort of wisdom, but it's not an ethical outlook that helps anyone else enormously. Only the idea of building a just society can really do that.

In the face of the collapse of utopian and totalitarian systems, which constituted a sickness in modern political thinking, and the vacuum left in modern philosophy by the disappearance of ethics, we're nowadays edging our way toward the very vague moral system that we call human rights, or humanitarian action. As a system, it's better than nothing, but it's still rather poorly defined. Humanitarian action, in the sense of going out to treat those in need and provide them with food supplies, is admirable, and I have the greatest respect for those who carry out such tasks. The trouble is that it's no use mopping up the blood from a wound without doing anything to close it up. There's little point in sending doctors to Liberia if we carry on letting the wretched bandits that head that country's various factions get away with what they're doing, and even provide them with arms. Only political reform can tackle problems at their source and really have some effect. From that point of view, the democracies' human rights policies – which amount to making a few half-hearted and vague declarations whenever we receive or go to visit a Chinese or Vietnamese leader, while at the same time throwing ourselves at their feet to get contracts – is woefully inadequate.

M. – You mention the pessimist philosopher Cioran as an example of a philosopher living in accordance with the way he thinks. But to my mind that's not at all the same as the truly wise teacher. For someone to be a sage, it's not enough just to live according to the way he thinks. The way he thinks must also correspond to an authentic form of wisdom that liberates the mind from all confusion and suffering and is then reflected in his human perfection. Otherwise, I'm sure you could find plenty of burglars who live just as they think – or dictators, even worse.

As for political systems, democracy is surely the healthiest for our time. No one, except those who stand to gain when democratic values are ridiculed, would disagree with that. But democracy is a bit like an empty house. You need to know what the people who live in it are going to do with it. Are they going to maintain the house properly, make it even more beautiful, or gradually let it collapse?

J.F. – That's very true.

M. – What's neglected in the idea of human rights is the individual's responsibility to society. The Dalai Lama often points out how particularly necessary universal responsibility is in our world, which has shrunk to the point that one can easily be on the other side of the world in a single day. It's obvious that unless a sense of responsibility develops in all the individuals sharing this planet, it'll be very difficult to apply any democratic ideals.

J.F. – What you're talking about is usually called public-spiritedness, or civic responsibility.

M. – Maybe, but what I remember being taught about civic responsibility at primary school was hardly very inspiring! So inevitably we come back to the need for individuals to work on improving themselves, through values coming from wisdom or from the spiritual path – and here, of course, I'm still talking about a spiritual path that isn't necessarily religious; it could be secular, too.

J.F. – Could you say more about what that might mean?

M. – Well, that leads us to the idea of altruism, which is often badly misunderstood. Altruism doesn't just mean doing something good or helpful to others from time to time. It means to be constantly preoccupied with, and concerned by, the well-being of others. It's an attitude that's very rare in our society. In a truly democratic system, a society has to maintain a sort of balance between individuals' desire to obtain the maximum for themselves and a general consensus that defines the limits beyond which such desires are no longer acceptable. But extremely few people are really concerned by others' needs. The same applies in the political domain. Those whose task it is to watch over the general well-being often see their mission as a career, at the center of which their own person occupies pride of place. Under such conditions, it's difficult for them to disregard the immediate term – especially their own popularity – and consider what would be best for everyone's good in the long term.

J.F. – As you say, that's rather rare among politicians!

M. – The goal of all those involved in political or public life shouldn't be to win others' praise and recognition, but to sincerely try to improve people's lot. In this respect, environmental protection is a very revealing example of the extent to which a sense of responsibility is generally lacking. Although the harmful consequences of pollution, the extinction of animal species, and the destruction of forests and other natural environments are undeniable and in most cases uncontested, the majority of individuals don't react until the situation becomes intolerable for them personally. Serious measures to combat the destruction of the ozone layer will probably only be put into effect when the average citizen can no longer sunbathe – which is already beginning to be the case in Australia – or when children have to be forbidden to look at the sky because the ultraviolet radiation is too damaging to their eyes – which is also beginning to happen, in Patagonia. These effects have been predicted for a long time, but they haven't yet represented an immediate threat to most individuals' own personal comfort. That's why I think lack of responsibility is one of the big weaknesses of our age. And it's in this sense, too, that personal wisdom and spiritual practice could be useful.

J.F. – I completely agree with you. Nevertheless, nowadays in the West human rights and ecological concerns are sometimes turned into '-isms' that have to some extent become a substitute for bankrupt socialist political ideals. People who've been on the left for a long time no longer have a coherent doctrine for transforming society, and so they've seized hold of humanitarian action and the environment in order to continue tyrannizing their peers.

M. – Let's not kill off ecology while it's still in the process of hatching. It certainly needs to grow in power and effectiveness. I remember Rachel Carson's *Silent Spring* appearing when I was fifteen, at a time when the few people who were passionately committed to the protection of nature were considered eccentric lunatics.

J.F. – I'm all for human rights and the protection of nature. But what's quite tragic is how the old ideologies, which have already been found to be bankrupt, continue to weigh down on these new causes. You can't help noticing what double standards those who make it their job to defend human rights and the environment are in the habit of using. For example, most people involved in humanitarian action are on the left. So they're very quick to denounce the existence of political prisoners in Morocco. Why? because Morocco is a traditional monarchy, in the camp of America and the West, and a capitalist country. On the other hand, they've taken a great deal longer to denounce the much more serious human rights violations committed in Algeria.

M. – Or in Tibet…

J.F. – Or in Tibet. I mention Algeria because it had the reputation of being a progressive country, which was of course no more than a bitter joke. And Tibet's occupied by China, another 'progressive' country. For ten years, two thirds of the French intelligentsia rollicked happily around the frozen and bloodstained feet of Mao Tse Tung. The same goes for the environment. Which nuclear power stations were the target of Greenpeace's demonstrations at the time of the Chernobyl disaster? Western ones, which were so much safer! But Greenpeace didn't organize a single protest against the Soviet Union. Greenpeace was certainly within its rights to take action and protest against French nuclear tests in the Pacific in 1995. But for the same organization to stay discreet – to say the least – about much worse pollution, Russian 'ex-Soviet' nuclear waste in the Arctic Ocean – an ocean into which, incidentally, I don't know how many millions of barrels of oil from leaking Russian pipelines have also been pouring – is too much, for me, to allow me to carry on believing in its honesty. As long as the struggle for human rights or against environmental pollution is biased by the old ideologies and prejudices, just because the 'ecologists' are mostly leftists, I don't think we'll get much in the way of results. Such struggles can only win people's respect if they're carried out according to the realities of the situation, and not just according to the bias of those who carry them out.

M. – I'd also like to put in an aside here to point out that we're always talking about *human* rights, but the fact that such rights are restricted to humans reflects the Judeo-Christian values that underlie Western civilization, even in democracies that see themselves as secular. That's where the idea comes from that animals don't have a soul and only exist for the consumption of humans. There are several religions that still hold that belief, but it's no longer acceptable in a global context. Our genes are ninety-nine percent identical to those of the great apes. Does that one percent justify the torture we subject animals to when, whether in the laboratory or the slaughterhouse, without a moment's thought, we treat them as mere objects?

J.F. – There is an association for the defence of animal rights in the West.

M. – But it doesn't seem to have enough power to change laws that see animals as 'agricultural produce' or 'laboratory material'. Let me quote what Leonardo da Vinci wrote in his notebooks: 'The time will come when people like me will think of the murder of an animal just as they think today of the murder of a man.' And George Bernard Shaw said, 'Animals are my friends, and I don't eat my friends.' It's not a matter of denying that there are differences in intelligence between animals and human beings, and that relatively speaking a human life is worth more than the life of an animal. But why should the right to live be the prerogative of humans alone? All living beings want happiness and try to avoid suffering. To assume the right to kill animals by the millions all the year round, therefore, is no more than the law of the jungle. Just a few centuries ago, the trade in 'black gold', slaves from black Africa, was considered acceptable. These days, there's still slavery in India, Pakistan, the Sudan; children are sold to work in factories or in the fields, and young girls for prostitution. But elsewhere, generally speaking, slavery is seen as an abomination. What do people do when they're exploited or oppressed? They get organized, form trade unions, protest and rebel. Animals are incapable of any of those things, so they're exterminated. I think it's a problem that ought to be completely rethought. And I'd just like to add how especially striking that blindness was during the 'mad cow disease' crisis. The British ministry of agriculture and its equivalents in the rest of Europe at first declared that they were ready to 'destroy', as they put it, millions of cows. If fifteen million cows had marched in the streets of London for their right to live, the government would definitely have revised its point of view.

J.F. – I'm not so sure of that!

M. – At the time, no one even knew for certain that the fifteen or twenty people who'd died of the nervous system disease thought to be caused by eating beef had really been infected by the meat of those animals. Even if they had, it wasn't the fault of the cows, but of the farmers who'd fed them such unnatural feed. As a whole, the life of one cow was judged as having a million times less value than that of a human.

J.F. – You're reasoning as if man was alone in killing animals. But animals kill each other, too. You only have to watch any film on marine life to see that they're all eating each other all the time. Each one lives in constant terror of being gobbled up by another! From a Buddhist point of view, how do you explain that?

M. – The suffering experienced by all the beings imprisoned in the world is the first of the four truths that the Buddha taught. In fact, the texts say exactly what you've just said. One of them says, 'The bigger animals swallow an incalculable number of smaller ones, while the smaller ones in large groups devour the bigger ones.' As everyone keeps on talking about the 'progress' of the so-called civilized world, it's my opinion that we could include in that progress some steps to reduce overall the suffering we inflict on other living beings for our own profit. There are other ways of feeding ourselves than the systematic slaughter of animal species.

J.F. – But while we're waiting for all Westerners to become vegetarians, which doesn't seem about to happen, we can at least do our best to make sure that domesticated animals are raised in better conditions than are current in modern industrial farming. It's a struggle that's begun, but there's a long way to go. Animals are so much worse off than they were in times of more traditional farming, like when I was a child in Franche-Comté. Cattle grazed peacefully in the meadows, and in the barns in winter they were fed on hay, never on artificial chemical feed – or processed sheep carcasses, which are what caused mad cow disease. Nowadays, the poor beasts are raised, kept, and transported in abominable conditions.

M. – Technological pseudo-progress in factory farming methods has worsened the sufferings of animals at the same time as creating, so it seems, new diseases for humans. It's a sorry kind of progress.

J.F. – I quite agree with you there.

~

ELEVEN

THE RED FLAG ON THE

ROOF OF THE WORLD

JEAN-FRANÇOIS – Let's go back to politics and ethics. As far as I know, traditional Buddhism didn't have any particular political doctrine. It's interesting to see how, while on the one hand Buddhism's influence and the personal influence of the Dalai Lama have begun to help fill the gap in Western thought once occupied by traditional wisdom, on the other the Dalai Lama's own participation in intellectual and moral debate in the West have led him to develop a more and more detailed political analysis of the relationships between democracy and violence within a Buddhist perspective. So, in the particular case of Tibet and China, what does he plan to do, to obtain some tangible results and not just keep on protesting into a vacuum?

   Matthieu – As the Dalai Lama often says, because of the Tibetan tragedy he's found himself exposed to the outside world, which has allowed him to explore new ideas for himself and to take a good look at the different political systems that exist today. He's now made the political system of the Tibetans in exile completely democratic, and has declared that if Tibet one day regains its freedom it'll have a democratic government. He's made it clear that he himself will withdraw from public life, like Gandhi did when India became independent, and that he won't take on any official function in such a future Tibetan government. His main reason for this decision is that as a Buddhist monk he wouldn't be able to support one party rather than another, while at present what he's fighting for is essentially the freedom and well-being of the Tibetan people as a whole – and of course the culture as well. But it's worth remembering, too, that in India at the time of the Buddha there were already some democratic systems in existence, that of the Licchavis, for example.

J.F. – Democratic in what sense? With elections?

M. – They were ruled by assemblies composed of experienced people, which deliberated and reached decisions by majority opinion.

J.F. – So they weren't necessarily tyrannies?

M. – No, not even monarchies. Decisions were taken in common, but I don't think they used votes. It must have been done by open discussion in which all those with anything relevant to say could take part.

J.F. – That's not a complete democracy. But it's true that even in the West universal suffrage is still a very recent phenomenon.

M. – The Buddha had quite a major social and political impact in his day, because he never stopped teaching that all living beings have the same rights to life and happiness. There was no question of any discrimination between people according to caste or race.

J.F. – Did he combat the caste system?

M. – Yes. He surprised some of his low-caste disciples, who didn't dare approach him to ask for his teachings, considering themselves untouchable. The Buddha told them, 'Come here, approach. You are human beings just like all of us. You have the Buddha nature within you.' So it was really quite an intellectual and social revolution to open his teaching like that to everyone. The idea that all beings have the same rights has impregnated all Buddhist civilizations.

J.F. – The equality of human beings is something that can only have been a declaration of principle. But now, the Dalai Lama's been compelled by the situation of the Tibetans in exile to make contact with more modern formulations of democracy and human rights. He's found himself involved in geopolitical problems and struggles between modern nation states. He has to live with the very real situation of being the spiritual and temporal leader of a country that's been invaded and colonized by an imperialist power set on destroying its culture. So he's been obliged to take political action and to take public positions, to make declarations expressing protest in all the countries of the world he's visited – but without closing the doors to negotiation, so as not to antagonize the Chinese giant to the point of making any solution impossible. Could this sequence of events be seen as Buddhism's initiation into modern diplomacy?

M. – Yes, certainly. The Dalai Lama's been able to combine very forthright political commitment with basic Buddhist principles, especially nonviolence. The way he refers to China is in striking contrast to the exasperated and vituperative Chinese outbursts against him. While they revile the 'Dalai clique' and call for a 'cutting off of the serpent's head', meaning the Dalai Lama himself, he always speaks in terms of his 'Chinese brothers and sisters'. He observes that China will always be Tibet's powerful neighbor, and concludes that the only durable solution is peaceful coexistence. He hopes for neighborly relations based on mutual respect. Such tolerance, however, remains to be reciprocated, and China still shows no signs of letting Tibet live as he proposes.

J.F. – Chinese repression in Tibet's getting worse day by day.[1] If they continue to be allowed to get away with it, in a few years' time they'll end up completely destroying Tibetan civilization, and perhaps the Tibetan people too. Would the Dalai Lama then be ready to reconsider the principle of nonviolence?

M. – Should the Tibetan people ever opt for violence by a democratically determined decision, he's made it clear that he would completely withdraw from political life. For him, it's obvious that nonviolence is the only realistic and acceptable approach.

J.F. – But what's the current situation in Tibet?

M. – The human genocide, which has cost a fifth of Tibetans their lives, has been accompanied by cultural genocide. At the moment, the communist regime is trying to dilute the native Tibetan population with a massive influx of Chinese colonists. Although population transfer isn't an explicitly declared policy, Beijing uses every imaginable means to incite Chinese colonists to settle in Tibet. There are now seven million Chinese to six million Tibetans in Greater Tibet.[2] What the Chinese would like to do is to repeat what's happened in Chinese Mongolia, where the indigenous people now make up only fifteen percent of the population. The populations of some of the large towns of former Tibet, like Xining in the province of Amdo, contain a large majority of Chinese. It'll soon be the same in Lhasa. Nevertheless, Tibetans are still in a majority in the countryside. More recently, the Chinese have started running courses of 'political reeducation' again in the monasteries and villages, for which the 'final exam' consists of signing a five-point declaration in which the 'student' recognizes that Tibet is part of China, renounces the Dalai Lama, pledges not to engage in any activity related to Tibet's freedom, undertakes not to listen to foreign radio stations, and so forth.[3] Monks refusing to sign this 'pledge of loyalty' face expulsion from the monastery and indefinite confinement to their village without the right to work or travel. Already, this program has rid monasteries so far visited of between fifty and eighty percent of their monks or nuns. On his side, the Dalai Lama has proposed holding a referendum, which would be easy enough to organize among the population of Tibetan exiles, of which there are a little over one hundred thousand in India, Nepal, and Bhutan; and although it would obviously be impossible to hold an open vote among the Tibetans inside Tibet, it's hoped that a clear idea of what they want can nevertheless be obtained. The question he'll put to the Tibetans will be, firstly, whether they want the Tibetan government to continue following the 'middle way' that he's been proposing for the last few years, or in other words a true autonomy in which Tibet would manage its own internal affairs but would leave China to control foreign affairs and defence. Tibet would become a neutral state, which would be a major contribution to peace in the region.

J.F. – It sounds more of an autonomous province, like Catalonia, than a neutral state like Switzerland or Austria.

M. – Yes, that's right. And that would already be a huge concession from the Tibetans' side, because according to all the commissions of jurists that have deliberated on the subject since 1950, according to international law Tibet is an independent country that has been subjected to illegal occupation by a foreign power.[4] In fact it's the challenge to their sovereignty over Tibet that irritates the Chinese the most and touches their most sensitive point, far more than the question of human rights. It's on the illegality of their occupation of Tibet that the emphasis needs to be put. Recently, the communist regime put the dissident Liu Xiaobo in prison immediately after he'd had the nerve to write that there ought to be 'negotiations with the Dalai Lama on the basis of the Tibetan people's right to self-determination'. That, for the Chinese, was a breach of the ultimate taboo. In reality, the 'Motherland' ought really to be called the United States of China, because China includes fifty-five 'minorities'. It's only the vice-like grip of the Communist party that holds the puzzle together.

The second option the Tibetan people could choose would be to insist on complete independence, to which Tibet has a right in terms of its own history. The Dalai Lama has stated that he'll adapt his efforts to the people's choice and would work to this end if they want him to, although in the present circumstances he himself favors the solution of internal autonomy as being more acceptable to the Chinese, and hence more realistic. The third solution would be violent resistance – to try to use force, terrorism, and so forth to force the Chinese to leave Tibet. The Dalai Lama has made it clearly known that if this were the Tibetans' choice, he himself would retire from public life to become a 'simple Buddhist monk'. There are Tibetans who would prefer a more aggressive policy. In fact, their position has often been singled out by Western journalists.

M. – How many Tibetans are in favor of more violent action?

J.F. – The Dalai Lama holds open discussions with the people who hold such opinions, who are free to express them. They've gained some ground in Dharamsala, the seat of the Tibetan government in exile in India, but represent only a small percentage of the total exile population. Their point of view isn't very realistic. If the Tibetans took up arms, they'd have no chance whatsoever in the face of China's machinery of repression. Their lot would just become even more wretched. Even countries that have used terrorism for many years have only seen their hopes answered the day they decide to negotiate a peaceful solution.

J.F. – Or when they receive help from a foreign power, like the Afghans from the United States when they were under Russian occupation.

M. – According to the Dalai Lama, nonviolence shouldn't be abandoned under any circumstances. All that he asks of the major powers is that they put pressure on the Chinese government to start real negotiations with himself and the Tibetan government in exile. But over the years the only response from the Chinese government has been, 'All right, let's discuss the return of the Dalai Lama to Tibet.' Which wasn't at all the goal of any discussions. Fifteen years ago, Deng Xiaoping issued a statement that 'Except the total independence of Tibet, anything else can be discussed.' But he never honored that statement, and he notably refused to discuss the five-point plan set out by the Dalai Lama in a speech to the American Congress in 1987.[5] It was in 1988, addressing the European Parliament in Strasbourg, that the Dalai Lama announced he'd agree to renounce Tibet's independence, although it was historically an independent country occupied by China since 1959, and offered to negotiate with China on the basis of an autonomy that would allow Tibet to manage its own internal affairs and leave China the control of foreign affairs and defence. Despite being offered this major concession, the Chinese have never agreed to hold talks with the Dalai Lama and the Tibetan government in exile.

J.F. – Alas, the Western democracies have hardly put any pressure on China to agree to discuss that five-point programme.

M. – Most Western leaders feel a great deal of sympathy for the Dalai Lama and the cause of Tibet. Their attitude justifies the incredible energy that he puts into his constant trips to different countries and regions of the world to talk about the Tibetan problem. Unfortunately, though, all that sympathy makes little difference as soon as it's a question of selling an Airbus or two, importing products manufactured in Chinese prisons or labor camps, or getting new markets in China. Anyway, the Dalai Lama says that he completely understands that countries have to look after their own economic well-being, and that no nation can be expected to put Tibet's interests before its own. But one might have hoped to see respect for democratic values inciting Western governments to take some slightly more concrete steps to help. The Chinese government, which is very cynical, rejoices in their spinelessness. Whenever any country supports Tibet, China threatens it with reprisals out of all proportion. Although it's obvious that none of those threats could ever be executed, it's enough to completely paralyze Western governments, who pathetically let themselves be taken in by them. Whatever the Chinese may pretend, they need Western investment much more than the West needs Chinese markets. There would certainly be ways of exerting pressure on them if the Western democracies wanted to.[6] The Chinese used to taunt America as a 'paper tiger', but nowadays they're the paper tigers, because whenever anyone ignores their threats they never actually carry them out.

J.F. – I understand that in the face of China, that colossus of one thousand two hundred million people, the king of Norway, a small country of only four million inhabitants, showed more courage than all the great Western powers together.

M. – Yes, China had threatened to break off diplomatic relations with Norway if the king, as custom dictates, personally handed the Nobel Peace Prize to the Dalai Lama at the prize-giving ceremony in 1989. The king replied, 'OK, go ahead, then, break them off!' And of course the Chinese did nothing at all. In 1996, the Chinese threatened to break off some major trade contracts with Australia if the prime minister and foreign affairs minister received the Dalai Lama. The ministers and the Australian people as a whole went on to receive the Dalai Lama in triumphant style, and that big balloon of Chinese threats just deflated. But whenever governments yield to China's blackmail, the Chinese rub their hands in glee and their contempt of the West just increases. In my more underhand moments, I think how tempting 'nonviolent terrorism' would be. For example, I've often thought of blowing up Mao Tse Tung's tomb in Tiananmen Square. There'd be no victim – Mao can't die twice – but what a big bang it would make in the communist church! In truth, however, there's no better approach than the nonviolent one.

J.F. – The agony of modern Tibet has a double dimension. On the one side, we all feel sorry for Tibet, as it's one of many countries that's suffered oppression and genocide at the hands of a communist power. On the other hand, we all think well of Tibet as a haven of Buddhism, especially since Tibetan Buddhism's influence is currently so widespread in the world, as we've already mentioned. Those two sides combined make it a very special case. You know, one thing that's quite striking in the history of Buddhism is that after it had had a very wide influence over all of India for almost two thousand years, it became a religion practiced more or less in exile from the land of its origins from the twelfth century onward. That uprooting of Buddhism has caused Buddhists enormous inconvenience and difficulty, but at the same time it's perhaps one of the reasons for its widespread propagation.

M. – The Dalai Lama often says, 'Tibet has no petrol for engines, like Kuwait, but it does have petrol for the mind, which should justify other countries coming to its rescue.' When the armies of communist China entered Tibet in 1949, the Tibetan government launched an urgent appeal to the United Nations Organization asking for help to resist the invasion. Britain and India advised the general assembly not to react, in order to avoid – so they said – conflict on a wider scale. But for most countries, China's invasion of Tibet was certainly an aggression. This fact became obvious during the UN General Assembly's plenary session debates in 1959, 1961, and 1965. The Irish representative, Frank Aiken, declared:

'For thousands of years, or for a couple of thousand years at any rate, Tibet was as free and as fully in control of its own affairs as any nation in this assembly, and a thousand times more free to look after its own affairs than many of the nations here.'

Only the countries of the communist bloc sided openly with China. Why on earth would the Chinese have felt the need to 'liberate' Tibet, as they themselves put it, if it belonged to them already? At different periods in its long history, Tibet was subjected to influence from the Mongols, the Nepalese, the Manchus, and the governors of British India. At other periods it was Tibet that exercised influence over neighboring countries – including China, for at one time the Chinese province of Xian had to pay taxes to the king of Tibet. It would be difficult to find a single nation state in the world that has never been subject to foreign domination or influence at one time or another in its history. But is France going to lay claim to Italy under the pretext that Napoleon conquered it for several years?

J.F. – I think Tibet's case was complicated by many factors, particularly its geographical location. It's not only the cowardice of Western democracies, great though that's been. Geostrategically, it's also very difficult to intervene militarily in Tibet.

M. – For that very reason, because of its geographical situation, the Dalai Lama points out the advantages to be gained in making Tibet a buffer state, a haven of peace in the middle of the major Asian powers. At the moment, the Indian and Chinese armies face each other along a frontier thousands of kilometers long. In 1962, the Chinese army annexed a third of Ladakh and parts of two northeastern Indian states in Assam.

J.F. – What democracies never understand is how vulnerable totalitarian systems are, particularly to the weapon they use so well against us – propaganda. And more than that: why are the Chinese so mad with rage every time some vague partisan of Tibet brings out a tiny flag to wave in front of a Chinese embassy? Why do they protest so much as soon as fifteen people get together at some tiny conference to call for Tibetan independence?

M. – And even more so when a hundred thousand young people attend a three-day concert of rock music dedicated to the cause of Tibet, as happened recently in California. Or again, when the Chinese threaten to forbid the building of a Disneyland in China unless Disney abandons the production of *Kundun*, Martin Scorsese's film on the life of the Dalai Lama. Mao versus Mickey Mouse – it's so ridiculous!

J.F. – It's because they're absolutely convinced of the illegitimacy of their own occupation of Tibet. A great historian and observer of politics, Guglielmo Ferrero, has shown in his book *The Principles of Power*[7] that illegitimate states are scared stiff of anything that might help to uncover the illegitimacy of the power they're exercising. But the democracies fail to use even the peaceful weapons available to them. What's more, as you said just now, economically speaking China needs the West much more than the West needs China. It would be quite possible to bring China to its senses and to avoid, at the very least, the most cruel of the extremes it's in the process of inflicting on Tibet.

M. – When people ask the Dalai Lama what he bases his hopes for a free Tibet on, he replies, 'On the fact that our cause is just and legitimate.' The truth, he says, has an intrinsic strength, while lies are but a fragile facade that can only be maintained at the cost of disproportionate efforts, and sooner or later are bound to fail. It's important not to forget that the future of Tibet concerns not only six million Tibetans but also a wisdom that belongs to our world heritage and deserves to be saved.

---

1. Since our dialogue took place, U.S. Senator Frank Wolf, the first House member to visit Tibet since Chinese forces moved in forty years ago, declared in a devastating report (August 1997): 'The clock is ticking for Tibet. If nothing is done, a country, its people, religion and culture will continue to grow fainter and fainter and could one day disappear. That would indeed be a tragedy. As one who visited a Soviet prison camp during the cold war (Perm Camp 35) and Romania before and immediately after the overthrow of the ruthless Ceaucescu regime to see things first-hand, I believe conditions in Tibet are even more brutal. There are no restraints

on Tibet's Chinese overseers. They are the accuser, judge, jury, prison warden and sometimes executioner rolled into one. Punishment is arbitrary, swift, vicious and totally without mercy and without recourse. I found that the People's Republic of China has a near-perfect record of vicious, immediate and unrelenting reprisals against the merest whisper of Tibetan dissent.'

2. Greater Tibet includes the whole territory of Tibet as it was before the Chinese cut it into five regions. The so-called 'Tibet Autonomous Region' only comprises about a third of Greater Tibet. The other regions have been annexed to several different adjoining Chinese provinces.

3. In more recent developments, Chen Kuiyuan, Tibet's hard-line Communist party chief (who was sent to Tibet in recognition of his successful crushing of the Mongolians' identity in Inner Mongolia), has declared that Buddhism is completely marginal to Tibet's culture and calls it a 'foreign import'. If twelve centuries or more is insufficient time for a tradition to have become part of the culture, Christianity's standing in Europe and America would logically be quite precarious, too – to say nothing of much more recent foreign imports like Marxism into China.

4. In particular, in 1960 a study of recent history led the respected International Commission of Jurists in Geneva to declare: 'Tibet demonstrated from 1913 to 1950 the conditions of statehood as generally accepted under international law. In 1950 there was a people and a territory, and a government which functioned in that territory, conducting its own domestic affairs free from any outside authority. From 1913–1950 the foreign relations of Tibet were conducted exclusively by the Government of Tibet, and countries with whom Tibet had foreign relations are shown by official documents to have treated Tibet in practice as an independent State.' Since the French edition of this book was published, the same Commission has recently (December, 1997) published a 365-page report on Tibet in which it declared: 'Under international law, the Tibetans are a people under alien subjugation entitled to the right of self-determination ... A UN sponsored referendum is needed to resolve the status of Tibet.' The report also warns that there has been a recent increase in violations of human rights in Tibet, including major transfers of Chinese population against the wishes of the native population, forced indoctrination in the monasteries, an increased use of torture, and repression of the Tibetan language and culture.

5. The Five Point Peace Plan, proposed by the Dalai Lama on September 21, 1987, to the American Congressional Human Rights Caucus: 1) The designation of the whole of Tibet (including the provinces of Amdo and Kham) as a zone of peace; 2) the abandonment of China's population transfer policy, which threatens the very

existence of the Tibetans as a people; 3) the restoration of the Tibetan people's fundamental human rights and democratic freedom; 4) the restoration and protection of Tibet's natural environment, and the abandonment of China's use of Tibet for the production of nuclear weapons and dumping of nuclear waste; 5) the commencement of 'earnest negotiations' on the future status of Tibet and relations between the Tibetan and Chinese peoples.

6. One recent positive development has been the appointment by the U.S. government of a special coordinator for Tibet, Gregory Craig. This provoked the usual cries of outrage from the Chinese authorities.

7. *The Principles of Power, the Great Political Crises of History.* New York, Arno Press, 1972.

≈

TWELVE

BUDDHISM: DECLINE

AND RENAISSANCE

JEAN-FRANÇOIS – There's no doubt that the spread of Buddhism in the West has been furthered by the tragedy of Tibet – by the fact that the Dalai Lama has been forced to live in exile, and that numerous Rinpoches, lamas, monks, and laymen have had to flee Tibet and make contact with other cultures, both in Asia and in all the other continents. Although by themselves these events wouldn't have been enough to explain the high level of interest in Buddhism today, they've certainly contributed. Buddhism has always shown a remarkable capacity to adapt, having been forced to exist outside its country of origin from the end of the twelfth century onward. By the third century B.C., the time of the Emperor Ashoka (himself a convert) a century and a half after the Buddha's *parinirvana*, the Buddhist teachings had spread throughout India and its neighboring countries. Buddhism was one of the two main religions of India, along with Hinduism, from the sixth century B.C. until the twelfth and thirteenth centuries – the period in which it was persecuted following the Muslim invasion of India. The intrusion of Islam into India was a considerable shock to everyone, and from the twelfth to the eighteenth centuries part of India fell under

Muslim domination. Hinduism nevertheless remained the dominant religion, while Buddhism was swept away. Why?

MATTHIEU – To start with the exile of the Tibetans, it's true that around 1960 there was an extraordinary concentration of Tibet's greatest spiritual teachers in the Himalayan foothills of India, Bhutan, and Nepal. All of them had fled the Chinese invasion. Had they stayed in Tibet, to meet them would have meant journeys on foot or horseback for months on end, and that's even supposing you knew anything of their existence in the first place. The tragic occupation of Tibet and exile of so many Tibetans was what brought the West the opportunity to make contact with these teachers and the thousand-year-old tradition they held. A number of them were old, and many of them are no longer alive today – which is part of what makes Arnaud Desjardins's documentaries so extraordinary.

More generally, Buddhism traveled far over the course of its history. Buddhist monks were, in fact, wandering monks right at the beginning. The Buddha himself traveled continuously from place to place and stayed put only during the three summer months for the 'rainy season retreat'. The monks would take shelter in temporary huts made of bamboo and foliage for the duration of that retreat period, before resuming their wandering for the rest of the time. Over the years, some of the Buddha's patrons had the idea of offering him places he and his monks could return to every year for the summer retreat. So they began to make solid buildings, still resembling, in form, those bamboo huts. Gradually, a few monks began to live the whole year round in such *viharas,* as they were called, and then whole communities established themselves there. That's how the first monasteries came to be. At first, for a long time, Buddhism remained confined to the country of Magadha, the present Indian state of Bihar. It subsequently spread and flourished throughout the whole of India as far as Afghanistan. There were even exchanges with Greece, as witnessed by a famous philosophical text which takes the form of dialogues between a Buddhist sage and the Greek king Menander, who ruled Bactria during the second century B.C.

J.F. – We should add, for the reader who might not be a professional historian of classical times, that the Hellenistic age in which King Menander lived covers the period between the age of the true Greek city-state, which came to its end toward the end of the fourth century B.C., and the age of triumph of the Roman Empire, in the middle of the first century B.C.

M. – The coming and going of merchant caravans must have allowed encounters between Buddhism and Greek civilization, which was very open to the flow of ideas coming from beyond its confines.

J.F. – Yes, and the conquests of Alexander accentuated such contacts, which notably gave rise to Greco-Buddhist art.

M. – It was in the eighth and especially the ninth century that Buddhism was brought to Tibet by Padmasambhava, at the invitation of King Trisong Detsen. The king, who already had a Buddhist teacher, wanted to build the first great monastery in Tibet. Following his teacher's advice, he asked Padmasambhava, the most respected sage of his time, to come to Tibet. Padmasambhava is now considered the 'second Buddha' by Tibetans, because it was thanks to his extraordinary energy and wisdom that Buddhism was really able to take root in Tibet. He supervised the construction of Tibet's first monastery, Samyé, and then set about organizing the translation of the Buddhist Canon into Tibetan from Sanskrit. He invited about a hundred great Indian Buddhist scholars, and sent a number of young Tibetans to India to learn Sanskrit there; then, for about fifty years, these Tibetan translators and Indian scholars formed a college, based in the monastery of Samyé, which translated the hundred and three volumes of the Buddha's own words, the Kangyur, and the two hundred and thirteen volumes of commentaries that had been written on them by great Indian Buddhist teachers, the Tengyur. Over the next two or three centuries, other Tibetan teachers traveled to India, often staying there for ten or twenty years, and brought back to Tibet with them texts that hadn't been translated in the first wave of translations. Several Buddhist lineages, of which there are now four main ones, were founded under the inspiration of particularly eminent masters. Buddhism continued to flourish without a break right up to the Chinese communist invasion.

J.F. – What had been happening meanwhile in India?

M. – By the end of the twelfth century and the beginning of the thirteenth, the Muslim persecution of Buddhism in India was at its height. Buddhism, in fact, had already been on the decline, and its enormous and highly visible monastic universities offered an easy target for the Muslim hordes, who sometimes mistook them for fortresses and were none too concerned with the details! In the great universities of Nalanda and Vikramashila, for example, many thousands of students had gathered under the direction of the greatest teachers of the period. They housed vast libraries of a richness comparable to that of the famous library of Alexandria. All these buildings were destroyed, their books burnt, and the monks exterminated.

J.F. – And was it Buddhism's particularly high profile, with all its universities, libraries, and monasteries, that explain why it was more easily stamped out than Hinduism, which withstood the onslaught much better?

M. – Not only. Buddhism had already started to decline in India, for reasons that are still not very clear. Even from the sixth century onward, the renewal of the Brahmanical traditions and the assimilation of many Buddhist concepts into the Vedanta – one of the principal Hindu metaphysical systems – had gradually been eroding Buddhism's influence. Buddhism's geographical spread, which had included the whole of India, shrank down again to the region of Magadha (present-day Bihar) and what's now Bangladesh. Advaita Vedanta, which emphasizes nonduality, had incorporated some important points from Buddhist philosophy, while still criticizing it nevertheless. This process of assimilation to some extent narrowed the doctrinal gulf between Buddhism and Hinduism. What's more, India was loath to abandon the caste system, which Buddhism deliberately disregarded.

J.F. – Are there certain Buddhist ideas that have lived on in Hinduism?

M. – Well, some of them were incorporated into it, despite the fact that Hindu philosophers continued to attack Buddhism on a doctrinal level.

J.F. – So Buddhism is one of the rare examples of a religion – let's call it a religion for the sake of convenience – that was wiped out of the geographical region in which it had been born, practiced, and spread for more than a thousand years. Another example of the same situation is that of the pre-Colombian religions, which were suppressed, extinguished, and partially eradicated as a result of the Spanish and general European conquest of Latin America.

M. – Buddhism also spread south to Sri Lanka, then to the east to Thailand, Burma, and Laos, in a form known as Theravada. Later it was taken north into China in the second century, in the form called the

Mahayana, whence it spread to Japan and evolved into different forms, especially Zen Buddhism, which emphasizes the sudden recognition of the nature of mind.

J.F. – In the fifties and sixties, Zen was the form of Buddhism that was best known and most fashionable in the West. The students at Berkeley in the sixties, in their movement against Western civilization, were quite obsessed with Zen Buddhism. Some even tried to put together a kind of syncretism, here again, of a political doctrine and Buddhism, inventing what they called 'Zen Marxism', which, I'm not sorry to say, didn't last long.

M. – Zen Buddhism is still flourishing in the West. But it's interesting that in Tibet all the different aspects and levels of Buddhism, called the 'Three Vehicles', were preserved and transmitted with great care in their entirety, which enables an individual to integrate those different levels of the teaching into his or her own spiritual path. The practice of the Theravada, the 'Words of the Elders', is based on lay ethics and monastic discipline, and on contemplating the imper-fections of the ordinary world and the futility of the preoccupations that underlie most of what we do. Such reflections inspire the practitioner's wish to be free from suffering and *samsara*, with its vicious circle of rebirths.

The Theravada's not without any notion of love of one's neighbor and compassion for those undergoing suffering, but it's the Mahayana, as found in Tibet, China, and Japan, that puts a central emphasis on love and compassion. According to its teachings, it's quite useless to liberate ourselves alone from suffering if all the living beings around us continue to suffer. The goal of the path, therefore, is in essence to transform ourselves internally for the sake of all beings. In India, and especially in Tibet, there developed a third vehicle, the Adamantine Vehicle or *Vajrayana*, which added to the two other vehicles a great variety of spiritual techniques that allow the Buddha nature present within us to be actualized still more rapidly, and the 'primordial purity' of phenomena to be realized. Transcendent though this vision certainly is, it deepens and strengthens compassion rather than stifling it. The combination of geographical and political circumstances, therefore, allowed Tibet to integrate all three vehicles of Buddhism into a single path.

J.F. – As a result of its tribulations Buddhism seems to have acquired an ability to transcend cultural boundaries, which will perhaps help its current development in the West. While it's not associated with any particular culture, it's found itself closely linked to several different cultures during its history. Tibet, a sort of geographical and spiritual fortress, was able to preserve all the component vehicles of Buddhism for a thousand years; but the Buddhist teachings also spread to civilizations as different as Sri Lanka and Japan. Has Buddhism taken on the flavor of the countries in which it's flourished?

M. – In a way, yes. In Tibet, for example, there was an indigenous religion, *Bön*, with some similarities to animist traditions but with a complex system of metaphysics, too. It still survives to this day. In the ninth century, metaphysical debates pitched *Bön* against Buddhism. Some *Bön* customs were adapted to and incorporated into Buddhism. Similar adaptations occurred in Thailand, Japan, and other countries, and will no doubt take place in the West. The essence of Buddhism, however, hasn't changed, and indeed has no reason to change.

J.F. – The teaching and practice of Buddhism must certainly have a universalist vocation. But a lot of religions claim to have a universal dimension. Christianity, of course, and especially Catholicism, whose name comes from the Greek for 'universal'; hence the right it has too often assumed to convert people by force. Islam, too, has a tendency toward universal expansion – by the might of the sword and the gun if necessary. In these religions, to become a believer you have to agree to have faith in a certain amount of dogma from the start. But that's not the case with Buddhism. Its universal vocation, we could say, could be extended to cultures other than the one in which it was born, but could never in any way mean that a new adept be required – even less, compelled – to submit to a particular faith.

M. – The Buddha said, 'Do not accept my teaching out of respect for me. Examine it and rediscover the truth in it for yourself.' He also said, 'I have shown you the path. It is up to you to follow it.' The Buddha's teaching is like a guidebook describing and explaining the path to wisdom that he himself took. To become a Buddhist in the true sense, you take refuge in the Buddha, considering him not as a God but as a guide and as the symbol of enlightenment. You also take refuge in his teaching, the Dharma, which isn't a dogma but a path. Finally, you take refuge in the community, all those who are accompanying you on that path. But Buddhism doesn't force things or try to convert people. It wouldn't make any sense.

J.F. – For the very reason that it doesn't resort to forced conversions, which from its own perspective would be unthinkable, Buddhism's implantation in a civilization fundamentally different from the one in which it took birth deserves to be studied – and, if it lasts, to be explained.

M. – Buddhism doesn't take a conquering attitude. It works more by a sort of spiritual influence. People who feel like getting to know more about it have to take the first step themselves and discover it through their own experience. It's interesting to see how Buddhism flourished in Tibet and China. Great teachers traveled to those places and their influence naturally attracted disciples to them, just as the nectar of flowers attracts bees.

J.F. – Throughout our conversations, I've noticed how extraordinarily rich Buddhist language is in metaphor. I like that. Plato, too, never stopped using images, myths, and similes when he talked. I'm all for the introduction of poetry into philosophy. But I'm not completely sure that by itself it's enough to answer all the questions one might want to ask.

M. – Well, I'll reply with one more image by saying that metaphor is like a finger pointing at the moon; it's the moon we're supposed to be looking at, not the finger. An image can often communicate more than a long description.

J.F. – The essential question for Western civilization is to know what sort of correspondence there might be between some of the needs that Western civilization experiences that aren't satisfied by its own spiritual resources, and the answers that Buddhism might be able to provide to those questions. The only thing is that the idea of a doctrine being adapted so as to meet some specific needs can also be a trap. Large numbers of people in the West belong to sects that are complete impostures, sometimes even criminal. So the question is one of the truth and authenticity of Buddhism as a science of the mind.

M. – Well, as for its authenticity, the main thing Buddhism's been investigating is the nature of the mind, and it only has two thousand five hundred years of experience in that particular field! As for its truth, what can I say? Perhaps it's its truth that gives it its strength. I think that's something that appears clearly in the facts and the people, and stands up to the test of time and circumstances. That's not the case with sects, which are only counterfeits of authentic spiritual traditions. Their facades collapse at the first opportunity. The fallacious nature of sects, which nevertheless attract numerous adherents, is generally expressed by all sorts of internal contradictions, scandals, and sometimes abominations – things we hear about quite often these days. By contrast, the growing interest in Buddhism in the West is more discreet. Buddhist centers are places where, for the most part, you can find friends who share the same aspirations and want to join in and help each other to study, practice, and translate texts and commentaries into Western languages. Their goal is to make an authentic and living tradition better known. They're generally seen in quite a positive light by the local population.

J.F. – I'd absolutely never compare a wisdom tradition more than two thousand years old with the sects that plague us nowadays. They're often monstrous and almost always absurd, and for the most part only exist to swindle people. That was far from what I was thinking. But I'm always suspicious of the impulsions of human nature, and so I simply wanted to point out that just because a certain number of people have a craze for a particular theory and for its teachers – who in their eyes acquire a certain prestige, but could also be impostors – that doctrine isn't thereby proved to be necessarily a good one. Some further demonstration is necessary.

M. – Such demonstration can only come from the long-term results of spiritual practice. As it's said, 'The result of study is mastery over oneself; the result of practice is that one's negative emotions diminish.' A passing craze is hardly worth anything.

J.F. – That's what I meant. It's obvious that if you stick to pure and simple observation of the facts, there's no comparison possible between Buddhism and sects. Nevertheless, it's important not to forget that sometimes even the most distinguished minds can be taken in by absolute nonsense. I've known eminent doctors who joined completely fraudulent outfits and believed in them for several years, bending themselves to all the demands of their sect. So it's no good taking the sincere aspiration that people might feel for some spiritual system as any proof of its authenticity; it might well be fake, because the sad fact is that human beings have an unfortunate tendency to feel strong inclinations for all sorts of strange things. For that reason, the burden of proof always rests on the person who's teaching.

M. – An authentic spiritual path implies making great demands of oneself, but being very tolerant toward others. In most sects, however, people are very demanding of others, but flagrantly contravene the ideals they profess themselves. It only needs one person with a little bit of charisma who decides to exploit his or her influence, for people to gather around and become mentally and physically enslaved without a moment's hesitation. But the fundamental difference is that sects are generally based on a mishmash of disparate elements and pseudo-traditional debris that have no real relationship to an authentic spiritual transmission, and aren't based on any true metaphysical principle. They therefore can't bring about any durable spiritual progress, and only engender confusion and disillusionment. Any true spiritual path must include two essential components – the means with which to perfect oneself, and the means with which to contribute something to others. From one tradition to another, there's plenty of variety in how those two goals are approached, but both those criteria have to be met.

~

THIRTEEN

FAITH, RITUAL,

AND SUPERSTITION

JEAN-FRANÇOIS – Most religions include an element of ritual piety, and from outside that's often seen as religious bigotry – blessed water, rosaries, palm crosses, belief in all sorts of indulgences and in the efficacy of the sacraments, or of particular prayers, or of lighting candles. Buddhism, however, is generally seen as being quite different, and as being particularly free of ritual and superstition. Indeed, it's that very idea of Buddhism that seems to be one of the reasons why intellectuals, among others, are attracted to it, while being put off by some aspects of the other established religions which seem to them too theatrical, formal, or irrational. Now, it seems to me that the image they have of Buddhism is rather idealized – the sort of image you might have looking at it from a distance, knowing something about what it teaches doctrinally but not having taken part in it in the way it's actually practiced from day to day. When you travel in Buddhist countries and get to see what's happening inside the monasteries, what you see is quite the opposite – an extraordinary panoply of practices, chanting, processions, prostrations, and so forth, which to an agnostic like myself appear to belong to the same sort of superstition or obsessive ritualism

as you'd find in Orthodox or Catholic Christianity, Islam, or Judaism.
I'd even go so far as to say that some of the practices going on here, in
the twentieth century, under our very eyes, are closer in spirit to
medieval Catholicism than anything in present-day Christianity. Isn't
there something rather irrational, external, and mechanically ritualistic about Buddhist practice that over the centuries has perhaps been
grafted on to the wisdom of the Buddha?

MATTHIEU – First of all, in Buddhism, as in all religious traditions,
you have to make the distinction between superstition and ritual. Faith
becomes superstition when it goes against reason and gets cut off from
any understanding of the deep meaning of ritual. But ritual does have
a deep meaning. The Latin *ritus*, in fact, means 'correct action'. It calls
for reflection, contemplation, prayer, and meditation. The meaning of
the words that are chanted always invites contemplation. This is particularly true in Tibetan Buddhism. If you look at the content of a ritual and at the texts that are recited in it, you'll find it's like a guide
containing all the different elements of Buddhist meditation – emptiness, love, and compassion, and so on. A ritual is a spiritual practice carried out in the inspiring setting of a monastery or temple. The serene
atmosphere is enhanced by sacred music, which is designed not so
much to arouse the emotions as to pacify them and promote mindfulness. It's seen more as an offering than as a form of artistic expression.
Certain rituals continue without a break, day and night, for a week or
more. The idea is that all the participants take part in an intense period
of group practice. In the meditation on a *mandala*, the emphasis is on
techniques of concentration, and a very rich symbolism is brought into
play.

J.F. – Could you say a bit more about what a *mandala* is? I only
have a very vague idea.

M. – A mandala is a symbolic representation of the universe and
beings, in the form of a perfect place and the deities that reside there.
The 'deities' of a *mandala* are not gods; as I've already said, Buddhism
is neither polytheistic nor monotheistic. They're archetypes, different
aspects of the Buddha nature. Meditation on the *mandala* is a training
in what's called 'pure perception', meaning the perception of the Buddha nature present in all beings. Such visualization techniques make it
possible to transform our ordinary perception of the world – a mixture
of pure and impure, good and bad – into a realization of the fundamen-

tal perfection of the phenomenal world. By visualizing ourselves, as well as the other living beings around us, in the form of these perfect archetypes that make up the pantheon of 'deities' in Tibetan Buddhism, we get used to the idea that the Buddha nature is present in each one. As a consequence, we stop discriminating between beings in terms of how they might seem from the outside – ugly or beautiful, friend or enemy. In short, such techniques are skillful means used to rediscover the primordial perfection inherent in ourselves and all beings. It's also important to point out that for Tibetan teachers such rituals only have a relative importance, and retreatants who dedicate themselves exclusively to meditation sometimes abandon all forms of ritual altogether. Some, like the great yogi Milarepa, even go so far as openly disparaging the use of ceremonies and ritual. The variety of spiritual techniques, therefore, corresponds to the variety of disciples, as well as to different levels of spiritual practice.

J.F. – Yes, but the other day in Kathmandu we were watching a crowd of Buddhist believers who'd come to pray around that huge monument – what's it called?

M. – A *stupa.*

J.F. – Yes. All those people were walking round the *stupa* in procession for hours at a time, always in a clockwise direction. On a previous trip to Bhutan I learned that when you want to walk round a temple or *stupa* you always do so clockwise, for reasons that escape me and for which I've never been given a satisfactory explanation. Isn't it just superstition, pure and simple?

M. – That's an important point. Aren't most of the things we do in ordinary life purely utilitarian and devoid of any deep meaning? Very often, walking is a question of getting somewhere as quickly as possible, eating is to fill our bellies, working is to produce as much as possible, and so on. But in a society where spiritual life impregnates everything, the most ordinary activities are given meaning. Ideally, nothing you do is any longer ordinary. While you're walking, for instance, you think that you're walking toward enlightenment. While you're lighting the fire, you make the wish that all beings' negative emotions might be burnt up. While you're eating, you wish that everyone might taste the flavor of contemplation. Whenever you open a door, you wish that the door to liberation might be opened for all beings. And so forth. In the case of a *stupa,* Tibetans feel that it's more enriching to walk around such a monument for an hour than to go jogging. A *stupa* is a symbol of the mind of the Buddha (the scriptures symbolize his speech and statues his body). Since the right-hand side of the body is considered the place of honor, they express their respect toward the Buddha and his teachings by keeping the *stupa* to their right as they walk around it – in other words, they walk around it clockwise. As they walk, their minds turn toward the Buddha and therefore toward what he taught, too.

J.F. – Why are there all those frescoes, apparently depicting supernatural beings of some kind? I thought there were no gods in Buddhism.

M. – Once again, they're not seen as gods in the sense of beings with some intrinsic existence. They're symbolic representations of various qualities of enlightenment. The single face of a 'deity' represents oneness, the absolute. His or her two arms are the wisdom of emptiness and the methods of compassion, united in one. Some deities have six arms, symbolizing six perfections – generosity, discipline, patience, diligence, concentration, and wisdom. Rather than looking at ordinary images, it's surely more useful to reflect on forms that are highly charged with meaning and remind the meditator of the different elements of the spiritual path. These archetypes also make it possible to use the power of our imagination as a factor for spiritual progress, instead of letting ourselves be carried away by our unbridled thoughts. One of the main obstacles to mindfulness, in fact, is the wild proliferation of thoughts. The techniques of visualization are skillful methods that allow people whose minds are always in turmoil, and who have trouble calming down the flow of their thoughts, to channel that flow toward an object. Visualization can be very complex, but instead of dispersing the mind it stabilizes it and makes it more peaceful. Correct visualization requires three qualities. Firstly, the ability to maintain a clearly visualized image, meaning that you have to keep bringing the mind back to the object you're concentrating on, over and over again. Secondly, awareness of what the object you're meditating on symbolizes. And thirdly, to maintain the perception of the primordial Buddha nature inherent in you.

J.F. – But I've seen people in the temples prostrating themselves in front of images of the Buddha. Surely, that's how people behave in front of a divinity, a god, or an idol – not in front of a sage.

M. – Prostrating in front of a Buddha is a way of paying respectful homage, not to a god but to ultimate wisdom and someone who embodies it. The Buddha's wisdom, as well as the teachings that he gave, have enormous value for the person bowing before him. To pay homage to that wisdom is also a gesture of humility. It acts as an antidote to pride, which is a hindrance to any deep-seated transformation. Pride prevents wisdom and compassion from emerging. 'Just as water doesn't collect on a mountain peak, true merit doesn't accumulate on the peak of pride,' says a proverb. Moreover, prostrations aren't just a mechanical movement. When you touch the ground with your two hands, two knees, and forehead, making five points, you aspire to purify the five poisons – hatred, desire, ignorance, pride, and jealousy – by transforming them into the five corresponding aspects of wisdom. As you get up again and slide your hands along the floor toward you, you think, 'May I collect all the sufferings of all beings upon myself and rid them entirely of them all.' In such ways, everything we do in daily life, far from remaining neutral, banal, and ordinary, brings us back to spiritual practice.

J.F. – In Christian monastic life the only reality is God. The world we live in – the 'century', as seventeenth-century French Catholics called it when they spoke of living within or without the century – is only a turning of one's attention away from the essential, God. Consequently, the religious life, the life of someone who withdraws from the world, whether Pascal at Port Royal or the hermits in a Carthusian monastery, consists of getting rid of all distractions – 'diversions', as Pascal called them – meaning everything that diverts attention toward all the futilities of our ordinary concerns, all the false values of success, all the satisfactions of vanity, wealth, and so on. The hours of which life in the century is woven are banished, so that one can concentrate all one's attention on the only relationship that counts, the relationship to the divine. The monks of the Grande Chartreuse withdraw from the world in order to be able to concentrate on God without interruption or distraction. But in Buddhism there's no transcendent God, so what is monastic life, or retreat from the world, directed toward? In a word, since Buddhism isn't a religion, why does it look so much like one?

M. – I think we've already said a little about that in the last few days. Whether you call it a religion or a system of metaphysics makes very little difference in the end. The spiritual goal Buddhism's directed toward is enlightenment, the very enlightenment the Buddha himself attained. The path consists of following in the footsteps of the Buddha. It requires a profound transformation of our current of consciousness. So it's understandable that those who aspire deeply to follow such a path should want to devote all their time to it. It's also understandable that, especially for beginners, the external conditions can either further or hinder such a quest. Only those who've attained enlightenment are invulnerable in all circumstances, because for them the phenomenal world is a book, each page of which is a confirmation of the truth they've discovered. A spiritually realized person is no more disturbed by the hubbub of a big city than by the peace of a mountain retreat. But beginners need to seek out favorable conditions that will enable them to develop their concentration and transform their thoughts. In all the tumult of ordinary life, that process of transformation would take much longer and runs a strong risk of being interrupted before it's complete. That's why Tibetan practitioners sometimes spend years in isolated retreat. Their aim is to dedicate themselves to the spiritual quest, without ever losing sight of their ultimate goal, which is to attain enlightenment in order to then be able to help others.

J.F. – How would you define enlightenment?

M. – It's the discovery of the ultimate nature of both oneself and phenomena.

J.F. – And can you make it clear what Buddhism means by faith?

M. – That's a word that has quite loaded connotations in the West. Buddhism distinguishes four different aspects of faith. The first is the feeling of clarity and inspiration that's aroused when you hear a spiritual teaching, or the life story of the Buddha or a great teacher. It's a kind of very keen interest. The second aspect is more an aspiration. It's the desire to know more, to put a teaching into practice yourself, to follow the example of a great teacher and little by little attain the same perfection. The third aspect is when faith turns into conviction, the certainty acquired by verifying for yourself the validity of the teachings and the effectiveness of the spiritual path, from which you obtain growing satisfaction and a sense of fullness. It's a bit like discovering a landscape that gets more and more beautiful the further you penetrate into it. Lastly, when you find that whatever the circumstances may be your conviction is never contravened or proved wrong, you attain a stability in your practice that makes it possible to use whatever happens in life, favorable or unfavorable, to progress. Your certainty becomes second nature to you and your faith becomes irreversible. So these are the four stages of Buddhist faith, which is not at all a leap that the intellect has to make, but is the fruit of progressive discovery and of confirmation that the spiritual path truly does bear fruit.

~

FOURTEEN

BUDDHISM AND DEATH

Jean-François – Withdrawing from the world, whether from a Buddhist or a Christian viewpoint, is also a sort of preparation for death. A consistent Christian, like Pascal, might well come to the conclusion that from the moment you've understood that the only reality is the Divine, it no longer makes any sense to live in the world. In this very life, you've got to get yourself into a fit state to appear before your Maker, which means living all the time as if you had only a few moments left to live. This idea keeps coming up in Pascal's *Pensées,* and in fact it comes from the Gospels. You never know just when the Lord is going to summon you – in ten years, or in five minutes. Philosophy, too, even without any religious connotation, often says of itself that it's a preparation for death. One chapter of Montaigne's *Essays* has the title 'That to be a philosopher is to learn to die'. I understand that the idea of preparing for death and making that transition plays a very important role in Buddhist teaching, too. Buddhism speaks of a transitional state after death called the *bardo,* I believe. Is there a treatise on the *bardo*?

MATTHIEU – Yes, there is. The thought of death is something that

Buddhists should keep constantly in mind. Far from being sad or morbid, such thoughts incite them to use every moment of life to bring about an inner transformation, and not to waste a single instant of their precious human existence. If you don't think about death and impermanence, it's all too easy to say to yourself, 'First of all I'll deal with what I have to do now, and bring my current projects to fruition. When I've finished with all that, I'll be able to see things more clearly and devote myself to spiritual matters.' To live as if we've got all the time in the world ahead of us, rather than living as if we've only a few more minutes, is the most fatal trap – because death can come upon us at any moment without warning. The moment of death and the circumstances that are going to bring it about are completely unpredictable. All the circumstances of ordinary life – walking, eating, sleeping – can suddenly turn into as many causes of death. A practitioner should always remember that. While a hermit lights his fire in the morning, he wonders whether he'll still be there the next day to light another one. Whenever he breathes out, he considers himself lucky to be able to breathe in again. Thinking about impermanence and death, therefore, is a constant spur to spiritual practice.

J.F. – Is death frightening for Buddhists?

M. – Buddhists' attitude to death evolves along with their practice. For beginners who haven't attained a mature level of practice yet, death is something to be afraid of – they feel like a deer caught in a trap, trying to get free from it in any way possible. Then, instead of wondering in vain how to escape death, people with some understanding of the path start to work on finding out what they need to do to pass through the *bardo* confidently and serenely. Later still, they come to feel like a farmer who's ploughed his fields, sown his crops and looked after them as they grow; whatever the weather, he doesn't worry because he's done his best. People who've worked all their life on changing themselves feel no regret and approach death with serenity. Finally, the best practitioners are joyful at the thought of death. Why should they be afraid of it? All attachment to their possessions, to any notion of a personal self, or indeed to any phenomena at all as having any true and solid existence, has vanished. Death has become a friend. It's no more than a stage in life, a simple transition.

J.F. – I wouldn't want to underestimate it, but that sort of consolatory view of death isn't very original. Does Buddhism have nothing more to add?

M. – The process of dying and the different experiences that ensue are described in great detail in Buddhist texts.[1] Once your breathing has stopped, there follow several stages of the dissolution of consciousness from the body. Then, when the material world fades from your eyes, your mind dissolves into the absolute state – the very opposite of the state of the conditioned world you perceive when mind and body are intermingled. At the moment of death, consciousness is absorbed for a very brief moment into what's called 'the luminous expanse of the absolute' before arising again to experience the intermediate state, the *bardo*, which leads to a new existence, or rebirth. There are meditations aimed at remaining in that absolute space, before the different experiences of the *bardo* appear, in order to attain in that very instant the realization of the ultimate nature of things.

J.F. – Yes, but even so … The history of philosophy and religion is full of all the ways of thinking about death that might help make it acceptable to human beings. Broadly speaking, they boil down to two types. The first is based on belief in survival. As soon as there's any idea of life after death, in which our spiritual principle or soul is immortal, it's enough for us to lead a certain type of existence conforming to particular rules – in Christian terms, avoiding all the mortal sins or confessing them to a confessor – for us to be sure of survival in quite pleasant circumstances in the hereafter. Death is then a sort of physical trial that has to be undergone, like a sickness, but that leads from this world to a better one. Priests who guide dying people help to lighten the fear and anxiety inherent in such a transition. The principle of this kind of consolation is that death doesn't really exist. The only question that still gives rise to any anxiety is whether we'll be saved or damned.

The other broad type of reasoning is purely philosophical, and is valid even for people who don't believe in any life after death. It's based on cultivating a sort of resignation and wisdom by telling ourselves that the destruction and disappearance of this biological fact that we call 'me', an animal among other animals, is an inevitable and natural event. Our only option is to learn to accept it. In relation to this theme, philosophers have shown a great deal of ingenuity in supplying sweetening arguments that make death easier to bear. Epicurus, for instance, uses a famous reasoning that goes like this. We don't need to fear death because in fact we'll never encounter it. As long as we're still here, it hasn't happened yet; and when it does happen, we won't still be here. So feeling afraid of death is pointless. Epicurus's main concern was to deliver man from useless fears – fear of the gods, of death, of natural phenomena like lightning, earthquakes, and so forth – so he tried to explain them in a very modern way, as phenomena which had causes and obeyed particular laws.

But in any case, as far as death is concerned there's no escaping one or the other of these two main kinds of explanation or consolation. I'd categorize Buddhism as being among the first group. Although Buddhism isn't a theistic religion, the spiritual technique that makes death acceptable is based on a metaphysical system according to which death isn't the end. Or else that when it becomes the end it's a beneficial end, because it means that one's free of the incessant sequence of reincarnations in a world of suffering. In the modern world, in the West, as has often been pointed out, death is hidden away as if it were something to be ashamed of. In the old days death was treated as an official event. It took place over several days. The whole family gathered around the dying person, his last advice and wishes were listened to, processions of priests came and went and administered the sacraments. The death of a ruler was a spectacle attended by almost the whole court. Today, death is evaded – it's a taboo subject. But at the same time we've become aware that silence isn't enough, and there are now therapists who help dying people and strive to make their departure more bearable.

M. – These days, faced with death and suffering in general, people often tend to look the other way. Our embarrassment comes from the fact that death is the only insurmountable obstacle to the ideal of Western civilization – to live as long and as pleasantly as possible. What's more, death destroys what we all care about most, ourselves. There's simply no material means by which that inevitable outcome can be altered. So we'd rather leave death outside our field of concern and preserve the sweet purring of an artificial, fragile, and superficial well-being for as long as we can. This solves nothing, and only postpones any confrontation with the true nature of things. We might claim that at least we haven't had to live in anguish. True, but during all that lost time our life has been running out, day by day, without our having used it profitably to get to the nub of the problem, and find out what the causes of suffering really are. We haven't been able to give meaning to life's every instant, and life has just been time slipping away like sand between our fingers.

J.F. – What does Buddhism suggest we do about that?

M. – There are, in fact, two ways of looking at death. Either the materialist view that our being is simply going to come to an end, like a flame being extinguished, or water being absorbed by dry earth; or else that it's a transitional stage, a passage from one state to another. Whichever the case, Buddhism can help people die in peace and serenity, whether or not they're convinced that the current of their consciousness is going to go on into different states of existence once it's separated from their present body. That's one of the reasons why Sogyal Rinpoche's book, *The Tibetan Book of Living and Dying*, has been so successful. A lot of it is all about preparing for death, helping people who are dying, and the process of death itself. Since death is the final, inevitable destruction of the very thing we are most attached to, he says, the Buddhist teachings on nonself and the nature of the mind can help. So as death approaches it's important to cultivate nonattachment, altruism, and joy.

J.F. – So would it be true to say that Buddhism combines both of the kinds of preparation for death that we've distinguished?

M. – In most religions, the perpetuation of consciousness or a spiritual principle after death is part of revealed dogma. In Buddhism's case, it's more a matter of direct experience, something that's borne out by people who are admittedly not ordinary but who are numerous enough for their testimony to be taken into consideration. But in any case, it's surely preferable to spend the last months or moments of life in joyful serenity rather than in anguish. What good is it to be tortured by the idea of leaving loved ones and possessions behind, or living in dread of the fact that the body's going to be destroyed? Buddhism helps us understand how to get rid of all these powerful attachments, which can easily turn death into mental torture rather than just a physical trial. But above all it teaches that it's no use waiting until the last minute to prepare for death, because just before you die isn't the ideal time to start practicing a spiritual path. We're constantly concerned about the future and spare ourselves no effort not to run out of money or food, or to fall ill. But we'd rather not think about death – although it's certainly the most significant thing that's ever going to happen to us. Thinking about death isn't at all depressing, in fact, if we use it as a reminder, to help us stay aware of how fragile life is, and to give meaning to every instant of existence. A Tibetan teaching says, 'If you constantly contemplate death, your mind will turn toward spiritual practice, your strength to practice will be renewed, and you'll see death as uniting yourself with absolute truth.'

J.F. – Death these days also brings up the question of euthanasia. In the West there's a whole problem as to whether or not we have the right to choose when to die. I'm not talking about suicide, which is another matter still. But when sick people feel beyond hope, or their suffering becomes intolerable, do they have the right to ask to die? Does a doctor have the right to help his patients die? It's a question that comes up in ethics, and even in law, and it's among the problems of society we spoke of earlier, along with abortion. Indeed, it's so prevalent a problem that the pope made a speech during a trip to Slovenia in 1996 attacking those he called 'the forces of death', meaning those who advocate abortion and euthanasia. Does Buddhism take any particular position on euthanasia?

M. – For a practitioner, every moment of life is precious. Why? Because each instant, whatever happens, can be used profitably to make progress toward enlightenment. Even having to cope with intense physical suffering can make it possible to meditate on the ultimate nature of things, because at the bottom of that very pain the nature of the mind, which is pristine awareness and peace, is untouched. The nature of the mind isn't affected by either joy or suffering. So someone with great strength of mind and a good stability in his or her spiritual practice can use even the most intense moments of suffering to make progress toward enlightenment.

J.F. – The title of one of Pascal's short essays is *On the proper use of sickness.* He was himself afflicted by illness.

M. – Pain can also serve to remind us of the sufferings that innumerable beings are going through, and to revive our love and compassion. And it can be used as the broom with which our negative karma is swept away. In fact, since suffering is the result of our past negative actions, it's better to pay off our debts while we have available the help of spiritual practice.

For all of these reasons, neither euthanasia nor suicide are acceptable. But that doesn't mean that life has to be pointlessly prolonged when there's no hope. The indiscriminate use of life support machines to prolong a dying person's life by a few hours, or to keep someone in irreversible coma alive, do more harm than good, because the person's consciousness is kept floating between life and death for a long time.

That can be very disturbing. It would be better to let dying people live out their last moments in a conscious and peaceful state.

J.F. – But what if the person's not a Buddhist?

M. – If someone feels suffering as an unbearable oppression that's annihilating the little bit of serenity that might be hoped for in the last moments of life...

J.F. – That's generally the case.

M. – Then it can be supposed that prolonging life is pointless and will only be torture. However, as I've just said, Buddhism takes suffering as being due neither just to chance, nor to destiny or divine will, but simply as the result of our past actions. Surely it's better to exhaust our *karma* than to carry it as a debt to the other side of death. Who knows what sort of life will follow death? Euthanasia doesn't solve anything.

J.F. – The ethics of euthanasia isn't just a question for people hoping to cut short their own suffering, but also for those helping them to die – who in so doing are killing a human being and taking life. There, I believe, Buddhism is quite categorical. Life should never be destroyed.

M. – Neither one's own, nor that of others. In fact, such a sad situation, the fact that anyone even considers resorting to euthanasia, is a reflection of the almost total disappearance of spiritual values nowadays. People find no resources within themselves and nothing to inspire them outside. It's a state of affairs that would be inconceivable in Tibetan society, where the dying are sustained by the teachings they've reflected on all their lives, and thanks to which they're prepared for death. They have all the reference points and inner strength they need. Because they've been able to give meaning to their lives, they know how to give meaning to their death, too.

What's more, they usually have the advantage of an inspiring and warm spiritual presence, their spiritual teacher. It's a striking contrast to the emergence of doctor-executioners like Dr. Kevorkian in the United States. Whatever the motivation behind the activities of such people might be, it's a miserable situation. The positive approach to death in the East is also in marked contrast to the sentimentality, the atmosphere of catastrophe, or the heavy physical and mental loneliness in which so many people die in the West.

J.F. – What do Buddhists think about organ donation at the moment of death?

M. – Buddhism's ideal is to put altruism into action by all possible means. So to donate our organs is admirable. It can make our death useful to others.

J.F. – And suicide?

M. – Whether you kill someone else or kill yourself, it's still taking life. Besides, wanting not to exist any longer is a delusion. It's a form of attachment that, destructive though it is, nonetheless binds you to *samsara*, the circle of suffering existence. When someone commits suicide, all they do is change to another state, and not necessarily a better state, either.

J.F. – Yes. That's the same as in Christianity, then. Are they damned, for the same reason?

M. – There's no such thing as damnation in Buddhism. *Karmic* retribution of actions isn't a punishment, it's a natural consequence. You're only reaping what you've sown. If you throw a stone up in the air it's no good being astonished if it falls back down on your head. It's a bit different from the usual idea of sin – although I find very interesting Father Laurence Freedman's explanation: 'The Greek for sin means to miss the target. Sin is what turns consciousness away from truth. Being the consequence of illusion and selfishness, sin includes its own punishment. God doesn't do the punishing.'[2]

I don't know if I've emphasized it enough already, but notions of good and evil in Buddhism aren't at all absolute. Nobody's decreed that to do this or that thing is good or bad in itself. Actions, words, and thoughts are made good or bad by their motivation and by their results, the happiness or suffering that they bring about. Suicide, from this perspective, is negative because it's a failure in your attempt to give meaning to life. By committing suicide, you destroy the possibility you have, in this life, of realizing the potential for transformation that you have within you. You succumb to an intense attack of discouragement which, as we've seen, is a weakness, a form of laziness. By saying to yourself, 'What's the point in living?' you deprive yourself of the inner transformation that would have been possible. To overcome an obstacle is to transform it into an aid to your progress. People who've overcome a major trial in their lives often draw from it a teaching and a powerful inspiration on the spiritual path. Suicide solves nothing at all, it only shifts the problem to another state of existence.

J.F. – To come back to the *bardo*, what are the different stages you go through in it?

M. – The meaning of the word *bardo* is an 'intermediate' or 'transitional' state. Several different ones are distinguished. First of all, there's the *bardo* of life, the intermediate state between birth and death. Then comes the *bardo* of the time of death, the time during which the consciousness is in the process of separating from the body. This includes two phases of 'dissolution', an outer dissolution of the physical and sensory faculties, and an inner dissolution of the mental processes. The first is the transformation of the body from a living organism into an inanimate object. It's described in terms of the dissolution of the five elements that make up the living, conscious body, each of which in turn merge into and lose any difference they had from the five elements that make up the inanimate, external world. When the 'earth', or solidity, element dissolves, your body feels very heavy, you have trouble maintaining your posture, and you feel oppressed by a great weight on top of you like that of a mountain. When the 'water', or liquidity, element dissolves, your mucous membranes dry up, you feel thirsty, and your mind feels confused and adrift, as if it was being carried off by a river. When the 'fire', or heat, element dissolves, your body begins to lose its warmth, and you find it more and more difficult to perceive the external world properly. When the 'air', or movement, element dissolves, you have trouble breathing, you can no longer move, and you lose consciousness. Hallucinations appear, and a sort of film of your whole life runs through your mind. Some people experience great serenity and see a peaceful, luminous expanse. Finally, your breathing stops. But there's still a subtle kind of 'inner respiration' that continues for some time before coming to an end in its turn.

In the second phase of dissolution, the continuing flow of consciousness goes through a series of more and more subtle states. You experience a state of great clarity, then one of great bliss, and finally one of complete absence of any thoughts. It's at this point that a seasoned practitioner, by recognizing and remaining in what's called the *bardo* of the absolute nature, can attain enlightenment. But in most cases that experience is over in a flash and the consciousness engages in the *bardo* of 'becoming', the intermediate state between death and the next rebirth. The different experiences the consciousness then undergoes depend on your degree of spiritual maturity. For people without any spiritual realization, the result of all their thoughts, words, and deeds during the life that's just come to an end will determine the degree to which the experiences in this *bardo* are frightening and unpleasant. They'll be swept along like a feather by the wind of their *karma*. Only someone with a certain amount of spiritual realization will be able to control what happens. Gradually, the details of the next state of existence begin to appear.

The process of rebirth is the same for ordinary and realized beings, but the former are reborn as a result of the strength of their past actions, while the latter, free of all negative *karma*, take rebirth deliberately in suitable conditions in which to continue helping others. That's how it's possible to identify the rebirth of a former teacher.

J.F. – Well, we don't need to go back to the problem of reincarnation at this point. But in the end, it seems to me that what attracts a lot of Westerners to Buddhism is also that it teaches how to master oneself, and that's a classic pattern in the history of philosophy.

M. – Mastery of oneself is essential, but it's only a tool. Tightrope walkers, violinists, judo experts – even some murderers – are all masters of themselves, but with very different motivations and results. Mastery of oneself, like so many other qualities, is only something of true value when it's based on the right motivation and metaphysical principles. According to Buddhism, mastery of oneself consists of not succumbing to the chaining together of negative thoughts, of not losing sight of the nature of enlightenment. It would be quite legitimate to speak of a 'science of the mind'.

J.F. – So it's a question of mastering one's spiritual being, while keeping one's sights on good. Mastering one's thoughts, one's feelings, and therefore everything one does in life. From ancient times, that's what's been called the behavior of the sage, resulting from inner practice and metamorphosis. In this context, there's a lot of curiosity in the West about all sorts of other techniques, particularly yoga. Could you say something about the relationship between Buddhism and yoga?

M. – The Sanskrit *yoga* means to unite, and its equivalent in Tibetan, *naljor*, to 'unite with the true nature'. It's a way of saying that we unite our mind with the Buddha's mind, or with the teacher's mind, in the sense of integrating their spiritual realization into our own experience. Hinduism, too, includes several forms of yoga. *Raja-yoga* consists of developing a great deal of strength of mind in the path of action. *Bhakti-yoga* is the path of devotion, *jñana-yoga* the path of gnosis, and the form best known in the West, *hatha-yoga*, uses exercises and physical postures which, combined with control of the breathing, bring about certain psychosomatic effects. Such exercises lead to a state of relaxation and inner calm that favor a serene outlook on whatever happens in life. Tibetan Buddhism also includes practices for controlling the breath and physical exercises that are taught during long retreats, although never to beginners or outside a context of specific spiritual practice. Nevertheless, some objective testimonies are available. During the Harvard symposium we've already mentioned, Professor Herbert Benson read a paper entitled *Mind/body interactions including Tibetan Studies*. Encouraged by the Dalai Lama, over the last fifteen years Professor Benson has studied the effects of meditation and certain other techniques on human physiology. In particular, he's investigated the effects of the practice of *tummo*, or inner heat, so vividly described by Alexandra David-Neel in her book *My Journey to Lhasa*:[3]

'I saw several of these masters in the art of *tummo*, sitting in the snow night after night, completely naked, immobile, and deep in their meditation, while the terrible ravages of winter spun and screamed around them. I saw, in the brilliant clarity of the full moon, the fantastic examination that their disciples had to take: several young men were led, in the heart of winter, to the shore of a lake or a river where, stripped of all their clothes, they had to dry sheets soaked in the icy water on their own flesh. Hardly had one sheet been dried than it was replaced by another. Stiffened by ice as soon as it emerged from the water, it was soon steaming on the shoulders of the rekyang candidate as if it had been placed on a burning stove. I myself trained in the technique for five winter months, wearing a novice's thin cotton robe at an altitude of 13,000 feet.'

Benson studied hermits from the exiled Tibetan community doing this practice in the Himalayas. Among his main findings were that, during this form of meditation, oxygen consumption could fall to as much as sixty-four percent of its normal level, blood lactate levels fell, respiratory movements slowed down, and so on. He filmed practitioners drying not only one but several sheets dipped into icy water at a temperature of one degree centigrade. Any normal person, he said, would have shivered uncontrollably and could even have died of cold. But the surface of these yogis' bodies, far from being frozen, was hot.

This isn't some sort of exhibitionism. I personally have a number of Tibetan friends who've trained in these techniques, which are practiced in order to gain mastery over the body and its energies through meditation, without being an end in themselves. Their purpose is to help practitioners make progress in understanding their minds. As it's said, 'The goal of asceticism is mastery of the mind. Apart from that, what use would asceticism be?'

1. For example, see *The Tibetan Book of Living and Dying,* op. cit.
2. Father Laurence Freeman, in *The Good Heart,* op. cit.
3. Virago, London, 1969.

~

FIFTEEN

The Supremacy of the Individual

JEAN-FRANÇOIS – Do you Buddhists ever wonder if the discoveries made by our Western human sciences, as they've been built up and evolved over the last century or two, might have any contribution to make to your own sciences of the mind? Or do you think that, having been established two thousand five hundred years ago, Buddhist psychology has nothing to learn from the West?

MATTHIEU – The Buddhist attitude is to be completely open to all ideas and aspirations. So there's no question of being closed to how the West sees the mind sciences. But don't forget that on the whole the West has become less and less interested in any contemplative science and has concentrated on so-called natural sciences. Curiously enough, until recently even psychology, whose name suggests that it ought to be a 'science of the mind', has avoided introspection altogether, considering it as not objective enough, and has tried to convert mental events into measurable phenomena. So it almost completely ignores the contemplative method, on principle and in practice. For Buddhism, however, it seems obvious that the only way to get to know the mind is to examine it directly, first of all analytically, and then by contemplation, or meditation – and meditation means a lot more than some vague mental relaxation, which is the image many Westerners have of it. What Buddhism calls meditation is a gradual discovery, over years of practice, of the nature of the mind and how mental events appear in it. Western psychology's approach therefore seems fragmentary and rather superficial, in the sense that it only deals with the mind's outer-most layer.

J.F. – As far as the exact sciences are concerned, on the other hand, I believe Buddhism is quite unequivocal.

M. – Yes, that's right. For instance, if some mathematical or physi-cal law has been proved clearly and beyond any reasonable doubt, the only thing to do is to accept it. The Buddhist attitude is to accept all valid knowledge and to relinquish whatever has been proved wrong. That's why Buddhism has no difficulty in modifying the way it per-ceives the physical universe, for instance in accepting the findings of modern astronomy – since the earth being flat or spherical doesn't make much difference to the fundamental mechanisms of happiness and suffering. The Dalai Lama often says that in Tibet he was taught that the earth was trapezium-shaped, but that he had no trouble understanding and therefore accepting that it was, in fact, spherical.

J.F. – In Western philosophy, that's called rejecting an 'argument from authority'.

M. – There is an ancient Buddhist cosmology, compiled by the Buddha's disciples and reflecting the image people had of the world in India in the sixth and fifth centuries B.C. An enormous mountain, Mount Meru, forms the axis of the universe, and around it the sun and moon circle and various continents are arranged. As cosmology, it belongs to what's called relative or conventional truth, meaning the truth for some particular moment. Interestingly, it considered the uni-verse not as an unchanging, finite sphere, like Aristotle, but as infinite and continually changing.

J.F. – Insofar as the sciences of matter and of life are concerned – biology, astrophysics, and evolutionary theory – Buddhists seem to have a much more open attitude than the Catholic Church and Chris-tianity in general, at least as things were until a few years ago. The Church accepted, as part of its dogma, explanations of the universe and the creation of life that were later gradually demolished by science, which it therefore saw as an enemy. Even in the nineteenth century, the theory of evolution of the species aroused very hostile reactions in Christian circles. The Church accepted it in the end, but it's taken a long time. For instance, even in the fifties and sixties, Teilhard de Chardin, a priest who tried to reconcile evolutionary theory with Christian dogma, was blacklisted by the Catholic Church because he took evolutionary theory as the starting point in his theological research. Even today, there are plenty of Christian groups in America who oppose the teaching of evolution, rather than creation, in school biology courses.

M. – Yes, it's true that Buddhist conceptions of the phenomenal world aren't treated as dogma, because the way we perceive the phenomenal world is seen as being quite variable, depending on the particular time and the kind of beings perceiving it. That must surely be what led Einstein to write, 'The religion of the future will be a cosmic religion. It should transcend a personal God and avoid dogma and theology. Covering both the natural and the spiritual, it should be based on a religious sense arising from the experience of all things, natural and spiritual, as a meaningful unity. Buddhism answers this description ... If there is any religion that could cope with modern scientific needs, it would be Buddhism.' Present-day descriptions of the cosmos correspond to the perceptions we have of the universe in our own time, and Buddhism accepts them as such. There's no question of rejecting science as a description of facts or natural laws. On the other hand, Buddhism can't accept any quasi-metaphysical claims that science or scientists may make of possessing an ultimate explanation, whether on a material level or not, of the nature of the world or of the mind. Nor does Buddhism have any reason to make fundamental changes to its point of view just to follow whatever direction the wind of scientific discoveries happens to be blowing at the moment. In any case, such discoveries neither validate nor invalidate the principles of spiritual life. That altruism is a cause of happiness, and hatred a cause of unhappiness, owes nothing to the earth being spherical or the universe starting with a big bang. I can accept in principle that successive scientific theories provide a more and more accurate view of physical reality, but it's worth remembering that during its history science has often adopted ideas diametrically opposed to preceding ones, speaking each time of a 'scientific revolution' and showing profound scorn for anyone who doesn't share the latest theory. I'm not saying that one has to hold on to the past, but I think it's important not to jump to conclusions about the future or disparage other views of reality. Remember that only twenty years ago, scientists were still not sure whether the universe was in a steady state or expanding after an initial big bang – rather a huge difference, you have to admit.

J.F. – Let's go on to the human sciences. You were telling me just now that the one that first caught your own attention was what we call political science, in other words the study of systems of government.

M. – Since the goal of Buddhism is to eliminate all forms of suffering, it's clearly of primary importance to have some knowledge of the principles of a just society, based on spiritual values and on ideas not only of human rights but also of the responsibilities of the individual.

J.F. – How can a just system of government be built? Or in other words, how can a society be organized so that its system of government guarantees the legitimacy of its power – the fact that its power really does come from the citizens that are supposed to be subject to it? And so that it also guarantees equality for all its citizens – at least, to begin with, in terms of their legal rights? In other words, what we call a state of law. Especially, how can the equality of citizens be guaranteed in terms of how they actually live – their situation in terms of economics, education, health, and all the other details, from housing to working and leisure conditions?

M. – The basic principles of democracy – to eliminate iniquity and ensure that everyone's well-being is taken into account equally – are, of course, admirable. But the principles underlying the organization of society have to be experienced by its members as being obvious and beyond all argument. In theory, some of the ideas of communism, too, like the sharing of wealth, are also admirable. It all depends on how they're applied.

Over the last few years, the Dalai Lama has imposed a democratic system on the Tibetan government in exile, rather a unique move for a political leader. He felt that the respect in which the Tibetans hold him personally, on both a spiritual and a temporal level, was holding back the establishment of a democratic structure which, once he's no longer alive himself, is the only system that will enable them to assert their rights in the eyes of the international community. So he had two constitutions drawn up, one for the Tibetan government in exile in India, where there are more than one hundred and thirty thousand Tibetan refugees, and another for Tibet when it regains either its independence or at least some degree of real autonomy. The members of the assembly who drew up those constitutions wanted to combine traditional values with the best aspects of democracy.

During one of the Dalai Lama's visits to Australia, the federal system in operation there, with states enjoying a degree of autonomy from the central government, caught his particular interest. It could correspond to what he's proposed to the Chinese. That is, a system in which Tibet would manage its own internal affairs, leaving external affairs to China – thereby renouncing, in view of the circumstances, the complete independence to which Tibet has a basic right. Let me just say, too, in passing, that despite all such concessions that ought to have allowed negotiations with the Chinese to get under way, he's found himself up against a wall of complete silence from their side.

The Dalai Lama's reforms are not an attempt to influence the opinion of an electorate or to maintain his own position, as he's already renounced the possibility of his holding any political office in a free Tibet. He simply wanted the best possible regime for present-day Tibet to be determined. That's why he's tried to introduce into the constitution not only the notion of individuals' rights but also the idea of individuals' responsibility toward society and the state's responsibility toward other states in the world.

J.F. – Yes, it's true that one aspect of what we could call the crisis of modern democracies is that in our own state of law the citizens feel that they have more and more rights and less and less responsibilities toward the community. In that context, I have quite an amusing story to tell. In 1995, a reader wrote to me and asked if I knew that during the French Revolution there wasn't only a Declaration of Human Rights, but also, in 1795, a Declaration of the Duties of the Citizen. Why, he wondered, had no one had the idea of celebrating its bicentenary? It is indeed a historical fact – one I had, in fact, completely forgotten. I wrote an article in *Le Point* to remind our readers of that anniversary. It was greeted with utter indifference, because people are a lot less interested in the question of citizens' responsibilities than in that of their rights. They're nevertheless two sides of the very same thing.

The Dalai Lama's current political thinking, and that of Buddhists in general, brings up an interesting point. There's a theory current in

Asia these days of the relativity of human rights and democratic principles. Countries like China, which of course is run by a totalitarian regime, and even countries that have been under authoritarian but not totalitarian regimes, like Singapore, claim that the West is just a nuisance to them with its whole thing about human rights and total freedom of opinion and expression, the freedom to unionize, and democracy based on multi-party elections. According to them, every culture has its own particular idea of human rights. There's an Asian concept of human rights, they say, which has nothing much to do with democracy, and a Western concept of human rights which we're kindly requested to keep for ourselves! This bizarre theory of the relativity of human rights has been particularly developed by the famous Lee Kuan Yew, a great statesman since it was he who created modern Singapore.

The same theory that human rights are relative and dependent on the culture was also ratified by the French president, Jacques Chirac, in a speech he made during his visit to Egypt in April 1996. Each country, he said, has its own way of conceiving human rights, which it applies in its own fashion. His speech was a way of doing a favor to President Mubarak, the essence of the message being that although Egypt's a country that has little to do with what's usually called democracy, that doesn't mean it has to be condemned in terms of its human rights record. It was shortly before the 1996 visit of the Chinese Prime Minister Li Peng to France, during which there were several episodes of friction about human rights. Anyway, whatever one might think of such a declaration, it does seriously raise the question as to whether there really is an Asian or an African notion of human rights which might be different from what democracy's great thinkers have always tried to defend. What would the Buddhist position be?

M. – According to Buddhism, all living beings aspire to well-being and have the same right to be happy. All aspire to be free of misery and have the same right not to suffer. Of course all those aspirations and rights have a universal value. So the nature and effectiveness of human laws and institutions needs to be examined in terms of whether they promote or hinder those basic rights. The East is more inclined than the West to think that society's harmony shouldn't be compromised by people using the notion of human rights to justify doing anything they like, at any time, however they want, as long as it's 'allowed'. For indeed, such an attitude is really a form of anarchy. It leads to an imbalance between rights and duties, between liberty for oneself and responsibilities toward others. The individual is supreme in Western societies. The individual can do practically anything, as long as it's within the framework of the law.

J.F. – And often even when it isn't. The rights of certain individuals and groups, in fact, often reach a level of permissiveness that goes well beyond what's legal. Rights outside the law.

M. – Yes, and behaving like that not only doesn't bring happiness or fulfilment to the individual, but is also a constant disturbance to society. The individual's responsibility is to consciously preserve the harmony of society. That's something that can only be done if individuals respect the law, not as an obligation, but in the light of an ethical sense, both spiritual and temporal. So it's easy to see why societies based on traditions of a more spiritual nature, like India and Tibet in the recent past, would attach more importance to the overall well-being of the community than to respecting individualism at all costs. The failure, and tragedy, of totalitarian regimes is that they blindly and violently oppose individualism by dominating individuals, and claim to ensure people's well-being in a way that's in gross contradiction to the actual facts. The point is not to restrain individuals' freedom but to instill in them a sense of responsibility. However, the Dalai Lama has stressed many times how important it is to guarantee equality in the rights of men and women, and equality in basic rights to life, well-being, and protection from suffering regardless of race, caste, or gender.

J.F. – Well, I'd certainly second that. But you know, frankly, I don't think there are any such spiritual considerations in the distinctions that Li Peng and Lee Kuan Yew are so fond of making between African or Asian and Western concepts of human rights.

M. – Li Peng's ideas about human rights, of course, have nothing to do with notions such as the individual's responsibility for the well-being of society. He's simply haunted by the fear of chaos – which he's ready to shed blood to prevent – and of any freedom which would destabilize the totalitarian regime.

J.F. – But to come back to the misuses of individual rights that you were describing just now, these are things that are happening all the time in the most democratic societies. How do they happen? Democratic societies lay themselves open to all sorts of maneuvers by which lobby groups – groups with a social or professional interest to defend, groups or individuals enjoying certain privileges – can try to extort special advantages from the community as a whole by passing them off as democratic rights.

European and American societies are currently involved in a debate about acquired advantage. There are corporate bodies who over the years have garnered for themselves advantages not enjoyed by ordinary citizens. They've often been able to do so in the name of particular conditions or difficulties that applied to them at a certain point in their history. Those special dispositions and advantages, which were therefore justifiable initially, have over the years become abuses and constitute privileges that they defend just as if they were in the general interest. In democracies, that sort of deterioration is going on all the time, and I'd say it was almost inevitable. To correct it, things would need to be leveled out periodically and the counter brought back to zero, the equality of all in the eyes of the law and in terms of the consumption of public spending.

The danger of particular groups and individuals getting together to obtain privileged treatment over and above communal laws, and exempting themselves from having to respect them, is one of democracy's old bugbears. It's very well described in Plato's *Republic*, showing how democracy, when it degenerates, can beget tyranny. As soon as so-called 'democratic rights' become no more than a mosaic of special interests that clash with one another while using the rhetoric of the general good, society is getting close to a state of uncontrollable anarchy that will almost inevitably arouse the temptations of authoritarian government. That's what happened in Italy in the twenties and Spain in the thirties. A dictatorial regime doesn't ever just appear from nowhere. There are always certain conditions in which it's incubated. Consequently, the dangers signaled by the idea of different standards of human rights for different continents and cultures, which to my mind is mistaken, come back to an old problem of democracy, to a problem continually cropping up in the best-behaved democracies. What Lee Kuan Yew and Li Peng mean is that a certain amount of authoritarianism is preferable to anarchy. Instead of solving the problem, they're obliterating it, in their own rather heavy-handed way.

M. – Let's take an example that keeps causing controversy, the exploitation of sex and violence in the media. In the States, whenever legislation to control the broadcasting of violent or pornographic images on television or the Internet is proposed, it arouses a storm of protest from intellectuals invoking freedom of expression. If human rights are considered on their own, without human responsibilities being taken into account, there's never going to be a solution to the problem. We're letting violence become our daily fare, to the point that an average American adolescent will have seen forty thousand murders and two hundred thousand acts of violence on television before reaching the age of nineteen. Violence is implicitly presented as the best way to resolve a problem, and sometimes as the only way. It's glorified, and at the same time it's dissociated from physical pain, as only visual images are involved.

It's an attitude that extends to plenty of other fields. The boxer Mike Tyson became the best-paid sportsman in history – seventy-five million dollars in one year. What for? For punching someone else. There's no denying that this general attitude to things in the media increases the use of violence in reality. Any control on such excesses is denounced as muzzling freedom of expression, but without any control we'll just see more and more violence. Surely, the problem is a lack of any sense of responsibility. The producers who broadcast those television programs or organize such contests know very well, at the bottom of their hearts, that what they're doing is far from helping the human race. But the public's fascinated by violence and sex, and commercially it works very well. The producers only see money to be made, while the legislators are paralyzed by the fear of even touching people's freedom of expression. The result is complete ignorance about responsibility and an inability to translate such a notion into either law or convention. In the end, a sense of responsibility has to come from the maturity of individuals, not from restrictive laws. And for individuals to attain such maturity, spiritual principles that make inner change possible have to be alive and well in society, instead of being cruelly missing.

J.F. – Notions of freedom of opinion and expression arise in a threefold context, political, philosophical-scientific, and religious. In the political context, freedom of opinion and expression means that everyone, under a liberal regime, has the right to express a political opinion, to support it, to present it to the electorate, to establish parties to defend it, and to have people elected who try to have it applied – as long as none of that compromises the rights of other citizens. In a philosophical context, those two freedoms have been asserted against religious censorship of the kind, for example, that once led the Christian Church to publicly burn books judged to be contrary to Church dogma. A more recent but very similar phenomenon has been seen under modern totalitarian regimes, who've also burned books and works of art, and imprisoned scientists because their research went against the philosophical dogma on which the totalitarian state was based. In the religious context, the problem seems quite similar these days, as certain theocratic states like Iran are based rather more on totalitarian political ideology than on actual religion, as well as being highly intolerant of other creeds and using ferocious methods of coercion and repression. All the main democratic societies today are based on freedom of political opinion, freedom in scientific and philosophical research, and religious freedom. But always on condition that there's no infringement of the rights of others.

Another very important aspect of that freedom of expression is that it must remain relative to its field. For instance, freedom of speech doesn't include incitement to murder. If I make a speech in the Place de la Concorde to say that everyone should go and kill Monsieur and Madame So-and-So, that's not freedom of speech. Incitement to murder is prohibited by the penal code and carries heavy sanctions. Similarly, laws have been passed against denying that the Holocaust, the extermination of Jews under the Third Reich, actually happened. Denials of the kind, disguised as freedom in historical research, really have nothing to do with historical research, because it's quite unjustifiable to come along now and contest the reality of facts that have been perfectly well testified by thousands of witnesses and hundreds of historians. Claims of that sort, far from being true historical criticism, are motivated by a concealed intention to harm particular human groups, and therefore contravene a well-defined article in the constitution that forbids incitement to racial or religious hatred. Nor is it necessary to resort to claims about some Asian concept of human rights in order to avoid such abuses. The spectacle of violence or degrading pornography in the media can itself be considered a violation of human rights, rather than something that should be protected by freedom of expression.

M. – Nevertheless, it's fear of limiting freedom of expression that makes us hesitate to pass laws condemning these purely commercially motivated abuses. Directors of such films and television programs stay

just below full-blown incitement to violence, but they glorify or trivi-
alize it, and therefore promote it at the same time. This has been well
demonstrated. In the end, attitudes of this kind boil down to a lack of
altruism.

J.F. – But the sectarian prohibitions of the Iranian ayatollahs aren't
any more altruistic.

M. – For the moment, Western nations have chosen to leave such
abuses well alone, while some oriental governments, like that of Singapore, have decided to put an end to them using authoritarian means.
Neither one of these solutions is completely satisfactory. A balance
between rights and responsibilities hasn't been reached. Through a
lack of wisdom and altruism, a lack of ethical and spiritual principles,
there's been no clear distinction made between the desirable aspects of
freedom of expression and those which directly or indirectly harm
other people.

J.F. – It would be impossible to define principles that would cover
all special cases. Some of Shakespeare's tragedies, for instance, where
there's a new corpse every five minutes, might be banned as too violent. And in the thirties one of the arguments used in right-thinking
circles against psychoanalysis was that it was pornographic. Why?
Because Freud showed that sexuality had a role in the origin of aspects
of human behavior that weren't themselves sexual. Here we're getting
into what I'd call the casuistry of applying laws, which requires a great
deal of finesse. Categorical, mechanical application is simply not feasi-
ble. But that's the distinctive feature of all civilizations. If civilizations
were simple, they'd be terribly tedious.

M. – But after all, as long as the predominant motive is profit
rather than the deepening of knowledge, and as long as the consequences are harmful, to argue on sacrosanct principles of freedom of
expression seems to me to be cynical deceit on the promoters' side and
a new form of superstition on the intellectuals' side.

J.F. – Yes, but don't forget what an important factor public opinion
is in democracies. Education of public opinion is the essential point. No
legislator can do anything without it. That's exactly where freedom of
information and freedom to exchange views play such an important
role. Nowadays there's a movement of public opinion against violence
on television and in the cinema. It's not led by legislators, but by spec-
tators who are beginning to feel disgusted.

I remember a conversation I had in 1975 with the then minister for culture, Michel Guy. At the time, the ministry was wondering whether to authorize X-rated hard porn films in ordinary cinemas, or perhaps to limit them to particular cinemas at particular times. When Michel Guy asked my opinion, I told him that I thought he ought to let them be shown unconditionally (except to underage viewers, of course) because they were so bad, so monotonous, and so vulgar that the public would just be disgusted by them. Now, I don't automatically think I'm right, but anyway that was what happened, and one after another we saw all the porn cinemas in Paris close down. There are hardly any left nowadays. There are only specialist ciné-porn shows, not in public cinemas but in sex shops where people go if they really want to. So the public took action much more effectively than any ban would have done.

To come back to the main point, then, we could say that along with Buddhism as a whole the Dalai Lama, of all the political and religious leaders in the East, accepts that democratic principles are universal and doesn't subscribe to that distinction – to my mind fallacious – between Eastern and Western ideas of human rights.

M. – Yes, but without forgetting that it's crucial to consider others' interests to be just as important as one's own.

J.F. – I don't think altruism could ever be laid down as a constitutional rule. The danger here is utopianism. As I've said in our previous conversations, utopians who've tried to set up constitutions starting from scratch tend to be seen in a rather touching light as being a bit unrealistic but as having good intentions. But that's not at all how it is. Utopians are the inventors of totalitarian systems. When you study the great utopias – Plato's *Republic,* Thomas More's *Utopia* in the sixteenth century, Campanella's *City of the Sun* in the seventeenth, the writings of Charles Fourier in the nineteenth, and finally the Marxist-Leninists, the most formidable of them all because they got the chance to put their theories into practice, with Mao Tse Tung and Pol Pot as extensions – you see that the utopians were all authors of totalitarian constitutions. Why? Starting from an abstract idea of what human beings should do, they apply their prescriptions in a completely ruthless way. That's not true political science. Utopians are a danger to the public.

True political science is based solely on the observation of how

THE SUPREMACY OF THE INDIVIDUAL

human societies function, their sociology, their economics, and their history. Lessons are drawn from those observations. What has actually worked well, in practice, and what hasn't? Starting from those sciences, and never *a priori*, a certain number of directing principles can then, with great care, be identified.

M. – But what principles are those human or political sciences based on?

J.F. – I should say right away that if it were only up to me I'd never have called them sciences, because to my mind they're not sciences at all in the strict sense of the word. Why? Because the human sciences are open to two dangers all the time. The first is what I'd call the danger of philosophy, in other words wanting to set out an overall system that claims to explain how human societies function, once and for all. A very large number of modern sociologists and anthropologists have fallen for that temptation. That is, the idea that they can supplant all the theories of their predecessors and render redundant all theories of their successors. That totalitarian temptation in sociology is still present in a number of important contemporary writers. Several sociologists of the structuralist school seem to me to have fallen into that trap, no less so than the Marxist sociologists. And that's the second danger, in fact – the danger of ideology. The human sciences are criss-crossed with different ideologies, and often with gossip and wit, too. Clearly, none of these disciplines should be taken as science in any categorical sense. Whatever discourses or writings they're made up of can only be essays, though they can be rigorous to a greater or lesser extent depending on the author's scruples, competence, working abilities, research talent, and above all honesty – not bending to any allegiance of school or clan.

M. – But you can't take liberties with history, you simply can't say such fanciful things as the Chinese do about the history of Tibet.

J.F. – No, you can't. There are some scientific principles that have been developed and asserted, or that have become clear as modern history has evolved. But there's no science of history as such. There are historians who show evidence of having scientific scruples, and others who show much less of it. I must say that among officially recognized, academic historians, I've often discovered distortions in what they've written, or even misinformation so tendentious that I could only qualify it as deliberate. I'm saying all this to make it absolutely clear to you how, in my opinion, Buddhists ought to approach the study of Western human and historical 'sciences'. There is in it all, nevertheless, a considerable mass of research and thought, as well as mistakes and aberrations, so inevitably it's the basis on which political thought is founded. Do Buddhists feel any curiosity about political thinking? Do they have any inclination for Western history?

M. – History means to observe, as rigorously as possible, the evolution of the human race. At the very most, it can describe events, identify tendencies, and analyze causes, but it doesn't set out principles by which to live. Most Tibetans, of course, aren't familiar with the details of Western history or sociology, but plenty of them have quite a clear idea of the basic orientations and priorities that distinguish cultures impregnated with spiritual values from those that neglect them. The Dalai Lama and the members of his government in exile, who think a lot about the future of the Tibetan people, are very interested in history and different political systems, both religious and secular, with their successes and failures. They're also well aware of what was wrong with Tibetan society before the Chinese invasion, and they're trying to work out what sort of system would be the most likely to ensure the proper functioning of society in the modern age while at the same time preserving Buddhism's basic values. Those values are far from being an obstacle to a democratic system. They would, in fact, increase its effectiveness, because they'd help people to understand that the law as a whole is underpinned by the principle of individuals' responsibilities toward society. They'd make a better balance between rights and duties possible.

~

SIXTEEN

BUDDHISM AND

PSYCHOANALYSIS

JEAN-FRANÇOIS – Let's move on to another Western discipline that Buddhism will certainly be confronted with – psychoanalysis. Psychoanalysis isn't really an exact science. It's more a direction in which to look. But it's played a huge role in the way human nature's been seen in the West over the last hundred years. At one time there was even talk of a general invasion of psychoanalytic ideas. In terms of the problem we're considering here, the aspect of psychoanalysis that Buddhism needs to look at is Freud's central thesis – that however hard human beings try to be inwardly lucid, however humble they might be, however much they wish to be sincere, get to know themselves, and change themselves, there's something that stays beyond the reach of introspection, and that's what Freud called the unconscious. In brief, there exist psychic formations, impulses, and repressed memories that maintain some activity and influence on the psyche, and therefore on our behavior, without our being conscious of them or having any access to them. The only technique that can allow us to discover them, and perhaps to dispel and gain mastery over them, is psychoanalysis. According to Freud, any claim that we can cross the barrier of repression that's buried these psychic forces away in our unconscious and access them using our ordinary intelligence alone is bound to be an illusion. We simply can't reach them just by looking inside ourselves or by any sort of spiritual exercise. For once, this isn't purely a matter of theory, because the experience of therapy has shown that the unconscious, inaccessible to classical introspection, actually exists.

MATTHIEU – It seems to me rather premature to claim that the barrier of repression can't be penetrated. That's just like William James's statement that the flow of mental associations can't be stopped because he'd tried it himself and couldn't do it. Conclusions of that sort only indicate that the person concerned has had no prolonged firsthand experience of introspection, of contemplating the nature of the mind directly. How did Freud try to go beyond that 'barrier of repression'? By using his brilliant intelligence to reflect on it and by using new techniques with which to approach it, certainly. But did he spend months and years concentrating solely on contemplative observation of the mind, like Buddhist retreatants do? How can psychoanalysts help others to realize the ultimate nature of the mind without having realized it themselves? In fact, Buddhism emphasizes how important it is to dissolve roughly what psychoanalysis calls the unconscious. The equivalent in Buddhism is called the 'habitual tendencies' or the 'layers of the mental state'. They're not present as the manifest content of consciousness, but they're what predispose us to behave in this or that particular way. You could say that Buddhism emphasizes the importance of these tendencies all the more because it sees them as going back not only to early childhood but to innumerable former lives. They're compared to layers of sediment that are gradually laid down on the riverbed of consciousness, known as the 'base consciousness'. In fact, eight different components of consciousness are distinguished, but I'd better not go into too much detail.

J.F. – Why not? It could be interesting.

M. – The 'indeterminate base consciousness' is the most basic component of the mind, the simple fact of being conscious and having an overall, indistinct perception of the existence of the universe. Then come five aspects of consciousness related to vision, hearing, taste, smell, and touch. Next is the aspect of consciousness related to thoughts or mental associations, and finally one related to the positive or negative emotions that arise from those thoughts. The first, the 'base consciousness', is the medium and carrier of habitual tendencies. When you try to purify the stream of consciousness by examining the nature of the mind, using introspection and spiritual practice – which Freud said were unable to reach the unconscious – it includes the dissolution of those tendencies. They are, in fact, harder to get rid of than the gross emotions, because they've been accumulating over a considerable time. It's like a sheet of paper that's been left rolled up for a long time. When you try to flatten it out on the table, it stays flat as long as you hold it down, but rolls itself up again as soon as you let go.

J.F. – So Buddhism accepts the existence of unconscious tendencies and representations – if there can be such things as unconscious representations. There must be, actually, because we refer to memories that are potential at least, to representations that have been repressed. So this unconscious baggage goes back not just to infancy but also, as you said, to former lives? In that case, the work of anamnesis, or re-remembering, which Socrates, too, recommended to his disciples, would have to go back well before the first few years of life. That gives our psychoanalyst colleagues plenty of work to do, a new field for investigation ... I hope it brings them plenty of business!

M. – The shock of being born is accompanied by the obliteration of any previous memories, except in the case of those capable of controlling their stream of consciousness between death and rebirth during the *bardo* experience. In ordinary beings, an oblivion occurs which is comparable, though it's not of the same degree, to the adult's forgetting of the events of early childhood. It's interesting, by the way, that long before Freud, the *Bardo Thödrol*, the *Tibetan Book of the Dead*, said that beings about to reincarnate, according to whether they're going to become male or female, feel a strong attraction to the parent of the opposite sex and an aversion to the one of the same sex. But what's very different is the way in which Buddhism sees the nature of that unconscious, and the method it uses to purify it. In terms of methods, Buddhism doesn't agree with Freud that spiritual methods can't reach those past tendencies or act on them in any way. The very goal of the spiritual path is to dissolve those tendencies, because all thoughts of attachment and aversion arise from previous conditioning. Working on the mind consists of getting to the root of those tendencies, examining their nature and dissolving them. That process can be called purification, not so much in a moral sense as in a practical one, rather like the elimination of the pollutants and sediments preventing a river from being clear and transparent.

In the presence of people who've undergone psychoanalysis, in the little experience I've had, I've always had the impression that they'd probably got rid of the most dramatic components of their problem by tracing them back to early childhood, but that they hadn't been able to dissipate the most deep-seated root of what was inhibiting their inner freedom. After so many years of trying, they don't really seem to radiate serenity and fulfillment. They often remain vulnerable, tense, and anxious.

J.F. – Unfortunately, I don't think you're alone in having that impression. In fact, some recent schools of psychoanalysis have renounced the Freudian idea that anamnesis equals cure, or even that the unconscious as a whole can be seen and brought to a state of clarity.

M. – The reason why it's so difficult to see the habitual tendencies, the equivalent of the unconscious, is that they stay latent, like the images on a film that's been exposed but not yet developed. All the efforts of psychoanalysis go into trying to develop the film. But Buddhism finds it simpler to set fire to it with the fire of wisdom, allowing the ultimate nature of the mind – its emptiness – to be realized and at the same time those tendencies to be eliminated without any trace. So it works at a quite different level. It's not enough just to identify some of our past problems. To relive a few events of long ago is only a limited remedy which no doubt allows some blockages to be whittled away but doesn't eradicate their primary cause. It's no use to keep on stirring up the mud from the bottom of a lake if you want to purify the water.

J.F. – No – but all the same, it's a bit more subtle than that! What do we mean by a neurotic? In theory, psychoanalysis is designed for people with some sort of difficulty. Take, for example, someone who's always putting himself into situations where he fails, almost deliberately. He undertakes some project or other, he's about to succeed, and just when everything's going well he commits some fatal mistake – so enormous, especially in the case of a clever person, that in rational terms it's completely inexplicable. I've had friends, very famous ones in fact, who at several periods of their lives have got into catastrophic sequences of behavior and have incomprehensibly destroyed everything they've built up with much skill, intelligence, and dedication.

There's just no rational explanation, and subjecting such people to any reasoning process is absolutely no use. They keep on getting themselves into similar situations without having any awareness that they're repeating the same mistakes. They can't untie such fatal psychological tangles by introspecting on their own. They need the leverage that intervention, analysis, transference, and so on, provide.

Freud's hypothesis, in any case, has quite often been verified. We have complete reports of some of his own analyses, and those of other analysts, too. It often does turn out that in early childhood there was some particularly dramatic occasion when the person was in conflict with his mother, for instance. To punish her, so to speak, he destroyed something, or deliberately got bad marks at school because he wanted to take revenge for what he considered to be a withdrawal of his mother's love. That pattern of lacking something, buried in the unconscious, continues to determine his behavior as an adult. He pursues that revenge against his mother by breaking up what he's just achieved. But he doesn't know that he's doing it. By becoming aware of the original trauma, in theory, he's liberated from being enslaved to an unconscious past event. Now, that doesn't mean that he's going to become a completely harmonious person in every possible way, but in certain cases it can decondition him from a specific neurotic pattern.

M. – I don't mean that Buddhist meditation can replace psychotherapy in treating neurosis, or any other mental illness; nor was I implying that Buddhist practitioners would never need psychotherapy. Of course people with psychological disturbances may need some appropriate form of therapy to help them find the stability necessary to undertake contemplation in the first place. They shouldn't expect meditation alone to cure them of their problem. In fact, to undertake deep and sustained spiritual practice one needs a strong and stable mental state.

Where Buddhism's approach and that of psychoanalysis diverge is in the means used to attain liberation. Psychoanalysis is correct, and works within the framework of its own system, but that system is limited by the very goals it sets itself. Take the problem of libido, for example. If you try to repress all the energy of desire, it's bound to come out via some roundabout route and be expressed in an abnormal way. So psychoanalysis tries to redirect it toward its proper object and give it back its normal expression. But according to Buddhist contemplative science, you neither try to repress desire nor give it free rein in its ordinary state – you try to be completely liberated from it. To do that, you use a progressive series of methods, beginning by applying antidotes that remove some of desire's strength, then by recognizing desire's intrinsic emptiness, and finally by transmuting desire into wisdom. By the end of the process desire can no longer enslave the mind, and gives way to an inner bliss, unchanging and free of any attachment.

While Buddhism aims at our freeing ourselves from the stagnation of thoughts like a bird taking off from the fumes of the city toward the pure mountain air, psychoanalysis, or so it seems, brings about an exacerbation of thoughts and dreams – thoughts that are completely centered on ourselves, in fact. Patients try to reorganize their small world, and to control it as best they can. But they stay bogged down in it. Plunging down into the psychoanalytic unconscious is a bit like finding some sleeping snakes, waking them up, getting rid of the most dangerous, and then staying in the company of the rest.

J.F. – And all the more so since a Buddhist isn't allowed to kill them … But what does Buddhism say about dreams?

M. – There's a whole series of contemplative practices related to dreams. First of all, you have to train yourself to recognize that you're dreaming while you're still immersed in the dream, then to be able to transform the dream at will, and finally to create different forms of dream whenever you want. The culmination of such practices is the complete cessation of dreams. An exceptionally accomplished meditator, it's said, doesn't have any more dreams, except for occasional prophetic ones. Gampopa, the disciple of the great hermit Milarepa, for instance, dreamed one day that his body had no head, which symbolized the death of his dualistic thoughts – and that was the last dream he ever had. The whole process can take many years.

To put it in a nutshell, the problem with psychoanalysis is that it doesn't identify the basic causes of ignorance and inner enslavement. Conflict with one's father or mother, and other traumatic experiences, aren't primary causes, they're circumstantial ones. The primary cause is attachment to the ego, which gives rise to attraction and repulsion, infatuation with and the desire to protect oneself. All mental events, emotions and impulses are like the branches of a tree. If you cut them, they'll only grow again. But if you cut the tree at its very root by dissolving attachment to the ego, all the branches, leaves, and fruit will be felled in one. The identification of disturbing thoughts and of their destructive or inhibitory effects is therefore not enough to dissolve them, and doesn't bring about the person's profound, total liberation. Only the liberation of thoughts, attained by tracing them to their very source – looking directly at the very nature of the mind – can lead to the resolution of all mental problems.

All techniques of meditation on the nature of the mind are aimed at discovering that hatred, desire, jealousy, dissatisfaction, pride, and so on, don't have the strength we wrongly suppose them to have. If you look directly at them, first by analyzing them and then through sheer contemplation, if you look at thoughts in all their nakedness until you see their primary nature, you see that they have none of the solidity and power to restrain you that they seemed at first sight to possess. Such examination of the nature of thoughts has to be repeated over and over again. But if you practice with perseverance, the moment will come when the mind remains in its natural state. It requires a lot of practice. As time goes on, you get better and better at liberating thoughts.

At first, identifying thoughts at the moment they arise is like spotting someone you know in a crowd. As soon as a desirous or hostile thought arises, and before it sets off a whole chain reaction of other thoughts, you have to recognize it. You know that, despite the way it might appear, it actually has no solidity, no true existence. But you don't quite know how to liberate it. The second stage is like a snake untying a knot in its own body. To do so, it doesn't need any help from outside. Another image used is that of a knot in a horse's tail, which comes undone by itself.

J.F. – All just metaphors!

M. – During this second stage, you acquire some experience in the process of liberating thoughts and you have less need to resort to specific antidotes for each type of negative thought. Thoughts arise and disappear by themselves. Finally, as a third stage, you completely master the liberation of thoughts. They can no longer do you any harm. They're like a thief in an empty house – the thief has nothing to gain and the owner has nothing to lose. Thoughts come and go without ever enslaving you. At that point, you're free from the yoke of present thoughts and the tendencies from the past that trigger them. By the same token you're free from any suffering. The mind stays in a state of clear and wakeful awareness, in which thoughts no longer have any disturbing influence.

In fact, the only good thing about negativity is that it can be purified and dissolved. All those sediments down in the unconscious aren't made of rock. They're just ice – ice that can be melted in the sun of wisdom.

~

SEVENTEEN

CULTURAL INFLUENCES
AND SPIRITUAL TRADITION

JEAN-FRANÇOIS – Buddhism's position with regard to psychoanalysis, then, is quite clear. Now, what about the lessons Buddhism might draw from history and sociology, the sciences that explore the evolution and structure of societies? All religions and philosophies arise within a particular cultural context. They tend to consider as eternally true a certain number of beliefs that in reality are just customs taken for granted in that particular society. The greatest minds of ancient philosophy, for instance, thought slavery was completely fair and natural, and accepted the prejudice that women were inferior to men as a fundamental truth.

MATTHIEU – And that animals were even more inferior, as if their right to live wasn't the same as that of any other living creature.

J.F. – So don't you think that Buddhism might need to examine itself a bit and explore the possibility that the fact of having arisen in a particular geographical zone, and within certain social, family, and other structures, might mean that some of the things it takes as universal principles are no more than local customs?

M. – Well, if the mechanisms of happiness and suffering are local customs, they're local everywhere – or, in other words, universal! Who isn't concerned by those principles? Is there anyone who doesn't care what ignorance or wisdom can bring about? All beings want to be happy and not to suffer. So if beneficial and harmful actions are judged not by the way they seem but by the altruistic or selfish intention behind them and the happiness and suffering that they bring about, then a system of ethics derived from such principles shouldn't be one heavily influenced by the cultural, historical, or social context.

J.F. – Yes, but the trouble is that when one's being influenced by something specific to one's own social system, one's generally not aware of it. The characteristic of a prejudice is that you don't see it as being a prejudice. There are good and bad prejudices, too. From the philosopher's point of view, the main thing is not to take them for anything other than products of a particular age. When religions or philosophies with universalistic ambitions incorporate some element derived from the society in which they arose or evolved, they're not at all aware that it's something conditional, specific to that particular social or cultural context.

M. – In the Buddhist tradition, there's a constant attempt to get rid of contingent influences of that kind. For instance, the motivation behind an act of charity needs to be examined very carefully. Am I being generous out of respect for social conventions, or am I really expressing a spontaneous altruistic impulse? To be perfect, giving should be free of any expectation of something in return, any reward, any hope of praise or gratitude, and even any idea of gaining 'merit'. To be a true source not only of merit but also of wisdom, an act of giving has to be free of three concepts: belief in the true existence of the subject, the person who gives; of the object, the person receiving the gift; and of the action, the actual giving. Authentic giving is accomplished with a purity of intention devoid of all attachment. So it's essential not to be attached to the outer aspect of an action, and in particular to be free of social and cultural conditioning, because as the Tibetans say – and the very same phrase comes up in the West, too, in Fénelon – 'Chains of gold are no less chains than chains of iron.'

J.F. – But is that really possible? Isn't there a danger of having the illusion of being free of conditioning while still being its prisoner?

M. – Well, that's a very Buddhist way of putting it. Perhaps it's better to have the illusion of being free than the illusion of being a prisoner! But joking aside, while there certainly is that danger, it's nevertheless important to understand the difference between cultural conditioning and spiritual tradition. A spiritual tradition is based on profound, living experience, not on any customs, and always emphasizes the danger that exists in being more attached to the form than the underlying basis. There's a Tibetan proverb that says, 'Remember where you're climbing to, and don't just stick to the ladder.'

~

EIGHTEEN

PROGRESS AND NOVELTY

JEAN-FRANÇOIS – There's one more big difference between Buddhist and Western cultures, which lies in the way those who belong to them behave and think about themselves. The whole of Western civilization is oriented toward history. It believes in historical evolution and in the productivity of time, or in other words – to use the term so especially favored in the nineteenth century – in progress. It's often been said that such belief in progress is naive. Indeed, belief in progress is the conviction that history can only bring improvement to the human condition, thanks to technological invention, science, increasing moral refinement, and the spread of democracy. Pascal likened mankind to the same person living forever and constantly learning as the centuries go by.

It's now clearer to us that such a belief, not in progress as such but in any automatic upward trend, is contradicted by events, notably by the somewhat somber history of the twentieth century. But that hasn't stopped the quality on which the West sets the highest price of all being that of novelty. One of the highest forms of praise in the West is to say of something, 'It's a new idea.' In science, that goes without saying – it's a discovery, so it's new. In art, and in literature too, you have to innovate to even exist. The worst thing you can say about a book, a painting, or a piece of music is that it's old hat, outmoded, academic, it's already been done. In politics, too, you have to have new or renewed ideas. In such ways, Western society is firmly set in the context of time – in the use of time as a factor for the permanent transformation that's considered an indispensable condition for any improvement in the human condition. The very fact of striving for perfection is felt to be dependent on historical progress, on the capacity to create new situations and new values. Does this overall mentality that I've rather briefly sketched here seem to you to be compatible with Buddhism and the part it might play in the Western world?

MATTHIEU – It doesn't make much sense to think that because a truth is an ancient truth it's no longer worth bothering about. If you're always looking for novelty, you're often depriving yourself of the most essential truths. The antidote to suffering and to the belief in a self consists of going to the very source of your thoughts and recognizing the ultimate nature of the mind. How could such a truth ever grow old? What novelty could 'outmode' a teaching that lays bare the very workings of the mind? If we get tired of such truths and run after endless ephemeral new ideas, we're only getting further from our goal. Attraction to novelty has one good side, and that's the legitimate desire to discover fundamental truths, to explore the depths of the mind and the beauty of the world. But in absolute terms, the novelty that's always 'new' is the freshness of the present moment, of nowness, of clear awareness that's not reliving any past or imagining any future.

The negative side of the taste for novelty is the vain and frustrating quest for change at any price. Very often, fascination with things that are new and different is a reflection of inner impoverishment. Unable to find happiness within ourselves, we desperately look for it outside, in objects, in experiences, in ever stranger ways of thinking and acting. In short, we get further away from happiness by looking for it where it simply isn't to be found. The risk with that is that we may completely lose any trace of it. At the most ordinary level, the longing for novelty arises from an attraction to superfluity, which erodes the mind and disturbs its serenity. We multiply our needs instead of learning not to have any.

If the Buddha and many of those who've followed him really

attained ultimate wisdom, what could we hope for that would be better and 'newer' than that? The novelty of the caterpillar is the butterfly. Everyone's goal is to develop the potential for perfection within. To attain that goal, we need to take advantage of the experience of those who've already trodden that path. That experience is far more precious than the invention of any amount of new ideas.

J.F. – Yes, but there's nevertheless a whole antithesis there. In Western civilization, we can see basically two different tendencies. On the one hand, there are a certain number of thinkers trying to formulate a wisdom that could allow any individual person, at any point in time, to shape for themselves an acceptable way of life, often through detachment from the passions, jealousies, and arrogance, which our own sages also single out as something to be combated. On the other, there's at the same time a conviction that the way – not to absolute salvation but to what could be called relative salvation with regard to the past – lies in a continuous or intermittent process of overall improvement in the lot of mankind, and that such an improvement depends on a number of innovations in the field of science and technology, as well as in law, human rights, and political institutions. That's something we're taking part in all the time. We're living today in a sea of computers that track almost everything in our private lives and companies' collective lives, something no one would have imagined thirty years ago. So that's in terms of technology, the most visible side.

But in other fields, too, particularly in politics – the transformation of societies and the adjustment of the way they're organized to the needs of an ever larger number of individuals – people in the West think that it's a matter of goals and processes that depend on the unfolding of time. Take culture, for example. We feel that what makes an artist authentic is that he or she creates a new work of some kind. We'd laugh at the idea of copying works from the Middle Ages – there are machines that can do that now. But that's not all. For the last fifty years or so, especially in the developed countries, cultural policies aimed at getting a growing number of people to participate in the joys of literature, art, and music have been devised. That's something that in the past was reserved for a quite restricted élite. I remember what it was like to visit a museum or an exhibition when I was young. There was all the space you could want, you could get in whenever you wanted, and you were never bothered by the crowds when you wanted to look at the paintings. These days, there are so many people interested in some exhibitions that you sometimes have to queue for hours. In Paris and New York, it's even begun to seem quite normal to reserve a place at an exhibition, or make an appointment to get in – like going to the theater. So that idea on the one hand that culture is perpetual innovation, and on the other that it ought to be extended to an increasing number of people, is very characteristic of Western attitudes. Temporal matter is used to bring about progress, and growing numbers of people share that general improvement. In other words, salvation is within time and not outside it.

M. – Salvation within time is the Bodhisattva's vow, the vow to keep working for all beings until all of them are freed from suffering and ignorance. The Bodhisattva will never give up, and will never abandon the responsibility he feels for all beings, until each and every one has taken to the path of wisdom and achieved enlightenment. Moreover, Buddhism completely accepts that there are teachings specific to different ages in human history, from ancient societies down to modern ones with their more materialistic outlook. According to the place accorded by society to spiritual values, certain aspects of the teachings are more or less emphasized. But the very nature of enlightenment, of spiritual wisdom itself, is outside time. How could the nature of spiritual perfection ever be subject to change?

It seems to me that the notion of novelty, the desire to keep on inventing things through a fear of copying the past, is an exaggeration of the importance given to the 'personality', to the individuality that's supposed to express itself in an original way at any price. And from the perspective of someone trying to do just the opposite – to dissolve any attachment to the all-powerful self – such a race for originality seems at best superficial. For instance, the idea that the artist should always be trying to give free rein to his imagination is clearly foreign to traditional sacred art, which exists to provide material for meditation and reflection. Western art often tries to create an imaginary world, while sacred art helps to penetrate to the nature of reality. Ordinary art's aimed at arousing the passions, sacred art at stilling them. Sacred dance, painting, and music try to establish a link with spiritual wisdom in the world of forms and sounds. They're arts whose goal is to link us through their symbolism with spiritual knowledge and practice. The traditional artist puts all his skill into the quality of his art, but he'll never just give his imagination free rein to invent completely new symbols or forms.

J.F. – That's clearly a completely different way of seeing art from the Western one, at least since the Renaissance.

M. – Traditional though such art may be, it's nonetheless not just fixed in the past. Spiritual masters are constantly enriching it with new elements derived from their experience in meditation. There are magnificent expressions of sacred art in Tibet. Artists put all their heart and talent into what they do, but their personality vanishes completely behind their work. For that reason, Tibetan painting is essentially anonymous. Art also serves as a medium of exchange between the monastic and lay communities. Several times a year in the monastery courtyard, the monks perform extraordinarily beautiful dances that correspond to the different stages of inner meditation. The local population never misses festivals of that kind. Similarly, art's to be found in every household in Tibet, because families commission icons, *mandalas*, and statues from the painters and sculptors. The people aren't cut off from art, but an artist who indulged in his own fancies wouldn't be much appreciated. When, in the West, artists paint an entire canvas blue, and because of their 'personality' their paintings are given enormous value and hung in museums, I think that the only problem is that nobody cries out, 'The king has no clothes!'

I read recently in a magazine that the Museum of Contemporary Art in Marseilles had exhibited an artist's work that consisted of thirty or so stolen articles, each labeled as such. In the end, the 'artist' was arrested and the museum was charged with receiving stolen goods. Several times, I've visited museums and galleries with Tibetans. They greatly admired classical paintings that showed great mastery, usually acquired through many years of effort. On the other hand, some very facile forms of art – an exhibit of squashed objects, or one of everyday objects set out or packaged in some unusual way – made them think of the difference between the great Tibetan spiritual masters, who taught in the light of the experience they'd acquired over years of reflection and meditation, and those who teach the spiritual path nowadays, without much authentic experience, whose talks are more just chats than the expression of any true knowledge.

Not to run after novelty, however, doesn't stop us being flexible and ready to face all sorts of new situations. In fact, someone who keeps the most essential truths in mind is better prepared than anyone else to adapt to whatever changes the world and society might undergo. The most important thing of all is to recognize those truths, to deepen and actualize them within oneself, and to 'realize' them. If one neglects that, what's the use of inventing something new at any price? So to summarize, I'd say that unlike running after novelty, the spiritual life makes it possible to rediscover simplicity, something for which we've rather lost the taste. To simplify our lives by no longer torturing ourselves in order to obtain things we don't really need, and to simp-lify our minds by no longer always turning over the past and imagining the future.

J.F. – I don't think you need to be a Buddhist to make observations like that. Lots of people in the West, too, including some who follow the arts very closely and are aware of all the latest developments, know that one whole side of Western art is about duping the public and daz-zling the naive. Fortunately, that's not the only side, and true invention and creativity do actually predominate.

M. – But what's often meant by creativity is the spontaneous expression of intimate feelings, which just goes round in circles within the arena of conditioning and habitual tendencies. It doesn't free us from ignorance, from desire, or from hostility. It doesn't make us bet-ter human beings, wiser or more compassionate. True creativity con-sists of gradually shedding the veiling layers of our ignorance and ego-centeredness so as to uncover the ultimate nature of both mind and phenomena. That's really the discovery of something new.

J.F. – But part of the reason why I wanted to point out the West's deeply ingrained preoccupation with novelty is that there are some areas of life that ought to be immune to the appetite for change, but seem to have succumbed to it nonetheless. For example, religions – which, in principle, are linked to dogma. A revealed religion is linked to a specific dogma, and one might suppose that the adepts of such a reli-gion practice it because it brings them something unchanging and is an expression of eternity, transcendent or divine eternity. Consequently, you'd think that this aspect of the history of human consciousness ought to be shielded from the imperatives of change and innovation that characterize activities belonging to the worldly, temporal context. But that doesn't seem to be the case. Take Catholicism, which is some-thing I can talk about dispassionately, not being a believer myself. The

Catholic Church is always being subjected to attacks from modernists who accuse it of not renewing itself enough, and demand innovative theologians so that the Church can adapt to the modern age. But one can only wonder, in that case, what the use of having a religion might be. If religion isn't the very dimension of human consciousness that shields that consciousness from the vicissitudes of temporal evolution and the need for innovation, what on earth could it be for?

Our appetite for novelty is such that even God himself gets asked to keep on renewing himself. By those who believe in him, at any rate. There are endless conflicts between the Holy See, guardian of theological orthodoxy, and the avant-garde theologians, who put forward theological innovations in just the same way as in other fields people put forward innovations in painting, music, or haute-couture. Even the idea of an avant-garde theologian is rather comic. In what respect can eternity be avant-garde or old hat? And the Vatican finds itself faced with a new dilemma. If it accepts these new theologies, it's obliged to accept modifications to some of its dogma's basic principles. But if it doesn't accept them, it gets accused of being out of date, reactionary, backward, and attached to outmoded forms of the divine. Do you think the influence of Buddhism in the West is going to subscribe to that insatiable appetite for change, or is it just the opposite, that Buddhism might provide a refuge for people who are fed up with the whole tyranny of novelty?

M. – Well, I hope it'll be the latter, of course. The principles can't change, as they correspond to the true nature of things. If you try to see where that thirst for novelty comes from, it seems to arise from neglect of the inner life. We stop going back to the source of things, and the idea occurs to us that by trying all sorts of new things we might be able to compensate for that feeling of lacking something.

J.F. – All the same, I'd also say that one of the worst threats to the human spirit has always been getting entrenched in routine. If we didn't aspire to look closely at all the notions handed down by our predecessors, not to be satisfied with ready-made ideas, not to take things at face value but to rethink them for ourselves, and to decide what to keep and what to reject in the light of our own reason and experience, then human thought would just be a huge, lazy slumber.

M. – I agree completely, and indeed that's central to the spiritual search, which wouldn't work at all if you didn't question everything.

It's a constant attempt to break out of and blow apart all the tight, encrusting layers of illusion. Spiritual practice is based on experiential exploration and discovery that has to be pushed just as far into the inner world as science pushes its explorations into the outer world. That experience is always fresh, and it's ceaselessly renewed. It also brings along with it no shortage of obstacles and happenings of all sorts. It's not at all a matter of using ready-made formulae but of experiencing the teachings in the present moment, knowing how to use life's good and bad circumstances, dealing with all the thoughts of all kinds that arise in the mind, and understanding for oneself the chain reactions they cause and how to set oneself free from that process. True innovation is to know how to use every instant in life for the goals one's set oneself.

J.F. – Personally, I'm inclined to accept one aspect of what you've been saying. Indeed, from another angle, how could anyone deny it? Certainly, some of the problems that beset mankind in terms of our lives, our history, and our environment are probably to be solved through what I'd call temporal creation. However, it's also true that especially since the eighteenth century the West has relied far too much for solutions to all mankind's problems on historical progress and the ability to innovate. The West has come up with the idea that all human problems – questions of personal happiness, personal development, wisdom, the ability to bear suffering or to be rid of it – could be solved through historical dialectic, as Hegel and Marx said. All the problems related to inner experience and personal accomplishment were therefore ideological fantasies, illusory remains of the belief that happiness and equilibrium could be attained on an individual level. That desertion of personal wisdom in favor of collective transformation reached fever pitch with Marxism. But while nothing can be created without time, time creates nothing on its own. For the last two centuries the West has been expecting mankind's salvation from solutions that are both historical and collectivist. It's an intransigent and dogmatic attitude, that overconfidence in collective, political solutions to be brought about simply by the unfolding of history – which is probably why the domination of that system of thought has created the dissatisfaction felt everywhere nowadays. To whatever extent Buddhism is spreading in the West, it's probably largely due to that lack, the vacuum left by the absence of personal wisdom and morality.

M. – For relationships with others not to be mainly motivated by selfishness, which only creates friction and disagreement, each person has to give meaning to their life and attain a degree of inner development. Every instant of the process of spiritual transformation has to be accompanied by the idea that the qualities one's trying to develop will help meet others' needs better.

J.F. – If Buddhism is to achieve a lasting success in the West, it'll be due to two factors. Firstly, Buddhism isn't a religion that requires an act of blind faith. It doesn't require people to rule out or condemn other doctrines. It's a system of wisdom, a philosophy marked by tolerance. This first condition is already satisfied. Secondly, and here the condition isn't yet completely satisfied, Buddhism will have to be compatible with the gigantic investment made by the West over almost two thousand five hundred years in scientific knowledge and in political thought and action. In other words, in the improvement of human life, here in the phenomenal world, through the improvement of societies and relationships within societies. I think that if Buddhism doesn't prove to be compatible with this second condition it's not going to have a lasting influence in the West. Our anchorage in what I'd call scientific, sociopolitical, and historical thought is far too strong to disappear.

M. – Once again, in principle Buddhism isn't likely to go against scientific knowledge, because it aims to recognize truth on all levels, outer as well as inner. It simply establishes a hierarchy in terms of priorities. Material development without spiritual development can only lead to the general feeling of discontent that we see today. In a society based on the education and development of wisdom rather than of information, the whole orientation is very different. Although it's an oversimplification, you could say that one is centered on being, the other on having. The fascination for always having more and the horizontal dispersion of knowledge are both things that take us away from inner transformation. Since the world can only be changed by changing ourselves, always having more of everything doesn't matter very much. A Buddhist thinks that 'those who know how to be content with what they already have are holding a treasure in their hands'. Dissatisfaction arises from the habit of seeing what's superfluous as being necessary. This isn't just a question of wealth, but also of comfort, of pleasure, and of 'useless knowledge'. The only thing one should never be satisfied with is one's wisdom, and the only efforts that one should never see as sufficient are the efforts one makes toward spiritual progress and achieving others' good.

J.F. – I'd like to conclude by quoting Cioran, a writer I greatly appreciate because he demonstrates very well to what point Buddhism so often crops up as a reference point in the works of Western writers. The quote comes from one passage of a preface he wrote for an anthology of character portraits in French literature. In his preface, he's called on to say something about the French moralists La Rochefoucauld, de Chamfort, and others, and of course about writers who use literary portraits of famous people to depict the shortcomings of human nature. Cioran, setting Pascal apart from and above the moralists, expresses the difference very accurately: 'The moralists and the portraitists depict our miseries, while Pascal depicts our misery.' Immediately afterward – and this is what's so striking – he's led to refer to Buddhism. Here are the few lines he puts into the middle of this text on classical French literature: 'When Mara, the God of Death, tries both by tempting and by threatening the Buddha to take the Empire of the World away from him, the latter, to confound Mara and divert him from his claims, asks him, among other things: have you suffered for wisdom?' This question, Cioran goes on, 'which Mara could not answer, is one that should always be used whenever the exact value of a mind needs to be assessed.' What's your comment on that quotation?

M. – Mara is the personification of the ego, since the 'devil' is nothing more than the belief that there's a 'me' that's a truly existing entity. As the Buddha sat under the *bodhi* tree at nightfall, on the point of attaining the perfect wisdom of enlightenment, he vowed not to get up until he had torn through all the veils of ignorance. Mara, the ego, tried first of all to sow doubt in his mind by asking him, 'By what right do you claim to attain enlightenment?' To which the Buddha replied, 'My right is based on the wisdom that I have acquired during numerous lives. I take the earth as my witness.' And at that moment, it's said, the earth shook. Then Mara tried to tempt the future Buddha by sending his beautiful daughters – symbolizing desire – to try to distract him from his final meditation. But the Buddha was perfectly free of any desire, and Mara's daughters turned into old women covered with wrinkles. Mara then tried to arouse hatred in the Buddha's mind. He made formidable phantom armies appear, hurling flaming arrows and shouting volleys of terrible insults. It's said that if the slightest thought of hatred had arisen in the Buddha's mind he would have been pierced by those weapons; the ego would have triumphed over wisdom. But the Buddha was only love and compassion itself, and the rain of weapons turned into a rain of flowers, the insults into songs of praise. At dawn, as the last shreds of ignorance faded away, the Buddha perfectly realized the absence of any true existence, whether of the person or of phenomena. He understood how the phenomenal world is manifested by the play of interdependence, and that nothing exists in an intrinsic and permanent fashion at all.

J.F. – What strikes me most in that quotation of Cioran's is that it reminds the West that wisdom is suffering, or at any rate can only be acquired through suffering. And that it's by its acceptance of that fact that the value of a mind can be measured. To me, it's a healthy reminder for Westerners who, more and more, imagine that it's possible to get rid of suffering right from the start so that everything happens happily ever after through dialogue, communication, and consensus, and in particular that education itself and the very fact of learning can take place without either effort or suffering.

M. – That's very much how the spiritual path is described. The pleasures of the world are very attractive at first glance. They invite us to enjoy them, and seem to be sweetness itself. It's very easy to get into them. They begin by bringing some ephemeral and superficial satisfaction, but you gradually perceive that they're not going to fulfill their promise, and it all ends up in bitter disillusionment. The spiritual search is completely the other way round. At the beginning, it's an austere business. You have to work hard on yourself, and confront what Cioran calls the 'suffering of wisdom', or the 'rigors of asceticism'. But the more you persevere in this process of inner transformation, the more you find that wisdom, serenity, and joy break through to you and impregnate your whole being – and that, unlike the pleasures of the world, they're completely independent of any outer circumstances. They can be experienced anywhere, at any time, and increase the more you use them. According to one saying, 'In spiritual practice the difficulties come at the beginning, and in worldly affairs they come at the end.' And another says, 'At first nothing comes, in the middle nothing stays, and in the end nothing leaves.' In fact, I'd add that the diligence required to acquire wisdom isn't, strictly speaking, 'suffering'. It's often defined as 'joy cast in the shape of effort'.

~

NINETEEN

THE MONK'S QUESTIONS

TO THE PHILOSOPHER

MATTHIEU – There's one objection you've raised several times. If Buddhism is aimed at unmasking the 'imposture' of the self, and if that self has no true existence, what's the point, you argue, of doing anything at all? And who, in that case, would be responsible for any action?

In actual fact, even though the notion of a 'person' doesn't refer to any real entity, every action inevitably gives rise to a result. Doesn't modern physics, too, reduce us to a collection of elementary particles, the famous 'quarks'? So now it's my turn to ask you a question. Since we're made of particles that as far as we know don't contain the slightest trace of our individuality, what's the point, in your opinion, of doing anything? What's the point of thinking, loving, worrying about happiness and suffering? After all, it's not the quarks that are suffering, is it?

JEAN-FRANÇOIS – Ah, yes, that's a very old piece of reasoning, even in some Western philosophical theories. If you look at a system like structuralism, it's rather the same sort of thing. Structuralism was a reaction, too – against existentialism, which had focused everything on freedom and personal choice and on the individual's ultimate responsibility. The structuralists said, no, man in himself doesn't exist, he's criss-crossed by structures that act through him.

M. – What do they call structures?

J.F. – Well, as they're philosophers, they don't actually define them very well! You could say, roughly, that they're entities of some kind that constitute or consist of laws and that generate organized behavior. The same sort of objection is found in Epicurus. We're composed of atoms, he said, and what we call the soul is just a collection of atoms. Consequently, we shouldn't have to take seriously any feelings we experience, any of our sufferings, desires, and fears. The argument that sets phenomena against the background of another, underlying world, which in fact is the only real one, is an old objection. The answer's always the same: none of that alters the fact that people experience certain perceptions and feelings that for them are their only concrete reality.

M. – That's exactly what Buddhism says. Even if suffering is an illusion, it's perceived as suffering, and it's therefore legitimate and desirable to dispel it. I don't understand the criticism leveled against Buddhism that argues: if this 'self', which we normally take as a constant of our existence, an entity that survives throughout all the changes in life, is really an illusion, how come we're so preoccupied with happiness…

J.F. – Then I'll explain it to you. Imagine that a rock falls on your house, destroying it and killing part of your family. You call out the emergency services, doctors, and an ambulance, but instead they send along a geologist who says, 'Listen, what happened is perfectly normal. You know, the earth is always evolving, and there are always shifts in the landscape, tectonic plates crashing into each other. There's nothing wrong.' In fact, what he says is true on a scale of several million years, which is the minimum time interval a respectable geologist can consider. But the two sides aren't talking about the same phenomenon at all. On the one hand, the impassive geologist is right. On the other, that doesn't alter the fact that you, the poor fellow whose house and family have just been destroyed, are living out a tragedy in terms of personal feelings. Neither of those two approaches can supplant the other. People get swept away by typhoons, and the fact that typhoons can be explained meteorologically by the patterns of wind in the upper atmosphere or whatever doesn't diminish the dangers and misfortunes of living in parts of the world susceptible to them. There are two realities there, and the one doesn't refute the other. Those two levels of experience should be kept side by side, because they're both real.

M. – So in fact, you agree – when Buddhism says that the self is just a puppet entity, devoid of true existence, there's no reason to interpret that statement as proof of Buddhism's indifference with regard to action, with regard to the happiness and suffering of our own selves and of others?

J.F. – The idea common to all systems of wisdom like Buddhism could more or less be summarized like this. The influence that I can have on the course of things is an illusion; it brings me enormous hopes and disappointments, and makes me live in constantly alternating joy and fear which torture me internally. If I can reach the conviction that the self is nothing, and that in fact I'm only the channel of a certain stream of reality, I'll attain a degree of serenity. Lots of systems of wisdom try to do that. It's the aim of all the reasoning of the Stoics and Spinoza. Alas, however, our actual experience rebels against such reasoning.

M. – That rebellion is the very thing that causes our torments. We're so attached to that self that we're incapable of realizing how, if we could just dispel the illusion of its existence, we'd solve all our problems. We're like someone with a wound who's afraid of having the stitches removed from the scar. The Stoics, it seems, managed a sort of passive resignation, but for Buddhists it's the absence of any self that's such a liberating experience.

J.F. – No, that's wrong. To be a Stoic consists of actively wanting what nature has decided to bring about. That's not passive. Stoics don't submit to what happens with some sort of fatalism, they identify themselves with the prime cause of the world, which is God at the same time. Spinoza takes up that aspect of it. 'God or nature', as he says. He's a pantheist. The way to attain wisdom is to stop being the passive plaything of cosmic necessity, and to espouse it actively within one's own subjective will.

M. – So, roughly speaking, that makes it more like the Hindu understanding of *karma*; the ideal way to live one's life and to view the world is to wholly accept the destiny allotted to us, without rebelling against it. But a Buddhist would take a different position. He accepts the present, because what happens is the result of past actions. But the future depends on him. He's always at a crossroads. To see that the self doesn't truly exist doesn't just make us go along stoically with whatever happens to us, it lets us act with enormous freedom, divested of all the constraints imposed by this 'me' that's so fond of itself and thinks it's permanent, substantial, and so on, producing endless chains of attraction and repulsion. To free ourselves of ego-centeredness gives us a much greater liberty to act. The past has already been played out, but not the future.

J.F. – I can understand how useful it is for the person who's acting to have the wisdom that enables him to stand back from his subjective particularities, his own passions, and thus from his own self, and to consider something wider than the self, whose reality he relativizes as much as possible. It guarantees that whatever he does will have a much greater mastery, will be more universal, will have more meaning for others, and that he'll be better able to understand the world and act on himself. I think, nonetheless, that all attempts to annihilate the self so as to anaesthetize forever the feeling of confronting adverse, irksome circumstances, the feeling that there are moral choices to be made, mistakes to avoid, that human action isn't always clear-sighted, lucid, and effective – in short, all the efforts human thought has gone to in order to calm us and get rid of that uncertain but responsible side of things – have always failed.

M. – The West seems to find it very difficult to understand how recognizing that the self has no true existence doesn't stand in the way of determination, strength of mind and action in the slightest. Instead, it opens our eyes wide to the causes of happiness and suffering. It's a recognition that makes action very precise. Belief in a self isn't what gives force to judgment, it's what blocks it. If our actions aren't always clear-sighted, courageous, lucid, and effective, as you say, it's because we're the plaything of our attachment to the self. It's said, 'The viewpoint of the sage is higher than the sky, and his discernment in terms of the laws of cause and effect is finer than flour.' You can't rebel against what you've sown yourself, but you can build the future by knowing how to distinguish between what leads to misery and what liberates you from it. That's very different from fatalistically espousing an inevitable future.

J.F. – There, I agree with you completely, in the sense that what the Stoics, and Spinoza too, wanted to do to make us more peaceful was to demonstrate that nothing could have happened other than what actually happens.

M. – We've spoken a lot of Buddhism as a way of giving meaning to life. But what is it that gives meaning to life for you, and for the trend of thinking that you represent?

J.F. – First of all, I don't represent any trend of thinking. I do my best to understand the systems that exist or have existed in the past, and that's already hard enough. But in trying to answer you, I'd like to fill in the background, as it were, of the diverse directions that Western thought has taken. Since the birth of Greek civilization – which is taken as the starting point of Western culture – there have been three main types of answer to the question of the meaning of life. The first is the religious answer, especially since the great monotheistic religions, Judaism, Christianity, and Islam have been predominant. This answer places the finality of existence in the beyond, or in a truth whose nature is transcendent, and therefore in all the steps to be taken and laws to be respected to ensure the personal salvation of the immortal soul. Each person will experience eternal life in the beyond depending on his or her merits in this life here below. Broadly speaking, this is the basis on which the West – with the help of religions which all, as it happens, came from the Middle East – has built its search for the meaning of life for the last several thousand years. It hasn't prevented each individual from seeking happiness in this world here below through the whole variety of actions that belonging to earthly reality, from the farmer trying to achieve a good harvest up to the king trying to bump off anyone who offends or challenges him, or the businessman trying to make money. You could say that apart from religious people in a strict sense – monks, or mystics, whose everyday life coincided with the ideal of salvation – all the rest sought happiness in a more or less empirical way, not excluding what religion calls sin, but nevertheless still seeking eternal happiness in the hereafter. The two goals were compatible, since the search for eternal happiness implied the notion of pardon, confession, absolution, and redemption for all the sins committed down below.

M. – Don't you think it's possible for spiritual values to impregnate the whole of daily life in such a way that there are really no 'ordinary' acts any more?

J.F. – In theory, that's what Christianity wanted to do. But man's capacity to act in a way that's completely the opposite of his ideals seems to be unlimited.

M. – But, surely, a religion that's lived out properly doesn't only make you live in the hope of an afterlife but also gives a meaning to everything you do now, in this life.

J.F. – In theory, yes. Christianity was first of all a set of precepts teaching people how to lead this life. It's according to how you conduct yourself in this life that you win your eternal salvation.

M. – But isn't there, as well as those precepts, some metaphysical view of existence that brings some inspiration and doesn't just operate in the field of people's behavior?

J.F. – Hold on! I'm still talking about what happened in the West. I'm not saying that according to the religious view of the meaning of life you could do whatever you liked in this life and nevertheless deserve eternal salvation – although most of the time this was actually the case. Spectacularly, the way Europeans lived for two thousand years was completely contrary to Christian morality. They murdered one another, reduced each other to slavery, stole, committed adultery, and gave themselves up to all the deadly sins, while still being nourished by the hope of getting to Heaven all the same, because they were offered expiation and redemption as long as they died confessed and with the last sacraments administered. Now, of course I'm not saying that all this was what they were being recommended to do. The clergy, those who directed people's conscience, the confessors, all spent their time reminding the faithful what sin was and what it meant to live solely according to the laws of the Lord. What I'm trying to point out is that the mere fact that they subscribed to a basically religious search for the meaning of life didn't prevent people, on an ordinary level, from seeking ordinary forms of happiness, most of which were anyway completely compatible with Christian morality. Establishing a household, having a family, rejoicing at a good harvest, prospering by legitimate means – none of these were forbidden. Plenty of other actions were perpetrated in clear violation of the Christian precepts. Nevertheless, as the Christian religion was one of sin, repentance, and absolution, it worked according to that dialectic.

M. – That being the case, it's perhaps worth looking at the varying abilities shown by the major religions and spiritual traditions to inspire conformity between theory and practice. No one would deny that human beings have the greatest difficulty in transforming themselves, and in actualizing their innate perfection. So a spiritual tradition could be assessed not only on the soundness of its metaphysical views but also on how effective its methods of inner transformation turn out to be in practice.

J.F. – It's true, a minimum of conformity between words and actions wouldn't do any harm!

Now, the second main way of giving meaning to life is what I'd call the philosophical way, in the sense used in ancient times. It's the search for wisdom and inner peace as the fruits of a point of view we've often discussed in these conversations, and which consists of freeing oneself from passions and superficial ambitions so as to reserve all one's energy for higher goals, whether intellectual, spiritual, aesthetic, philosophical, or ethical, and thus to make one's relationships with others and the functioning of the community as human as possible. It's the view of things we find in most of the great thinkers of the ancient world. Sometimes, as in Plato, with a more religious and metaphysical emphasis; and at other times, like in the Epicureans and Stoics, tending more toward a perpetual serenity and inner balance of the human faculties, by keeping one's distance from all the passions of the community, politics, love, and the whole diversity of other appetites. This is the wisdom to be found, for instance, in Seneca's *Letters to Lucilius* and, in its modern version in Montaigne, for example, when he gives us precepts by which to achieve a sort of inner freedom and detachment. It's not an approach that completely stops you enjoying the pleasures of life, particularly mental pleasures. This second, philosophical way was dropped, more or less everywhere, from the seventeenth and eighteenth centuries onward. Philosophy since then, through the dialogue it's had with modern science – which had just been born in the seventeenth century – has been more and more oriented toward pure knowledge and the interpretation of history, abandoning the management of human life and the search for its meaning.

M. – You mean, it's been more oriented toward 'factual' knowledge.

J.F. – Yes. Thanks to the emergence of science, the conviction that something exists that we can call objective became more widely accessible. This was knowledge open to everyone, not only the sage.

M. – Spiritual knowledge is open to everyone willing to take the trouble to explore it. That's how you *become* a sage. Otherwise, 'objective' knowledge, immediately accessible to anyone without them putting any effort into it themselves, can only be knowledge's lowest common denominator. You could call it a quantitative approach rather than a qualitative one.

J.F. – Let's say, rather, that in the West there's been a move from a culture of belief to one of proof.

M. – The fruits of spiritual practice – serenity, awareness, clear-mindedness – and its outer manifestations – goodness, nonattachment, patience – are actually more a matter of proof than of belief, too. It's said that altruism and self-mastery are the signs of knowledge, and that to be free of the negative emotions is the sign of meditation. These qualities end up taking root in our being and being spontaneously expressed in our actions.

J.F. – Historically, from the eighteenth century onward, belief in science replaced belief in wisdom. That was a first step, the philosophy of the Enlightenment. The 'light' of the Enlightenment was the light of reason, making it possible to understand how reality works, and dispelling all illusions, passions, absurd beliefs, and superstitions. From then on, personal achievement of inner wisdom had to happen by way of objective knowledge. To use the terms current at the time, it's the 'torch of reason' that sheds light on the problem of human happiness.

M. – Buddhism speaks of the 'torch of knowledge'. Without wisdom, reason will just argue about human happiness without ever actually bringing it about.

J.F. – If you like, the new idea that first appeared in the eighteenth century, and continued to be current throughout the nineteenth, was that progress – a vague term including ethical advances as well as scientific progress – flows from reason, which can explain the hidden moving forces behind the universe and the way people function. Reason and progress together are what will bring us happiness. In a certain sense, that's not untrue. Science has brought about considerable improvements in human life. It's important not to forget that even in 1830 the expectation of life in France was twenty-five years. Hardly any disease could be cured. It was rare that anyone had any teeth left by the age of thirty – if they lived that long. The discovery in England in the eighteenth century of vaccination against smallpox, a disease that claimed many lives, created an enormous impression. Voltaire speaks of it at length. Finally, things were really starting to change. You'd no doubt tell me it was just quantitative. And yet, those improvements, practical and material though they were, meant a great deal to the great mass of people. The message was that we were beginning a new age, and that the world wasn't as the ancients had thought, a perpetual repetition of the same thing. It could change, and it would be the progress brought by science and the elucidation of the laws of nature that would make possible a complete transformation in how man lived.

M. – So that approach is aimed more at changing the conditions of life than at giving it meaning. But why should one side be developed to the detriment of the other?

J.F. – Thanks to those changes in living conditions, each human being has much more chance of gaining access to personal wisdom. It's all very well to preach philosophical wisdom to hordes of illiterate peasants who die of cold in winter and fall like flies in the slightest epidemic. But if they're going to benefit from Seneca's teaching, the first thing they'd need would be to survive to an age at which they could apply it. The idea of seeing material benefits due to scientific progress as being in opposition to the sublime spiritual accomplishments that an individual can attain is, to my mind, reactionary. It's a completely false antithesis. When people in the eighteenth century spoke of progress thanks to reason, they certainly weren't thinking that science alone was going to solve all the problems of their personal happiness. They were thinking that it would give them more chance of having the right conditions in which to attain some degree of serenity, even if that just meant a little bit more time. Stoic wisdom, which was only accessible to the emperor Marcus Aurelius and a few courtiers or parasite philosophers living in his court, was all very well, but it was extremely élitist.

M. – Let's go back to your point about the freezing peasants. It makes me think of the nomad clans in Tibet, who are exposed to an extremely cold climate and live in great material simplicity. Now, those same nomads have a view of life that gives them a *joie de vivre* absolutely not restricted to any élite. Even nowadays, those freezing peasants have access to a wisdom touching everything in their daily life. I myself have spent months at a time in remote valleys in Bhutan and Tibet, without roads or electricity, where there's nothing to show that you're in the twentieth century. But the quality of human relationships in such places is in the greatest contrast to the big cities in the West. At the opposite extreme, when excessive material development leads to the manufacture of things that are completely unnecessary, everyone gets caught up in the system of superfluity. Without spiritual values, material progress can only lead to catastrophe. It's not a matter of advocating some utopian going back to nature – or to what's left of it – but of understanding that while our 'standard of living' has considerably improved, in the materialistic sense that's now understood by the term, the actual quality of life has considerably deteriorated. Tibetan nomads and Bhutanese farmers might not earn as much as American businessmen, but their lives have a dimension quite beyond any accountant's spreadsheet.

J.F. – That criticism of the consumer society, as people called it in the sixties, has been much talked about within present-day Western culture. But it's a debate that implies some previous success. Once again, the philosophers of the eighteenth century didn't say that science would solve the problems of human destiny or the meaning of life. Indeed, they too, especially Rousseau, advocated a return to primordial nature and more faithfulness to it. But their view of things was accompanied by a belief in the effectiveness of education, in the ability to learn about the whole range of options between different ways of life, different doctrines, different religions, and to choose freely among them. Whence came the idea of tolerance, which arose, or at least developed to its full extent, at that period. When you talk about Tibetan farmers who experience happiness thanks to Buddhism, it's not as if anyone's ever offered them anything else. They can't go down to the library to read about things and decide one day to convert to being a Presbyterian, or to follow Heidegger's philosophy. Like Christianity for a European peasant in the Middle Ages, their hand's rather forced. A Tibetan Buddhist nomad may well be very happy, and I'm very glad for him, but you can't say we're dealing with people who've freely chosen a particular system of wisdom. They've taken what their society offered them. If that makes them happy, all the better, but it's not at all the same situation.

M. – I'm not really so convinced that you have to try out everything before you can understand something's value. Take the example of pure, fresh, thirst-quenching water. Someone drinking it can appreciate how good it is without having to taste all the other different sources of water to be found in the locality. It's just the same with the joys of spiritual practice and its values – those who've tasted them don't need any other confirmation than their own personal experience. The happiness that flows from them has a strength and inner coherence that can't be a lie. I'd like to quote here a few verses of a song of spiritual realization by a Tibetan hermit, himself from a family of nomads:

Today I climbed behind
This excellent retreat place, I raised my head, looking up,
And saw the cloudless sky.
I thought of absolute space, free from limits,
I then experienced a freedom
Without center, without end—
All biased views
Completely abandoned.

I lowered my head to look in front of me,
And saw the sun of this world.
I thought of meditation—
Luminous and unobscured.
I then experienced a nondual, empty clarity.
All meditations that focus the mind
Completely abandoned.

I turned my head, looking south,
And saw a pattern of rainbows.
I thought of all phenomena—
At once both apparent and empty.
I then experienced a nondual, natural clarity.
All nihilist and eternalist viewpoints
Completely abandoned.

Just as no darkness exists at the center of the sun,
To a yogi, universe and beings all arise as deities—
And the yogi is content.

Just as no ordinary stones exist on an island of gold,
To a yogi all sounds resound as mantras—
And the yogi is content.

Just as a bird crossing a clear, empty sky leaves no trace,
To a yogi all thoughts arise as the absolute—
And the yogi is content.[1]

The person who wrote these verses had absolutely no need to travel round the world, taste the pleasures of the seedier parts of New York, or contemplate in a Presbyterian church to have a clear idea of the truth of his experience. I'm also not so sure that the freedom of choice in modern society is as wide as you're assuming. This didn't escape the Dalai Lama, who said, 'When you look closely at life in a city, you have the impression that all the facets of individuals' lives must be defined with great precision, like a screw that has to fit exactly in its hole. In one sense, you have no control over your own life. To survive, you have to follow that model and the rhythm you're provided with.'[2]

J.F. – But if the West's now feeling a new enthusiasm for spiritual wisdom, which is why it's been so interested in Buddhism recently, surely that's because it can compare its past and present experiences. The philosophy of the Enlightenment was accompanied by hope based not only on the expansion of science but also on the necessity for widespread education. That's where the idea came from of compulsory schooling, secular and free to everyone, which was actually achieved a century later. Secular didn't mean antireligious, but simply nonreligious, representing no specific doctrine. All of which, combined with a developing tolerance of free choice, should have well and truly given a meaning to life. It's of course true, incidentally, that this material culture of applied science and industry has created some superfluous, immoderate, and artificial needs. Even in his time, Epicure said that each satisfied need creates new needs and multiplies our feeling of frustration. That's why there's such a growing demand nowadays for the philosophies of ancient Greece, just as there is for Buddhism. Each is discovering again that it has something to say.

M. – At the same time, education needs to be more than just the accumulation of knowledge, whether scientific, technical, historical, or whatever. It should really be education in how to be.

J.F. – True. Anyway, let's go on to the third main section of the West's attempts to find answers to the question of life's meaning from the eighteenth century onward. This is where we find the great profusion of utopias about the remaking of society, or in other words the notion of revolution, which took off with the French Revolution. Until then, the word was only used to denote the revolution of heavenly bodies round the sun. The idea of revolution in the sense of first destroying a society so as to reconstruct it, from top to bottom and in all its aspects, economic, legal, political, religious, and cultural, was above all the 'idea of '89', or of 1793 at least. Including the revolution-aries' conviction that they had the right, in the name of their superior ideals, to use terror and liquidate everyone who opposed the great clear-out. Without always going to such extremes, though sadly they were only too frequent, it was then that the idea took root that mankind's happiness could only be achieved by a complete transfor-mation of society. And from that point of view it was useless to try to work out a recipe designed to make each individual human being good and lucid. Society had to be dealt with wholesale. The answer to the meaning of life was therefore no longer a personal matter.

M. – How can one hope to have a whole that's good, if its parts aren't good? You can't make an ingot of gold with a packet of nails.

J.F. – Because the whole was supposed to act on its parts. That's typical of utopias. All social theories of this kind are utopian – all theo-ries that think that the improvement of human beings, or the produc-tion of human beings, happens by improving society from top to bottom, not gradually or partially but suddenly and totally. That when society as a whole becomes just, each of its human members will become just and happy, too. In those utopias, the two elements of the philosophy of the Enlightenment came together. On the one hand, the ideal that scientific progress would ensure material prosperity and free human beings from all the troubles of want. And on the other, the ideal of just and fair social relationships. Each individual member of society would benefit from that justice and would himself or herself adopt a more moral attitude. The raising of individuals' moral standards and their happiness would both come about through the transformation of society as a whole. The individual person no longer had any true exis-tence, he or she only existed as a component of the social machine. There are lots of passages in Lenin and Stalin about man as the 'nuts and bolts' of the machine that communism constructs.

M. – So, in your view, what's happening at the end of the twenti-eth century? What sort of situation are we in now, if we're not particu-larly drawn to being a cog in the machine?

J.F. – Well, of the three ways of finding some meaning in it all, religions, or at any rate Western religions, are simply no longer truly practiced. The pope, perhaps, still has a large audience. He writes books that are very widely read. There are still people who have a lot of respect for certain other Church leaders, and consult them about lots of things – though mostly not religious questions. In fact, priests are our last Marxists. The Catholic Church shelters some remarkable intellectuals. But people no longer go to Mass and no longer feel like applying the Christian precepts. They want to be Christians without having to keep the rules, which they find reactionary. And there are very few people now who have the calling to be priests. It's no longer possible to maintain that the hope of an afterlife can compensate for social suffering, unemployment, and the disorientation of youth. There are no longer any priests who can go and gather together the young on the public housing developments and tell them that if they're good they'll be spared two years of purgatory. That doesn't work any more, it's over.

M. – So what can those young people, and older ones, too, actually be offered?

J.F. – People still believe in science and have high hopes of it, in terms of material progress and improvements in health. But there are problems. On the one hand, it's now obvious that science brings harmful repercussions like pollution, chemical and biological weapons, and all sorts of contamination that gets worse and more widespread all the time; in short, environmental destruction. And on the other, it's also obvious that science doesn't bring personal happiness. We live in a world transformed by science, and perhaps made more comfortable by it, but the questions of our individual lives and destinies are still just as they were in Roman times. By the way, it's striking that one of the best-selling recently republished classics in France is actually Seneca's complete works.

Then, finally, there were the social utopias, whose total collapse has been the main theme of twentieth-century history. It turned out that they simply didn't work. That they only produced harmful results. That their societies lost the contest – even in the area where their hope was to introduce the greatest equality and happiness for everyone, for their adventures ended in manifest failure. The standard of living in communist societies was ten to fifteen times lower than in capitalist ones, and the inequalities, camouflaged though they were, were even wider. They were a complete failure in terms of ethics, in terms of human freedom, and in material terms.

M. – As George Orwell said, 'All animals are equal, but some animals are more equal than others.'

J.F. – That's it. That slogan from *Animal Farm* was an ironical comment on the fact that communist leaders led a very comfortable and opulent existence, while the masses didn't. In impoverished societies there's always an aristocracy that lives in luxury.

M. – In Tibet, for example, the Chinese leaders travel around the impoverished countryside in luxurious four-wheel drive vehicles that the Tibetans nickname 'princes of the desert'. The cost of one of those cars would be enough to build five small village schools.

J.F. – That's typical of communist regimes. But over and above all those sad details, there's now no doubt whatsoever that the idea of rebuilding society from top to bottom to make it perfect has not only been discredited, it's also been drowned in blood by the history of the twentieth century. So what's left? A return to wisdom according to the good old recipes of the past. Which explains, as we've already pointed out during our conversations, the success of some recent books by a younger generation of philosophers turning back, very modestly, to some useful precepts by which to live. They've reached a huge audience, when forty years ago the same books would just have been laughed at.

M. – In the end, we more or less agree that what gives meaning to life isn't just an improvement in material conditions, as we're not just machines. Nor is it just some rules of conduct, as a facade alone isn't enough. It's a transformation of our being through wisdom.

J.F. – Not quite. I believe that all the systems of wisdom with which we try to make life bearable have their limits. The biggest limit of all is death. I think it's important to distinguish wisdom doctrines that believe in the hereafter, something after death, some form of eternity, from those that start from the principle that death is the total annihilation of the being and that there is no hereafter. My own personal conviction is the latter. Within that framework, the search for wisdom is always precarious and temporary, since it can only take place within the limits of this present life – the only one we know about and the only one we consider real – and it can't contain any hope of a higher solution. That always brings us back to the fundamental difference between wisdom doctrines or quests for life's meaning with a secular connotation and those with a religious one.

M. – To me, that distinction doesn't seem as fundamental as you make it out to be. Even accepting that there's a succession of lives before and after this one, those other lives are essentially of the same nature as this present one. So if you find the wisdom that gives meaning to this present life, the same wisdom will give meaning to future lives. In that way, knowledge and spiritual realization are to be applied in every instant of life, whether life's long or short, and whether there's only one or several. If you find a meaning in life, you don't need to wait for death to benefit from it.

J.F. – Well, yes, I do in fact think that the problem of wisdom is today, here and now. I have to try in any given circumstance to conduct myself according to the rules that I feel – by experience, reflection, and whatever I've learnt from the great thinkers – will be the most effective. But I still think, all the same, that there's a huge difference between that attitude and the idea that your existence can be prolonged into future lives. That implies a totally different view of the cosmos.

M. – Of course, but it would be a mistake to say it doesn't matter if I'm not happy now, because I'll be happy in a future life. It's true that attaining a profound spiritual realization has much greater repercussions for those who think the benefits of wisdom will go on for themselves and others over numerous future lives, than for those who only think it's going to affect the few years they have left to live. Nevertheless, qualitatively it's the same thing. Think of all the people who know they've got a fatal illness. Quite often, instead of losing all courage, they discover a completely new meaning in their lives, however little time they have left to live. Giving meaning to life through wisdom and inner transformation is to achieve something outside time, just as valid in the present as it will be in the future, whatever that might be.

J.F. – What you say is doubtless true for Buddhism, which isn't a religion based solely on the hope of an afterlife. But it's obvious that a Muslim only lives in the idea that he'll go to Paradise if he respects the divine law. Like all Christians by definition, whether Catholics or Protestants. Belief in the immortality of the soul to a large extent explains the precepts of Socratic wisdom, too. The significance of what Socrates and Plato say only reaches its full extent, in the end, because it hinges on a system of metaphysics according to which, although the world we live in is only a world of illusion, there's another world to which we can gain access straight away through philosophical wisdom, philosophical contemplation, theory – *theoria* etymologically means contemplation, the fact of seeing – after which, the immortality of the soul having been proved to us, we can at last experience fulfillment. That's very different from the forms of wisdom that are essentially based on accepting the idea of mortality.

M. – But don't you think that there could be some wisdom or knowledge that would be just as valid for the present moment as for the future? A truth that would in no way be diminished if this life alone was taken into account, or, even more extremely, the present moment alone? It seems to me that understanding the nature of being, the nature of the mind, of ignorance and knowledge, of what causes happiness and suffering, has a value that's both immediate and forever. In your opinion, what sort of wisdom would be liable to give a meaning to life outside any temporal contingence?

J.F. – There are systems of wisdom that can be structured around a metaphysical view of future lives and at the same time around the hypothesis that the life we're now living is the only one we'll ever have. Parts of Buddhism are one bit of that wisdom. Stoicism is another example. Stoicism was based on a cosmic theory of eternal return, which was a view of the universe. But the Stoics, in their wisdom and common sense, distinguished what they called esoteric Stoicism, accessible only to a few thinkers who could master a knowledge of cosmology and physics, from exoteric Stoicism, which was more a sort of recipe book – and I say that without any scorn – that contained precepts for conducting oneself well in life. Epictetus's *Manual*, for instance, is a practical treatise on virtues that should be put to use, designed for people one would never expect to be able to dedicate themselves to a detailed study of the whole cosmos. So there's a distinction between two levels. A doctrine of that type should contain a sufficiently extensive proportion of precepts that can be applied quite independently of any hypothesis of immortality, if it's to have the double function you're thinking of.

M. – That gradation between exoteric and esoteric exists in most traditions, including Buddhism. It matches people's different needs, aspirations, and capacities. But you were saying that now, at the end of the twentieth century, the problem of wisdom is coming up again in the West. How would you define the sort of wisdom that would bring everyone fulfillment?

J.F. – I don't believe in the immortality of the soul, so I actually don't think any true fulfillment's possible. I don't think that any human being who knows himself or herself to be mortal and who doesn't believe in an afterlife can experience a feeling of total fulfillment. Relatively, perhaps, it's possible, in terms of some temporary objectives that don't rule out a degree of consummation. But I think that complete solutions to the meaning of life simply don't exist – outside the great transcendent solutions, whether religious, para-religious, or political, in which I myself can't believe. The utopians building a socialist society said to themselves, 'I'm dying, but I'm dying for a great cause. After my time, there'll be a wonderful world.' That was a form of immortality.

M. – Do you not think that transcendence, defined as ultimate know-ledge of the nature of things, can be perceived or realized in the present?

J.F. – No.

M. – Why not?

J.F. – Because transcendence, by definition, signifies that life has no limit, and that you continue living after your physical, biological death.

M. – Knowledge of the nature of the mind, for instance, is ultimate knowledge, because it's the mind that has the experience of the phenomenal world, in all possible states of existence, present and future.

J.F. – That would be coming back to happiness through science.

M. – Through science, if it's a science focused on the knowledge of reality. Don't you think that to know the ultimate nature of the mind is a form of immanence?

J.F. – No … I think that the solution here depends on the attitude of each and every human being, and on their personal choices. I don't think you can say it's a solution that can be imposed on everyone. There'll always have to be some emphasis there, either on the idea that we're one stage in a continuity that's going to be perpetuated beyond death, or on the idea that we'll no longer exist after death. There's a quote attributed to Malraux that I've always found rather absurd: 'The twenty-first century will be religious, or it will not be.' Whatever happens, the twenty-first century will be.

M. – Didn't he say 'spiritual' rather than 'religious'?

J.F. – Spiritual is a bit less false, but a bit more vague. To seek spirituality without transcendence just isn't coherent. It's no good! There are two kinds of wisdom. One of them, once again, is based on the conviction that we each belong to a flow of which our present life is just one stage. The other I'd call the wisdom of resignation, which doesn't mean one of sadness, and is based on the opposite idea – the feeling that this limited life is all we have. It's a wisdom of acceptance, and consists of building oneself up in this present life using whatever means are the least unreasonable, the least unjust, and the least unethical, but knowing perfectly well nonetheless that it's only a temporary episode.

M. – Phenomena are transitory by nature, but knowledge of their nature is unchanging. I think that it's possible to acquire wisdom, fulfillment, and serenity, all of them arising from knowledge, or from what could be called spiritual realization. I think that once one's discovered the ultimate nature of the mind, that discovery is timeless. What often strikes me in the biographies of great Buddhist teachers is that they all say death makes no difference. Death, like rebirth, doesn't alter spiritual realization at all. It's true that Buddhism adheres to the idea of a continuity of successive states of existence, but true spiritual realization also transcends life and death, it's the unchanging truth that we can actualize within ourselves – fulfillment that no longer depends on becoming.

J.F. – Well, there you are. And since your hypothesis is more optimistic than mine, I'm sure our readers will feel better if I let you have the last word.

1. From *The Life of Shabkar, the Autobiography of a Tibetan Yogi*, translated by Matthieu Ricard, SUNY Press, Albany, 1994.

2. *The Good Heart*, op. cit.

THE PHILOSOPHER'S
CONCLUSION

W HAT lessons have I drawn from these conversations with Matthieu? What has their result been for me? I have become more and more appreciative of Buddhism as a system of wisdom, and more and more skeptical about it as a system of metaphysics. Our conversations have also helped me begin to perceive more clearly why it is that Buddhism arouses so much interest in the West nowadays. First and foremost, it is because Buddhism fills a gap left vacant by the desertion of Western philosophy in the area of ethics and the art of living.

From the sixth century B.C. until the sixteenth century A.D., philosophy in the West was made up of two main branches – the conduct of human life and knowledge of nature. Toward the middle of the seventeenth century, it lost interest in the first branch and abandoned it to religion, while the second was taken over by science. All that remained within the province of philosophy was the study of what lies beyond nature, metaphysics – a field that at best is full of uncertainties.

During the earlier periods of Greek philosophy, it was not theory that predominated. For Heraclitus, judging from fragments B40 and

129, it is quite clear that being learned is not enough by itself to make anyone wise. For a philosopher of the time the goal was to become a good person, to attain salvation and happiness by living a good life, and at the same time, as much by example as by teaching, to show the path of wisdom to all those wishing to follow it. The Greeks sought wisdom for its pragmatic value. The wise man is not only good, he is judicious and resourceful, too. To have that ingenious sagacity was the sign of a 'sophist' – a word originally devoid of any pejorative connotation. Philosophy, therefore, was not just one discipline among others, nor even the highest discipline governing all the others. It was an integral metamorphosis in one's way of living. But that whole territory has been abandoned and left without an heir by Western philosophy. It is that vacant ground that Buddhism now occupies, all the more easily in the absence of any local competition.

Presumably from the time of Socrates, Plato, and Aristotle onward, in the fifth and fourth centuries B.C., theory became predominant as the indispensable support of wisdom as well as its intellectual justification. Knowledge and wisdom now went hand in hand, but the legitimacy of the former lay in leading to the latter, which remained the most important of the two. The good life existed; knowledge of the truth implied an understanding of the world and, if necessary, of what lay beyond the world. That conjunction of intellectual contemplation of truth and the attainment of happiness through wisdom, with justice in mind, continued in Stoicism and Epicureanism, and was only seen for the last time at the end of the seventeenth century in Spinoza's *Ethic*.[1]

From that time on, Socrates' question, 'How should I live?', was abandoned. In modern times philosophy has gradually been reduced to a theoretical exercise, a field in which, despite all its pedantic pride, it cannot of course compete with science. Science, meanwhile, has gone its own way and evolved independently, but without giving rise to any system of ethics or wisdom. Whatever it has been twisted into saying about such matters is just nonsense, and anyone can see that scientists are no less lacking in clarity of vision and scruples than the average person.

Politics, from the seventeenth century on, was the major focus of new works – key insights that still nourish modern thought. However, it also became the refuge for a certain despotic tendency that had been present in philosophy, a spirit of dogmatism and domination. Philosophy, in fact, had already resigned its role in directing conscience, and as the supreme monarch of all knowledge had been usurped from its throne. Now it was the turn of justice, happiness, and truth – all that still remained within in its remit – to give way in its eyes to the authoritarian or totalitarian building of the perfect society. The absurd nineteenth-century claim to have found a 'scientific' socialism was a clear manifestation of how collective constraint, justified by some scientific mumbo-jumbo, had been substituted for the attainment of true individual and social autonomy. Aristotle's 'political animal' was no longer a man but a pitiful monkey, trained to imitate his masters on pain of death. As I suggested several times in these conversations, the collapse of the great political utopias that were our century's disastrous experience is, in my view, another factor that could explain why people are now turning back to the quest for personal wisdom.

The trouble with so-called scientific socialism, in fact, was not that philosophy was undertaking to reform society – that has always been its right, and even its duty. The trouble was that it was a utopia. Utopias, by their very nature, confront human reality with a model that is rigid, ready-made, planned in the abstract down to the last detail, and conceived without taking account of anything empirical. So human reality finds itself forced by the utopia, right from the start, into a role of resistance to the model, a role *a priori* of conspiracy and treason. Now, intolerance, Buddhism teaches, is never a vehicle of good, whether in politics or ethics. Constraint, proselytizing, even propaganda, are to be strictly avoided, it tells us. In the post-totalitarian age in which we live, that is perhaps another reason why the West is so attracted to it.

There's no doubt that for classical thought politics was part of philosophy, and depended on morality and wisdom, on justice and the serenity of the soul, all of which merged together, at least until Kant made happiness the antithesis of virtue. Also, from pre-Socratic times, 'the needs that thinkers sought to satisfy were felt to be social needs.'[2] The image of the classical sage egoistically and serenely indifferent to all the turbulence of public affairs is an unfounded cliché. And one side of Buddhism, the importance of which I have newly discovered during these conversations, is precisely the way it is projected into the political sphere. In what sense? In a sense that, to my mind, is quite close to that of the Stoics, who believed in a universal law, both rational and moral, that the sage must internalize and that forms the basis of a 'citizenship of the world'. That cosmopolitanism, literally speaking, is the crowning achievement of political philosophy, but does not authorize the sage to feel the least indifference or disdain toward the day-to-day politics of his own society. 'The sage of Chrysippus is a committed person.'[3] Ernest Renan, in a moving chapter of his history of early Christianity,[4] brings alive the way in which wisdom and power were united during the Antonine period, the most civilized age of the Roman empire. He recounts 'the efforts of philosophy to improve civil society'. It's true that sages, whether Greek or Buddhist, must avoid any compromise with the sort of intrigues that in present-day language we condemn as 'politicking'. But to what degree should the sage intervene? That is an age-old debate. 'Should the sage get involved in politics? No, reply the Epicureans, unless forced to do so by the urgency of the situation. Yes, say the Stoics, unless prevented from doing so in one way or another.'[5]

In this field, Buddhism has a great deal to teach us, much more than many might suppose if they have succumbed to the common misrepresentation of Buddhism as a doctrine of inaction, of *nirvana* taken to be some sort of vegetative lethargy – a long-standing misrepresentation based on trivial interpretation and flagrant mistranslation. In reality, Buddhist quietism is just a myth. For me, this was one of the unexpected discoveries of our conversations. I would add, for here is concrete proof if ever there was, that the Dalai Lama's humble, practical, and courageous sagacity, respecting an ethical ideal even in the tragic circumstances he has to work with as spiritual and political head of a martyred people, seems to be in a completely different dimension from the ineffective omniscience of so many career statesmen.

On the other hand, what my opposite number in these conversations did not manage to convince me of is the validity of that part of Buddhism I call metaphysical (since Buddhism is not a religion, despite the religious behavior it includes). To state it plainly, the theoretical background of Buddhist wisdom seems to me unproved and unprovable. And while I highly appreciate that wisdom for itself, and appearing as it does just at the right moment in a West whose own tradition has been lost, I myself feel disposed to welcome it only in its pragmatic form, as I do in the case of Epicureanism and Stoicism.

For me, the situation can be summed up as follows. The West has triumphed in science, but no longer has plausible systems either of wisdom or of ethics. The East can bring us its ethics and teach us how to live better, but these are devoid of theoretical foundations – the only exception being perhaps in psychology, which in any case, like sociology, falls short of being a science. If by wisdom one understands an alliance of happiness and morality, then to live according to wisdom is certainly more difficult if that wisdom is constrained within purely empirical limits, with no help from a background of metaphysics. Yet such limits have to be accepted. Wisdom will always be a matter of conjecture. Ever since the Buddha and Socrates, man has struggled to turn it into a science, but in vain. It would be vain, too, to try to derive a system of ethics or an art of living from the kind of knowledge that has become demonstrable. Wisdom is not based on scientific certitude, and scientific certitude does not lead to wisdom. Both, nevertheless, exist – forever indispensable, forever separate, forever complementary.

1. I should emphasize that I am speaking here of *intellectual* contemplation, not mystical contemplation. The former is the primary meaning of the word 'theory'. The Greek *theoria*, in Plato, means 'direct perception' of the truth, as does Descartes' term 'direct perception', which has nothing to do with guessing or divination, and comes from the Latin *intueri*, 'to look into'.
2. Michael Frede, in *Le Savoir grec* (*Greek Knowledge*), edited by Jacques Brunschwig and Geoffrey Lloyd, Flammarion, Paris, 1996.
3. Malcolm Schofield, in *Le Savoir grec*, op. cit. Chrysippus (280–207 B.C.) was the third head of the Stoic school.
4. Ernest Renan, *Histoire des origines du christianisme*, 1877, republished by Laffont, Paris, 1995. English translation: *The History of the Origins of Christianity*, Mathieson and Co., London, 1890. The passage mentioned is in the volume on Marcus Aurelius, chapter II, 'The Reign of the Philosophers'.
5. Malcolm Schofield, op. cit.

THE MONK'S CONCLUSION

WHAT might best fulfil human needs? Science? Spirituality? Money? Power? Pleasure? No one can answer such questions without also asking themselves what mankind aspires to most deeply, and what the very purpose of life might be. Buddhism's answer to that question is to point out that finally what we all seek in life is happiness. But it is important not to misunderstand the apparent simplicity of that observation. Happiness, here, is not just some agreeable sensation but the fulfillment of living in a way that wholly matches the deepest nature of our being. Happiness is knowing that we have been able to spend our life actualizing the potential that we all have in us, and to have understood the true and ultimate nature of the mind. For someone who knows how to give meaning to life, every instant is like an arrow flying toward its target. Not to know how to give meaning to life leads to discouragement and a sense of futility that may even lead to the ultimate failure, suicide.

Happiness necessarily implies wisdom. Without wisdom, it would be impossible to put right the principal cause of what we perceive as unhappiness – that is, persistent dissatisfaction dominating the mind.

That dissatisfaction comes from an inability to overcome the mental poisons of hatred, jealousy, attachment, greed, and pride, which arise from an ego-centered vision of the world and from the attachment to the idea of a self that is so powerful in us.

The other essential component of happiness is summed up in three words: altruism, love, and compassion. How can we find happiness for ourselves when, all around us, there are others suffering all the time? Our own happiness is intimately linked to the happiness of others.

Over the last twenty years, after centuries of mutual ignorance, a real dialogue between Buddhism and the main currents of Western thought has started. Buddhism can now take its rightful place in the history of ideas and the sciences. But, interesting though it may be that Buddhism in its time developed a theory of the atom more detailed and coherent than that of Democritus, its value does not just lie in a few points of epistemology. Buddhism offers us a science of the mind, a contemplative science more in tune with our times than ever, and one that will always be so – since it deals with the most basic mechanisms of happiness and suffering.

Why a contemplative science? Is it not enough to try to relieve all our problems materially? The conditions that the external world affords may well be vital to us in terms of our well-being, our comfort, our health, our longevity – our very lives, even. The techniques and remedies that work through material, external circumstances are important in bringing us certain kinds of happiness. But none of them can bring us true, inner well-being. Here, it is the mind that counts, for the mind plays the essential role in satisfaction and dissatisfaction, happiness and suffering, fulfillment and failure. The mind is behind every experience in life. It is also what determines the way we see the world. The mind is the window from which we see 'our' world. It only takes the slightest change in our minds, in our way of perceiving people and things, for that world to be turned completely upside-down.

Behind what might initially look like its exotic forms, the Buddhist path, like all the great spiritual traditions, is designed to help us become better human beings. Science has neither the design nor the means to help us attain that goal. Its primary purpose is to elucidate the nature of tangible phenomena, and then, in the light of those discoveries, to harness phenomena for our use. Science, therefore, can improve the conditions we live in. If we feel cold it can provide us with warmth, if we fall ill it can cure us. From that viewpoint all on its own, the ideal would be to live for hundreds of years in perfect health. But whether we live thirty or a hundred years, the question of the quality of life remains the same. The only way to live life with true quality is to give it an inner meaning.

It is no good expecting that Buddhism in the West will be practiced as it was in the East, and the lifestyle of monks and hermits in particular is unlikely to become as widespread here as it is in many Buddhist countries. Nevertheless, Buddhism seems to be able to provide the means necessary to instill in all of us a degree of inner peace. It is not a question of creating a Western form of Buddhism, reduced to an insipid 'lite' version by numerous concessions to everyone's different wants, but of using Buddhism's fundamental truths in such a way that the potential for perfection we all have within us can be actualized.

Once we are committed to a spiritual path, it is essential to check that over the months and years we are actually freeing ourselves from hatred, grasping, pride, jealousy, and above all from the ego-centeredness and ignorance that cause them. That is the only result that counts. The discipline that makes that happen deserves to be called a 'science,' in the sense that it is a form of knowledge, and, far from being useless information, constitutes true wisdom.

I must admit that I was at first surprised by the interest that Buddhism arouses nowadays in the West. When the idea of these conversations was first suggested I was not at all sure that a free-thinker of my father's calibre would want to engage in a dialogue with a Buddhist monk, even if that monk happened to be his son. But my father enthusiastically agreed to the idea, and chose the tranquil setting of the Nepalese hills for our talks. All the necessary circumstances for a real dialogue were thus created.

In our conversations, my wish was to share and explain, and my father's was to analyze and compare. That is why the philosopher asked the monk questions, more than the other way round. However, it was also important that the monk should question the philosopher about the meaning of life in the eyes of a modern Western thinker, and this gave rise to the last chapter of our dialogue, conducted this time on the coast of Brittany.

My affectionate relationship with my father has never weakened in the course of all my wanderings. But although we had often discussed the tragedy in Tibet, we had never had the occasion to talk deeply about our ideas. We were both overjoyed, therefore, to have so much time to talk about the principles that had inspired our lives, and to compare those ideas. But no dialogue, however enlightening it might be, could ever be a substitute for the silence of personal experience, so indispensable for an understanding of how things really are. Experience, indeed, is the path. And, as the Buddha often said, 'it is up to you to follow it,' so that one day the messenger might become the message.

ABOUT THE AUTHORS

Jean-François Revel, who is a member of the Académie Française, was born in 1924. His books, including the bestsellers *Without Marx or Jesus* and *How Democracies Perish*, have gained worldwide recognition. A former editor of the French weekly newsmagazine *L'Express*, he lives in Paris.

Matthieu Ricard was born in 1946. He received his doctorate in molecular biology at the Institut Pasteur in Paris and moved to India in 1972 to study with a series of Tibetan masters. A Buddhist monk for the past twenty years, he is the author of *Journey to Enlightenment* and translator of many Tibetan texts. He lives at the Shechen monastery in Nepal.

∽

Jack Miles, who won a Pulitzer Prize for his book *God: A Biography*, is Visiting Associate in the Humanities at the California Institute of Technology.